CULTURAL TRANSFORMATION AND RELIGIOUS PRACTICE

The book sets out to address and answer three questions from the point of view of Christian theology: From where does theology speak? What are the mechanisms whereby cultures change? How might we conceive the relationship between the contemporary production of theological discourse and the transformation of cultures more generally? Drawing upon the work of standpoint epistemologists, cultural anthropologists and social scientists, the book argues that public acts of interpretation are involvements in renegotiating the future direction of cultural change. Though the enquiry is conducted from one particular standpoint – Christian theology – the observations and suggestions it makes regarding cultural transformation and the defence it makes of syncretism have more general application.

Graham Ward was formerly Dean of Peterhouse, Cambridge, and is now Professor of Contextual Theology and Ethics at the University of Manchester.

D1607855

CULTURAL TRANSFORMATION AND RELIGIOUS PRACTICE

GRAHAM WARD
University of Manchester

CAMBRIDGE
UNIVERSITY PRESS

PUBLISHED BY THE PRESS SYNDICATE OF THE UNIVERSITY OF CAMBRIDGE
The Pitt Building, Trumpington Street, Cambridge, United Kingdom

CAMBRIDGE UNIVERSITY PRESS
The Edinburgh Building, Cambridge CB2 2RU, UK
40 West 20th Street, New York NY 10011-4211, USA
10 Stamford Road, Oakleigh, VIC 3166, Australia
Ruiz de Alarcón 13, 28014 Madrid, Spain
Dock House, The Waterfront, Cape Town 8001, South Africa
http://www.cambridge.org

© Graham Ward 2005

First published 2005

Printed in the United Kingdom at the University Press, Cambridge

Typeface in 11/12.5pt Adobe Garamond system Advent 3b2 8.01 [TB]

A catalogue record for this book is available from the British Library.

Library of Congress Cataloguing in Publication data

Ward, Graham, 1955–
Cultural transformation and religious practice / Graham Ward.
p.   cm.
Includes bibliographical references (p. 175) and index.
ISBN 0 521 83326 4 – 0 521 54074 7 (pbk.)
1. Christianity and culture.   2. Social change.   I. Title.

BR115.C8W37 2004
261–dc22   2004052685

ISBN 0 521 83326 4 hardback
ISBN 0 521 54074 7 paperback

Contents

Acknowledgements

This book began as a short essay on interpreting culture from a theological perspective conceived whilst on holiday during the lavender harvest in Provence. Over the subsequent months it grew and grew. I had opportunities to develop and try out some of my thoughts when invited to give seminars at the universities of Manchester and Cambridge. It was given a tentative form when I delivered the Gunning Lectures at the University of Edinburgh in the autumn of 2000. I wish to thank here my friends Marcella Althaus-Reid and Alistair Kee for their perceptive remarks whilst I lectured in Edinburgh. Throughout the project, the questioning and comments by others were fundamental. Their interventions made me change the direction of my research and opened new possibilities for approaching cultural transformation. The complexity of what I had become involved with began to increase such that there were times when trying to examine critically and articulate the dense webs of interrelated practices that constitute and keep any culture in motion seemed to me like attempting to discern figures in ectoplasm. Only when I began to understand the exact questions I was asking with respect to the discursive practices of Christian theology did an overall design emerge. There were two people in particular whose conversations were invaluable at that time. One was Charles Taylor, who argued with me about the role and nature of the social imaginary, and even found time to read through the final draft and make significant comments. The second was my friend and colleague at the University of Manchester, Dr Michael Hölzl. I would like to dedicate this book to both of them with the ultimate line from Aristotle's *Nicomachean Ethics*:

> *Legomen oun arxamenoi*
> 'Let us make a beginning of our discussion.'

Introduction

The origins of this essay lie in the struggle to write the sequel to *Cities of God* (Routledge, 2001), a book concerned more closely with examining Christian social practice in the context of the contemporary city; a book attempting to rethink Christian social ethics in an age characterised by radical pluralism, strong public narratives, global economic interests, cyber-realities and post-secularism. In order to clarify how Christian practices relate to (or are marginalised by) what is commonly held to be true or possible,[1] I increasingly recognised that it was necessary to provide a model for how cultures change. I needed to have some understanding of how discourses of truth become credible;[2] how such discourses and their accreditation are produced and transform or fail to transform their cultural milieu. The question I am trying to sketch an answer for is: what makes a belief believable?

I recognise this is a question at the heart of several continental projects – Michel de Certeau's, Michel Foucault's and Pierre Bourdieu's, to name a few. I will in part be drawing upon their work for my answer. But it is necessary to recognise in their work, as in the social sciences more generally, that the framework within which their thinking is done is a secular one. In some respects it is a framework not neutral to the discourse of theology, but antithetical. For each of these continental projects stands within a tradition of critique that has been handed down to the social scientists by Kant, Marx and Nietzsche. And as Marx understood in his 1843/4 essay 'Towards a Critique of Hegel's *Philosophy of Right*', the central

---

[1] One might call this 'public opinion', rather than public truth. See Jürgen Habermas, *The Structural Transformation of the Public Sphere: An Inquiry into the Category of Bourgeois Society*, tr. Thomas Burger (Cambridge: Polity Press, 1989), pp. 236–50.

[2] This evidently differs from accounts of truth as adequation, insofar as it emphasises the roles of interpretation, rhetoric and power in the production and dissemination of knowledge, and their inseparability from what Foucault termed 'governmentality'.

object of such critique is religion.[3] The resources that are theology's own –
liturgies, sacred texts, creedal statements, Church council documents – are
not analytical tools. They are not fashioned for theology's engagement with
its contextualising cultures and only partially fashioned to facilitate theology's own self-reflection.[4] Theology needs to borrow, then, tools honed in
the social and human sciences, in order to understand the processes of
enculturation and accreditation that situate and govern any theologically
orientated project. The analysis issues from a Christian question; a question fundamental to theological notions such as mission, apologetics, the
divine telos of being human, doctrines of time, history, *parousia*, eschatology and ecclesiology: how do we read the signs of the times? So the critical
question about what makes a belief believable becomes more specific: in
understanding the operation of cultural forces in the production of public
truth, within any given social context, how do the discursive practices of
Christianity fare, and why do they fare in that way rather than in any other
way? Only by demonstrating how this question might be answered can an
account be given of the relationship between Christian living (and talking)
and the implicit values of public consciousness. Only by being able to give
an account of this relationship can a space be cleared for rethinking the
gospel's specific transformative practices of hope in the new urban land-
scape. And so theology has to engage with social, political and cultural
theory, cultural anthropology, philosophy, hermeneutics, contextual

---

[3] '[T]he criticism of religion is the prerequisite of all criticism.' *Karl Marx: Early Writings*, trs.
Rodney Livingstone and Gregor Benton (London: Pelican Books, 1975), pp. 243–57. The goal of
such critique, whether it is voiced in Kant's *Religion within the Limits of Reason Alone* or Nietzsche's
Genealogy of Morals, is freedom from constraining dogmatisms, priestcraft and superstitions. It is
important to recognise that the operation of such critique that these constraining dogmatisms are
what Kant called 'self-incurred tutelage – chiefly in matters of religion' ('What is Enlightenment?').
The 'ecclesiastical despotism' ('What is Enlightenment?') that requires critique is man-made and
man-imposed. Foucault, in an essay responding to Kant's, entitled also 'What is Enlightenment?',
defines critique as 'a historical investigation into the events that have led us to constitute ourselves
and to recognise ourselves as subjects of what we are doing, thinking, saying … seeking to give a
new impetus, as far and as wide as possible, to the undefined work of freedom' (tr. Catherine Porter
in Paul Rabinow (ed.), *The Foucault Reader* (Harmondsworth: Penguin Books, 1991), p. 46). He is
following Kant, Marx and Nietzsche here. Religion is an historically constitutive event, an event in
the past (though its after-effects remain).

[4] It might be objected that the Scriptures have been used to pass judgements on wider cultural issues –
for example the use of Romans chapter 1 in the judgement of homosexual behaviour. But 'the
passing of judgement' is not an analysis. It is a ruling. And the ruling can only gain credence and
conviction among those who agree it is a ruling they wish to be constrained by. Furthermore, as the
debates by theologians on the issue of human sexuality have shown, to employ a first-century text as
a rule-book for twenty-first-century living begs more questions than it resolves – and the begging of
questions requires that there be analysis and demonstrates that of themselves the Scriptures cannot
provide such analysis.

accounts of epistemology, social semiotics and performative notions of gendered subjectivity (among a few of the contemporary 'sciences') – while remaining theological.

The burden of this essay is a description of that engagement. It is an engagement that is only made possible where the cultural conditions have allowed new objects for critique to emerge. As I said, the object of early critique was religion and the effect of that critique was to discredit religion and privatise its sentiments and practices. While such cultural conditions remained theology could not engage in a cultural hermeneutics. Where rapprochements were made in the past they either radically disengaged theology from its cultural context (Catholic antimodernism; conservative Protestantism) or said they were the same thing (Protestant liberalism). But a new public visibility for religion has led to its deprivatisation and calls for rethinking theories of secularism.[5]

Religion that was once the object of critique is now presented with an object for its own critique – the secular logics of Western global capitalism. Theology is in a new place, with questions to ask, and must attempt to fashion methods for analysing and answering the questions about where we stand.

In *Cities of God*, after considerable indecision, I eventually situated its theologically driven methodology in the opening chapter. It could have come at the end or even in an appendix since it articulated a level of thinking that emerged only after all the analyses composing the other chapters were in place. It was a metadiscourse, in all the complex senses of that Greek prefix. It was not the theory that subsequently would be demonstrated. No idealist intention lay behind posting it at the beginning. In fact, the argument of that book rejected the dichotomy of theory and practice, idealism and materialism, in the name of incarnational theology, while recognising the need to make some specific observations at a meta-level of generalisation heavily dependent upon various forms of social and cultural theory. The methodology was reflexively understood *through* and *after* the specific analyses. However, I finally opened the book with these observations on heuristic grounds: I hoped it would enable the readers to understand the approach I was taking to theology's relationship to the new

---

[5] See here the significant work of Robert Wuthnow, *After Heaven: Spirituality in America Since the 1950s* (Berkeley: University of California Press, 1998); Jose Casanova, *Public Religions and the Modern World* (Chicago: University of Chicago Press, 1994); and Peter L. Berger (ed.), *The Desecularization of the World: Resurgent Religion and World Politics* (Grand Rapids: William B. Eerdmans, 1999).

urban environment. In trying, in the sequel to *Cities of God*, to identify the place where a more methodological and reflective section should come, I decided against opening the volume with a meta-account of the processes whereby any culture comes to believe certain things and reject others. I considered, once more, moving the section to the middle of the book – as an interlude – or placing it in an appendix. But, as this account grew and became more detailed in its attempt to become as comprehensive as possible (an impossible task to execute), it seemed best to separate it altogether from the sequel, establishing it as an independent, reflective essay on what is the focus of my own theological project: the negotiation between Christian living and thinking and the contemporary world.

The essay is divided, for clarity, into three sections; each section attempts to answer one question. The first section attempts to answer the question, from where does the theologian speak? And it attempts to do this by reading with and against Karl Barth's rejection of apologetics and demand for a purely theological discourse. The second section attempts to answer a wider question opened by the conclusions that follow from the examination of Karl Barth's work. That is, what are the processes by which cultures and, thereby, the public perceptions of reality change? I choose to emphasise cultures rather than societies for I am uncertain how we would define a 'society' today that would not also be a definition of a 'culture'. The neo-tribal understanding of societies (in Bauman and Maffesoli) and the description of the imaginary nature of society (in Anderson and Castoriadis), both tend towards the conflation of society and culture. I wish to argue for and retain a strong notion of the 'social' as the sphere of human interaction and affiliation – I want to resist the apocalyptic fantasies of the posthuman as the cyborg – but reflections on the 'social' are only mediated through the cultural. So my question is how cultures change, while recognising that such changes affect understandings of the social. To answer this question I draw upon a number of leading critical thinkers from de Certeau and Bourdieu, to Adorno, Taylor and Bernstein, to the work by a number of feminist philosophers on standpoint epistemology and Žižek's brilliant (though sometimes exasperating) explorations of the cultural imaginary. While, inevitably, the discussion of subjectivity, agency, intentionality, praxis and hermeneutics here is abstract, I attempt to anchor some of the thinking with respect to aspects of my own standpoint within the Christian tradition. But the main negotiation between the nature of theological discourse (the focus for section 1) and the processes of cultural transformation and transmission (the focus for section 2) takes place in part three. For in section 3, on the basis of the two previous examinations, I attempt to answer the question of the relationship between Christian discursive practices and the production and transformation of public truth or shared knowledge. The answer to this question, it seems to me, will provide a new way of looking at theological discourse and therefore open up questions concerning theological apologetics and mission.

But there are several words, already employed in this introduction, that are not introductory and need some elucidation before we can proceed with the analyses and the argument of this essay. Specifically, what do I mean by culture, discourse/discursivity and practice? These are slippery and much contested terms. Most of the other terms will be discussed in what follows, but these are key terms that we need some grasp of before we can begin. (And they are often the subject of questions raised by those who have patiently listened to the working papers I have given on the way to writing this text.)

The most difficult of the terms, because historically it is the richest, is 'culture'. The critical theorists I am writing both with and against use the word in different ways. For example, Pierre Bourdieu and Theodore Adorno have a 'high' understanding of culture that associates it with social hierarchies and involves the production and appreciation of 'artistic' goods: painting, music, literature. Although neither would hold to a divorce between the social and the cultural, both would maintain the importance of a distinction between them in order to examine their structural relations to class and power. On the other hand, Michel de Certeau, Michel Foucault, Stephen Greenblatt, Clifford Geertz and James Clifford understand culture much more loosely in terms of certain semiotic systems that produce shared knowledges and values among groups of people, constituting their beliefs about the nature of reality. For each of these theorists, in different ways, the social is profoundly encultured. Neither can be rendered too distinct from the other, for each cultural grouping or system not only comprises a social body, but holds beliefs about the nature of what the social is or should be. I am employing the word 'culture' in this second way, as a symbolic world-view, embedded, reproduced and modified through specific social practices.

This understanding of culture has the advantage of being able to see multiple notions of the social being negotiated continually within and between various cultures that are simultaneously in operation and production. The motility of cultures and the exchanges within and between them are important to the construal of transformation that I wish to argue for; the fundamental syncretism that I view as bearing the projects of hope.

Cultures are polyphonic, hybrid, and fragmentary, always being composed and recomposed. They are sites of displacement and newly fashioned affiliation. They are dialogic entities, in the way Mikhail Bakhtin understands 'dialogic'. They are not monolithic and homogenous, though some cultures and views of the social are often more officially legitimated than others. Subject positions can be viewed not as belonging or aspiring to belong to a cultured, usually bourgeois, elite, but as belonging to several groupings and so moving across various cultures, each organising and practising levels of meaning and value, establishing goals and systems of belief.

The danger of treating culture in terms of semiotics, as Bourdieu has pointed out, is the pantextualism that results. That is, that everything is viewed in terms of a text and the circulations of signs composing these texts. This form of analysis can diminish the importance of agents and institutions; underestimating, on the one hand, the freedom to invert, divert and pervert the accepted while, on the other, underestimating the cultural domination and shaping effected by sanctioned social institutions and their power-bases: schools, courts of law, medical practices, churches, etc. We will have to treat this criticism, for cultural hermeneutics as a theological task cannot renounce agency or institutionalism – theologians speak from somewhere (as do social scientists, though some of them, even the most self-reflexive, forget that).

The second word is 'discourse' and the adverbial/adjectival form 'discursive'. Discourse is an act of communication, but usually refers to a spoken or a written act. Given the orientation of this essay towards cultures as semiotic systems, discourse refers not only to spoken and written acts by subjects but to other forms of composed communication – music, painting, architecture, liturgy, gesture, dance, in fact any social action. Both Charles Taylor and Paul Ricoeur speak of the text or text-analogue as the subject of hermeneutics, and I would speak of discourse in this sense: that expressive act that intends or means and is therefore immediately caught up in the receptive processes of translation and interpretation. Discourse as *expressive act* becomes inseparable from practices, and practices from hermeneutics.

The third word, 'practice', must be understood in relation to 'poetics', *poiesis* and praxis. 'Poetics' is the name given to Aristotle's text on 'poetry in itself and its various kinds'. The purpose of 'poetics', for Aristotle, was to examine poetry's 'essence and its several species and the way in which plots must be constructed if the poem is to be a success; and also with the number and character of the constituent parts of a poem'. He added, rather more vaguely, that 'poetics' would examine 'all other matters proper to this inquiry'.[6] But when he came to down to the specificities of epic poetry, tragedy, comedy, dithyrambic poetry and the music of the flute and the lyre, he located what to him is the general object of his enquiry: 'modes of imitation'.[7] 'Poetics' then can be understood as an enquiry into modes of creative action, practices of production (for Aristotle literary and/or musical production). It is an enquiry into the general principles of their structure or the distinctive features of their composition. The word became fashionable more recently with structuralist approaches to literature where structural linguistics referred to the textual organisation of signs – among which would be the language's grammar, use of synonyms and antonyms, employment of narrative temporalities, genre, etc.

Poetics, then, is the organisation of the fashioning of the text. We can, I will demonstrate, examine the poetics of an action, particularly the cultural poetics, in order to see how certain forms of action transform or fashion. *Poiesis* names the fashioning itself. The Greek word means 'making' as in 'creating' and relates directly to the verb *poieo*, to produce, perform, execute, compose or, more generally, be active. Put in structuralist terms, 'poetics' is a synchronic, ahistorical explanatory map, while *poiesis* is a diachronic, historical operation concerned with creative action. As such, *poiesis* would constitute one aspect of a theory of action – cultural action – and in this way it is associated with praxis, from the Greek verb *prasso* meaning to act, manage, do or accomplish. For Aristotle there appears to have been a distinction between a specific form of making or production (*poiesis*) and the more general notion of doing and being involved in an activity (*praxis* or *pragma*). *Praxis* would relate to ethics and politics, for example.[8] I am wishing to view *poiesis* in a complex sense that would not over-distinguish aesthetic production from political and ethical activity. It is social behaviour more generally and the practices of everyday life. Furthermore, in English, Aristotle's term came to be translated in the Renaissance period as 'poesy' and with this translation – as Sir Philip Sydney's *An Apology for Poetry: or Defence of Poesy* (1581) makes evident – a new characteristic of *poiesis* was brought to the fore that will be significant

---

[6] *Poetics*, trs W. Hamilton Fyfe and W. Rhys Roberts (Cambridge, Mass.: Harvard University Press, 1991), 1447a.

[7] Ibid.

[8] For a brief but useful introduction to the notion of 'praxis' see Richard J. Bernstein, *Praxis and Action* (London: Duckworth, 1972), pp. ix–xiii. For a more advanced meditation see Giorgio Agamben's excellent essay, 'Poeisis and Praxis', in *The Man Without Content*, tr. Georgio Albert (Stanford: University of Stanford Press, 1999), pp. 68–93.

for this investigation. 'Poesy' named the act of creating anew.[9] That is, given that according to Christianity the world was fallen – and Sydney, in particular, as a Protestant believed that – then what an act of poesy did was to refashion the world in a way that reorientated it to the paradise that was lost. Poesy did not simply mirror nature; it could recreate it.[10] This will become important in what I wish to suggest about Christian activity in the world and cultural ethics in the final section of this book. For now, let it stand that *poiesis* differs from social behaviour more generally, with respect to its power to create anew, to transform; it announces a production not a mindless reproduction.

By practice, then, I am naming the way in which any act of meaning or communication operates within, and is invoked by, certain sets of social and cultural forces. Any act is an embedded act that will be received and interpreted differently by the various other actants within that context. Some of these actants may be more powerful than others (and we will have to define the basis of that power later), but any act of meaning has to find its place (or disappear as irrelevant) within the wider productions of public truth. Attention to practice is then an attention to cultural *poiesis* – an attention to those other discourses that give rise to the need to act and that subsequently determine that action's orientation, position, meaning and possible value. Cultural *poiesis* involves also, necessarily, an attention to cultural politics, for as an operation it is empowered and works with respect to other power relations. The grid of forces within which it operates either lends or withdraws credibility from any creative act. By speaking in terms of actants and practices I am wishing to introduce faces and an historical materialism into cultural *poiesis*. It is not a matter of the circulation of anonymous cultural forces but of intentional acts done from specific subject positions with respect to defined institutions.

Finally, let me emphasise what I am and what I am not trying to do here. I am *not* attempting to discover a formula for the successful promotion of the Christian faith in contemporary culture. In fact, 'Christian theology' in this text could be replaced with any other cultural practice. Like Clifford Geertz's interpretative anthropology, this study is not an attempt to predict or engineer a future, but rather it seeks to diagnose a certain condition that embedded discourses take in any

---

[9] It is closer to what Robert Miner distinguishes as 'creation' rather than 'crafting'. See his theological account of such creativity, *Truth in the Making: Creative Knowledge in Theology and Philosophy* (London: Routledge, 2004).

[10] *An Apology for Poetry*, ed. Geoffrey Sheperd (London: Thomas Nelson, 1965), p. 101.

culture.[11] Sandra Harding, a feminist epistemologist whose work I will be examining in section 2 of this essay, writes concerning feminist stand-point theory that defenders of standpoint believe 'that social progress is desirable and possible and that improved theories about ourselves and the world around us will contribute to that progress...They debate what those theories should say...and who should get to define what counts as social progress.'[12] What I *am* pursuing and examining is the space for theological discourse and a Christian standpoint to be involved in such debates. I am investigating, from a theological perspective, how religious faith negotiates a position with respect to the other fields of symbolic production (to employ a metaphor from Bourdieu). In brief, I am seeking to elucidate the bases upon which one can conduct an examination of the social representation of Christian theology, and open a space for engaging with this social representation theologically. What is at issue, I believe, is the question of apologetics.

Why does the possibility of Christian apologetics matter? Any attempt to answer this question requires considering the nature and significance of theological discourse, and that consideration in turn requires thinking through the context in which such discourse arises. For whom is theology written and for what purpose? Or, who does the theologian address and what is the task undertaken in the address? Christian apologetics situates the theological task with respect to the gospel of salvation in Christ freely offered to the world; a world not divorced from Christ but whose meaning is only known with respect to Christ as the one through whom all things were made and have their being. The 'world' is not separated as nature from grace; secularity does not ontologically secure the world as independent of God. As such, apologetics orientates theological discourse towards a specific cultural and historical negotiation concerning public truth. Its task is evangelical and doxological. Upon the basis of apologetics rests, then, the Christian mission not only to disseminate the good news, but to bring about cultural and historical transformations concomitant with the coming of the Kingdom of God. This is why the possibility for Christian apologetics matters – for its task makes manifest the polity of the Christian gospel, its moral, social and political orders. Its task is Christological insofar as it is the continuation of, and participation in, the redemptive work of Christ. Without the orientation of Christian apologetics towards

---

[11] See 'Thick Description: Toward an Interpretive Theory of Culture' in *The Interpretation of Cultures* (New York: Basic Books, Inc., 1973), p. 29.
[12] *Whose Science? Whose Knowledge?* (New York: Cornell University Press, 1991), p. 186.

the world, the theological task is merely an exercise in navel-gazing. And while reflexivity has necessarily to be intrinsic to theological work – for the theologian attempts to speak in the name of Christ, and that is a presumption the theologian must continually be scandalised by – that reflexivity cannot be the telos of the theological work.

The possibility for a Christian apologetics then is fundamental to the theological task. Apologetics has a theological warrant for the work it undertakes in the operation of the Word in the salvation of the world. But it has no unmediated access to that Word such that it can be wielded like a weapon or used like a tool. The basis upon which apologetics engages the Word with the world requires an understanding of both the character of that Word and the character of the world. This dual understanding involves an immersion in the words and works that bear witness to the Word and the words and works that characterise any particular cultural context. And here lies the risk, the dialectical risk that theology must run. On the one hand, in understanding the world theology comes to understand itself (what it has to say, what the *charism* is that it has been given to deliver). On the other, though the theologian is situated within the world, the revelation of Christ comes from that time and place 'before the foundations of the world' (John 17.5). The eternal makes provision for and maintains the temporal, challenging all that is fallen and misconceived. Being situated in the world at a particular time, in a particular cultural situation, the theologian takes up the theological task with the resources of the tradition and a mind-set formed in and through the words and works that constitute this *habitus*. The theologian can only understand the faith held and practised by the Christian Church, the theological task this enjoins and the people to whom this task is addressed through what is culturally and historically available. The theo-logic of theology itself, the faith that seeks understanding, is then constituted in a cultural negotiation between the revelation of Christ to the Church (rooted in the Scriptures, the sacraments and the tradition of their interpretation and application) and the 'signs of the times'. Both the danger and the possibility of apologetics lie in the degree of critical difference that can be maintained between the Christian *evangelium* and the ways of the world. But, and this remains fundamental, neither can be accessed without the other. The secular world is never confronted as such, without first being constructed as a homogenous cultural order from the standpoint of Christian difference; while the Christian difference is never defined as such without also being constructed as a homogeneous religious culture from the standpoint of the irreligious or de-divinised world-view.

And so Christian theology must continually examine its place in the world in order to be able to recognise itself and carry forward the tradition of its revelation-based claims. This essay is an attempt to expose something of the grammar of its cultural engagement with respect to the grammar of all cultural engagement. Marx was only half right: religion is a social production, but the social is also a religious production. In understanding the grammars of these co-implicated productions, in understanding the operation of a fundamental syncretism, we may come to recognise the ways of cultural transformation and the structures of hope that operate in social interaction.

CHAPTER I

The governing question I: from what place does theology speak?

In order to begin an enquiry into the relationship between Christian theology, cultural transformation and the formation of public accounts of what is true, I wish to pose and examine a specific question in this opening section: from where does theology speak? Since we are concerned here with the effects of discursive practices – writing sermons and treatises, church attendance, the living out of a Christian ethic, liturgies, acts of piety, etc. – then there are two aspects to answering this question.

The first is the personal – that is, it is persons who do these things in the context of and in relation to other persons. Even the solitary reading of the Bible or the act of lighting a candle is rendered meaningful only with respect to wider relational fields: my reading of the Bible is a discipline my tradition first informs and then (it is hoped I discover) is necessary for my salvation, for example; or I have been taught that my lighting a candle can be a significant part of an act of intercession or remembrance. These solitary acts only make sense to the persons doing them when they are viewed contextually, that is, in terms of wider intersubjective practices and the institutions that structure and facilitate them. As such solitary acts have public meanings and communal significances. They are not divorced from the institutions that have judged these acts significant, and disseminated this judgement among those attached to and constituting these institutions. They are not divorced from the knowledge that other people do them and regard them likewise as important.

The second aspect of that question concerning the whence of theology is, then, social – that is, the positioning of these discursive practices with respect to other practices that also have their sites of significance and organs for the dissemination of those significances. These other practices may amplify and supplement the significance of the theological act – the lighting of a candle is now a political action found in secular contexts of resistance to forms of hegemony: claiming the streets at night for women; vigils on behalf of Amnesty International and CND; protests against the war in Iraq. These other practices may deny the significance of the theological act, so that in certain academic circles the teaching of Christian theology is an embarrassment in an institution committed to so-called objective strategies for teaching and learning knowledge. As a teacher of philosophy of religion, I was once told by an eminent analytical philosopher of mind that he saw what I was doing as harmless nonsense. Because, as far as he was concerned, there was no object to which the word 'religion' corresponded, and so philosophy committed to examining such a chimera was not philosophy at all. On the other hand, these other social practices may enhance or extend the theological significance of the act – lending to the contingency of a public protest a transcendent value.

To answer the governing question of this opening section, then, we will begin by examining these two aspects of any discursive activity: the personal and the social. Of course, this division between the personal and the social is heuristic: they are not purely isolatable positions. But the distinction between the personal act and the social event, in theological practices as in any set of practices, maintains an emphasis upon agency and inter-subjectivity. It will become increasingly important for my argument that, in the examination of what Foucault called the 'micro-physics of power'[1] and I would call cultural politics, we never treat anonymous and deterministic forces.

But it is at this point that a third aspect of the question 'From where does theology speak?' presents itself. For my examination so far has dealt with theology as a social and cultural activity; not as an activity claiming divine warrant for its undertaking. In other words, part of the self-understanding of those who practise Christian theology, any theology, is some account of their calling to be among the faithful and some appeal to the foundation of all theological discourse: a revelation that opens up a radical exteriority, a transcendent horizon. In Christian theology this is explicitly the revelation of God in Jesus Christ. In order then to understand as fully as possible the relationship between Christian discourse and public beliefs in what is true we need also to give an account of the basis of the Christian account of truth: revelation. For the social activity of Christian practice is given its most comprehensive meaning only when viewed in terms of this transcendent origin and destiny; that is, the work of redemption in the world and the truth of the gospel. Of course, the social activity has other more local meanings – I light this candle in a prayer for this friend in this situation,

---

[1] *Discipline and Punish: The Birth of the Prison*, tr. Alan Sheridan (Harmondsworth: Penguin Books, 1991), p. 26.

I read this passage of Scripture because I have been asked to preach on it next Sunday, etc. – but these local and contingent meanings become ultimately significant on the basis of what is believed about the operation of God with respect to the individual, the Church and the world. Furthermore, in the Christian tradition, this appeal to revealed truth is not simply an appeal to Scripture – though the question of the relationship of revelation to *sacra pagina* is not at all irrelevant at this point. But Christian *doxa* has never held that the Scriptures gave direct access to the revelation of the divine and were themselves divine.[2] The Scriptures bear witness to but are not themselves the Word of God. However, neither has orthodox teaching simply held that the revelation of Jesus Christ is a past event attested in the Scriptures. The Christian tradition maintains that Christ reveals Himself today, in and through the work of the Church; which, following the Ascension and Pentecost, became the body of Christ. Revelation is an ongoing activity, unfolding with the world. The coming to an understanding of what is 'revealed' – which would include the discernment of one's calling to a specific Christian practice – is inseparable then from a triple hermeneutical activity. First, with respect to interpreting the Scriptures; secondly with respect to the teaching of the Church; and thirdly, with a discernment of the contemporary work of Christ in the context of any activity undertaken. In other words, and this is the point I wish to labour, the coming to an understanding of what is 'revealed' in Christian theology, the arrival at the conviction of what one is called to do or the site from which theology speaks, is an interpretative undertaking. As such, it is an undertaking not divorced or even differing from other social activities in which one is involved. The belief in the transcendent operation of God in, through and upon the immanent orders of the world does not translate the enunciative site from which theology speaks *out of this world*. In brief, we cannot simply state that theology speaks from God. Christian teaching would accept a pneumatological and Christological basis for that speaking, that the Spirit leads us into all truth (John 16.13), but it would also accept an ecclesiological and anthropological basis for that speaking and recognise the limits and horizons of both those bases. Limits because of the finitude of human being and the operation of sin and ignorance in all human cultures; horizons because all human being is embedded in specific cultural and historical situations. On the other hand, one cannot reduce the

---

[2] There have been believers in the verbal inspiration of Scripture, particularly among conservative Protestants, but these have been a minority. They do not constitute a continuing tradition in Christian orthodoxy.

theological practice to just a social activity. There remains that within it that justifies and legitimates by referring the local action to what is 'ultimately significant'. The practice even provides a theological account of the relationship between the particular and the universal in the doctrine of all things existing in, that is participating in, Christ. Any Christian action (and for the Christian there can be no action which is not a Christian action) is undertaken 'in the name of' that which transcends the social, but it is conducted, examined and made sense of only in and with respect to the social. The very word 'action' indicates as much. The site from which theology speaks therefore has an ultimacy that can only be gauged, recognised, shared and comprehended in negotiation with all the other social activities (and the public truths they assert and contest) that inform it.

The interpretation of what has been revealed is interrelational. This does not necessarily compromise the truth of revelation – i.e., in the sense Emmanuel Levinas uses the word 'betrayal' when he describes the betrayal of the Saying in the Said.[3] Revelation would only be necessarily compromised if it were totally 'other' and external to the social and interrelational such that the division between truth and its cultural expression was both ontological and epistemological. But the revealed truth in Christian discourse is itself a historical (that is, social and cultural) event. The revelation was never merely other than the world, but given in and to the world – a world made and maintained by the goodness of God. The operation of faith as a hermeneutical activity with respect to this incarnate revelation, therefore, integrates that which is ultimate and transcendent in theological discourse with social activity and its cultural horizons.

To develop this analysis further, clarifying what is involved in the way social activity is implicated in cultural negotiation and undertaken by theological discourse, let us become specific by examining the work of one particular Christian and one kind of theological activity: Karl Barth and the academic pursuit of theology. This choice is obviously determined by my own interests and preoccupations (as is the question I have raised). But because his work was a major public undertaking still highly influential today other biographical and contextual information is also available. In examining the question 'From where does theology speak?' with reference

---

[3] See *Autrement qu'être ou au-delà de l'essence* (The Hague: Martinus Nijhoff, 1974), pp. 16–20, 64–7, 78–86, 239–53. I would not wish to disagree with Levinas's account of the Said and the Saying completely. In particular, I believe Christian theology has much to learn and revisit in its own tradition by examining what Levinas terms the pass 'from the Said to Saying or the wisdom (*sagesse*) of desire' (p. 239).

to Barh we have then access to the personal, social and cultural aspects of his work. We can therefore render visible aspects both external and internal to his published work that manifest its involvement in wider cultural negotiations; its implication in a wider politics of discursive knowledge. Nevertheless, I am only taking him as an example, and it should be possible to extend the analysis to other kinds of persona in other kinds of theological roles: the parishioner and the priest. Barth has also been chosen because his work opens up, by offering a stern challenge to, a second part of the question that we will come to investigate. For he explicitly refutes the idea that theological discourse negotiates a place with respect to other cultural discourses. He denies any apologetic role for Christian theology at all. We shall see the impossibility of such a boast: cultural negotiation is always syncretistic. In fact, the very hope for cultural transformation lies within this syncretistic process.

HABITUS AND THE PRODUCTION OF A THEOLOGIAN

'Barth' names a place from which theological activity issued. It might seem peculiar to talk of persons in terms of places; to employ a spatial metaphor for a particular individual. I do so here in order to resist both the Romantic notions of the subject – the gifted genius, struggling against hostile forces to proclaim the truth – and the atomistic view of the subject in a contract-society (which goes back to the sixteenth and seventeenth centuries). To put this in highly mechanistic (and Marxist) terms: Barth names a production site for a grand theological enterprise. I admit this depersonalises, even dehumanises, Karl Barth, but it is only a heuristic strategy for opening up a series of questions about Barth as an author of numerous theological tomes. Questions such as: does the theologian speak simply on the basis of self-appointment? Is the theologian one who is trained in the discipline of theology and, having reached a certain point, decides to ply that acquired skill in the market-place? Who is the theologian? Who designates this person or that *as* a theologian? On whose behalf does this theologian presume to speak? Who legitimises that speaking – calls it heresy or orthodoxy? Who positions that speaking alongside the speaking of other theologians, comparing this one to that, making critical judgements about the theological work done, situating the work with respect to schools of opinion or the tradition? Barth authored the *Church Dogmatics*, but who or what authorised his authoring? Why did Barth see himself *as* a theologian? What did he see when he saw himself as a theologian?

Who gave him this image of what a theologian was and what a theologian did and what a theologian's relations were with 'significant others'? Who were these 'significant others' who were addressed by the theologian?

I begin with Karl Barth because he gives us a concrete answer to the complex question 'From where does theology speak?' In examining this one concrete example it will also immediately become evident that there are as many specific answers to this governing question as there are theologians. And what does that then say about the nature of theology? With regards to Barth, there have been a number of excellent contextual studies of his work,[4] but the examination I offer differs from theirs. Mostly they are concerned with Barth's political views or with the influences upon the development of his theology, but, for my purposes, it is not simply that any thesis or argument will reflect or have social and political assumptions and consequences. In a small but perceptive appreciation of Barth's work in America, Marty E. Martin points to how Barth's theology 'will live as fashions come and go'.[5] He reflects upon how, as a consequence of World War II, Barth's thinking was pre-eminent, but by the early 1950s and the ascendance of the affluent society, despite the Cold War, McCarthyism and the Korean War, 'we worked in an atmosphere not then conducive to Barth studies'.[6] It is what defines and structures these 'atmospheres' and the fashions that are conducive and non-conducive to the reception of certain ideas that I wish to examine. I want to examine how the assumptions and consequences that are embedded as hidden possibilities in a project can, because the project itself is embedded in the complex forces between different fields of cultural production, gain a cultural legitimacy, authority, even hegemony – or else become irrelevant. But let us proceed systematically, by first mapping out the making of this subject-position

---

[4] See Friedrich-Wilhelm Marquardt, *Theologie und Socialismus: Das Beispiel Karl Barths* (3rd edn; Munich: Chr. Kaiser Verlag, 1985); George Hunsinger (ed.), *Karl Barth and Radical Politics* (Philadelphia: Westminster Press, 1976); Ralph P. Crimmann, *Karl Barths frühe Publikationen und ihre Rezeption* (Bern: Peter Lang, 1981); Simon Fisher, *Revelatory Positivism? Barth's Earliest Theology and the Marburg School* (Oxford: Oxford University Press, 1988); Bruce McCormack, *Karl Barth's Critically Realistic Dialectical Theology: Its Genesis and Development* (Oxford: Oxford University Press, 1995); Timothy Gorringe, *Karl Barth: Against Hegemony* (Oxford: Oxford University Press, 1999).

[5] 'Barth' in Donald Kim (ed.), *How Karl Barth Changed My Mind* (Grand Rapids: Wm. B. Eerdmans, 1988), p. 107.

[6] Ibid., p. 105. See also Paul S. Minear, 'Rich Memories, Huge Debts' in the same collection (pp. 47–51). Minear confesses he was more allergic at first to Barth than attracted, but 'the cumulative impact of the Depression and World War II . . . disclosed the bankruptcy of liberal Protestantism and its reliance on historical reason' (p. 48).

from which Barth spoke as a theologian. I cannot go into too much detail here, though I will point to where these details are available. Only a sketch is required to demonstrate my point and illustrate my approach.

To facilitate this sketch I wish to draw on the work of the anthropologist and sociologist Pierre Bourdieu. In particular I wish to make use of three terms that he has developed and employed – *habitus*, field and capital – to investigate the construction of a public space from which a theologian speaks. We will treat these terms as and when we require them. With *habitus* Bourdieu refers to that 'system of dispositions'[7] we both inherit and into which we are socialised. As such, a sociological analysis of *habitus* can involve a number of quite distinct social scientific approaches – social theory, social field work, cultural anthropology, history, biography, discourse analysis, even psychology. For example, Bourdieu's analysis of the literary work of Flaubert draws heavily upon the cultural history of nineteenth-century France, literary criticism, biography and collections of letters by authors or artists,[8] in order to define what he refers to as 'a community of dispositions'[9]. Bourdieu points out that, 'If agents are possessed by their habitus more than they possess it, this is because it acts within them as the organising principle of their actions, and because this *modus operandi* informing all thought and action (including thought of action) reveals itself only in the *opus operatum*.'[10] But what Bourdieu's approach to examining culture facilitates is an analysis of the organising principles of an action – with respect to Flaubert, a discursive action. And so we are able to grasp something of the place from which Flaubert's work (in this case *L'Education sentimentale*) speaks. Now the danger with such a description is determinism, that is, that there is little room left for assessment of the personal contribution made by the author. But keeping in mind this danger, and wishing to avoid it by focusing significantly upon the work of this one man, Karl Barth, we can proceed as Bourdieu did to uncover the cultural and social conditions for the possibility of certain thoughts, practices, values and evaluations. For the examination of *habitus* allows Bourdieu access to what he calls the governing social 'structures' that organise the space from

---

[7] Pierre Bourdieu, *The Field of Cultural Production*, tr. Randal Johnson (Cambridge: Polity Press, 1993), p. 71.

[8] See *The Rules of Art: Genesis and Structure of the Literary Field*, tr. Susan Emanuel (Cambridge: Polity Press, 1996), esp. pp. 1–112.

[9] *Outline of a Theory of Practice*, tr. Richard Nice (Cambridge: Cambridge University Press, 1977), p. 35.

[10] Ibid., p. 18.

which one acts. In a lecture given in 1986, Bourdieu speaks of his project as 'genetic structuralism' which is 'designed to understand both the genesis of social structures . . . and the genesis of the dispositions of the habitus of the agents who are involved in the structures'.[11] I suggest that we can employ his approach, then, to enable us to see something of the place from which theology speaks with respect to a particular theologian, Karl Barth.

The man

We have resources now for approaching Karl Barth's *habitus* in some depth. There are a number of studies of both Wilhelmine and Weimar culture[12] and of Christian socialism in both Germany and Switzerland throughout the formative years when Barth was making a reputation for himself as a theologian. There is the biographical work, of course, of his last secretary, Eberhard Busch.[13] There is also a psychological study of Barth by Wolfgang Schildmann,[14] the publication of his letters to Thurneysen, Bultmann, Harnack, Miskotte, Rade and Zuckermayer, alongside an

[11] 'Field of Power, Literary Field and Habitus', tr. Claud DeVerlie, in *The Field of Cultural Production: Essays on Art and Literature*, ed. Randal Johnson (New York: Columbia University Press, 1993), p. 162.
[12] Most significantly for English-speakers: George Rupp, *Culture-Protestantism: German Liberal Theology at the Turn of the Twentieth Century* (Missoula, Mont.: Scholars Press, 1977); W.R. Ward, *Theology, Sociology and Politics: The German Protestant Social Conscience, 1890–1933* (Bern: Peter Lang, 1979); Peter Gay, *Weimar Culture: The Outsider as Insider* (New York: Harper Torchbooks, 1968); Keith Bullivant (ed.), *Culture and Society in the Weimar Republic* (Manchester: Manchester University Press, 1977); T. Kniesche and S. Brockmann (eds.), *Dancing on the Volcano: Essays on the Culture of the Weimar Republic* (Columbia: Camden, 1994); Mark D. Chapman, *Ernst Troeltsch and Liberal Theology: Religion and Cultural Synthesis in Wilhelmine Germany* (Oxford: Oxford University Press, 2001).
[13] The following have been consulted: *Karl Barth: His Life from Letters and Autobiographical Texts*, tr. John Bowden (Philadelphia: Fortress Press, 1976); 'Autobiographical Sketches of Karl Barth' in *Karl Barth – Rudolf Bultmann: Letters 1922–1966*, ed. Bernd Jaspert, tr. Geoffrey Bromiley Edinburgh: (T&T Clark, 1982; 'Memories of Karl Barth' (an interview made in November 1985) in Donald Kim (ed.), *How Karl Barth Changed My Mind* (Grand Rapids: Wm. B. Eerdmans, 1988), pp. 9–14; 'Theologie und Biographie: das Problem des Verhältnisses der beiden Grössen in Karl Barths Theologie', *Evangelische Theologie* no.6 (1986), 325–9; 'Deciding Moments in the Life and Work of Karl Barth', trs. Martin Rumscheidt and Barbara Rumscheidt, *Grail*, no.2 (1986), 51–67; 'Gelebte theologische Existenz bei Karl Barth' in Heidelore Köckert and Wolf Krötke (eds), *Theologie als Christologie: Zum Werk und Leben Karl Barths: Ein Symposium* (Berlin: Evangelische Verlagsanstalt, 1988), pp. 170–92. See also Hans Frei's essay 'Eberhard Busch's Biography of Karl Barth' in George Hunsinger and William C. Placher (eds.), *Types of Christian Theology* (New Haven: Yale University Press, 1992), pp. 147–63.
[14] *Was sind das für Zeichen? Karl Barths Träume im Kontext von Leben und Lehre* (Munich: Chr. Kaiser Verlag, 1991).

assortment of letters, both personal and open, from 1945–68, and the biographical excavations of Renata Köbler and Suzanne Selinger.[15] The letters point to a disposition Selinger views as fundamental to Barth's theological thinking – his need of dialogue partners, even, as with Brunner, if these partners are to be critically assailed.

In 1986, Busch published the first attempt to correlate biography and theology, but its attention to personal history does not examine the 'schemes of *habitus*', those internalised 'signs, indices and sanctions'.[16] At the beginning of his thorough study of Barth's early theological development, Bruce McCormack raises the question, 'What was it that drove Barth?' He answers it by developing an answer given to that same question by Dieter Schellong: 'Expectation joined with an eschatological conditioned longing.'[17] This is, of course, a theologian's answer. For Barth's massive productivity also attests to an ambitious man driven by a passion to excel. In 1957, his son Markus can still write of his father's 'furious energy'.[18] Conscious, half-conscious, unconscious, theologically interpreted dispositions are negotiated with respect to other culturally nurtured ones. As Tim Gorringe points out, 'Barth came from a well established middle-class family, with many notable nineteenth century preachers and theologians among his ancestors.'[19] Though this statement can seem fairly anodyne, it in fact sums up any number of internalised values about education (of a certain conservative Protestant, that is, Pietistic kind),[20] social, economic and professional expectations, and particular images and associations of what a preacher's work and what a theologian's work were. The kind of theology Barth developed cannot be separated from the internalisation of the cultural values and systems that nurtured him and his response to those of which he was conscious. His Christian socialism, for example, may have first surfaced when he encountered 'the miserable living conditions of the working classes'[21] in his Geneva assistant pastorship or when he arrived at the industrial village of Safenwil as its pastor in 1911

[15] Renata Köbler, *Schattenarbeit: Charlotte von Kirschbaum. Die Theologin an der Seite Karl Barths* (Cologne: Pahl-Rugenstein Verlag, 1987); Suzanne Selinger, *Charlotte von Kirschbaum and Karl Barth: A Study in Biography and the History of Theology* (Pennsylvania: Pennsylvania State University Press, 1998).

[16] Bourdieu, *Field of Cultural Production*, p. 133.

[17] McCormack, *Karl Barth's Critically Realistic Dialectical Theology*, pp. 31–2.

[18] *New Christian Advocate*, no.8 (May 1957), p. 16.

[19] *Karl Barth: Against Hegemony*, p. 24.

[20] See Eberhard Busch, *Karl Barth und die Pietisten: Die Pietismuskritik des jugen Karl Barths und ihre Erwiderung* (Munich: Chr. Kaiser Verlag, 1978).

[21] McCormack, *Karl Barth's Critically Realistic Dialectical Theology*, p. 80.

and began reading the Religious Socialism of Werner Sombart and Hermann Kutter, but it was also in part the legacy of his father Fritz[22] – also an academic theologian. Furthermore, it was no accident that this socialism was awoken on his return to Switzerland, for the *Kulturprotestantismus* of Wilhelmine Germany was not fertile soil at the time for the development of Religious Socialism.[23] In fact, Busch observes how being Swiss had important implications for Barth's later thinking and acting when back in Germany – impeding certain forms of political engagement and fostering a detachment from Weimar culture and its turbulent politics. Models of what theology was and what a theologian did were on hand – from his father, to his influential catechist, Robert Aeschbacher,[24] to his revered teacher, Wilhelm Herrmann,[25] to the fiery socialism of Leon Ragaz and the Blumhardts, Christoph and Johann.[26]

Of course, *habitus* is not static. Other values and beliefs about social reality emerge, changing or challenging established patterns. McCormack dates an important theological change that takes place in Barth and is reflected in his sermons of 1913. Barth's vision becomes darker and more apocalyptic.[27] Of course, war is being rumoured throughout Europe, and Barth is being stirred by the activism of the Swiss socialist movement, but McCormack forgets to mention two significant biographical and psychological factors. First, in 1912 Barth's father had died suddenly, the man of whom Barth later said 'I undoubtedly owe [to him] the presuppositions of my later relation to theology'.[28] Secondly, it was the year of Barth's marriage to Nelly Hoffmann, a marriage that was 'troubled and unhappy almost from the start'.[29] It was a marriage 'largely engineered by his mother'[30] and as it gets worse so Barth begins to write more theology.

---

[22] Fritz Barth knew the father of the Religious Socialist movement, Hermann Kutter, while Kutter studied for his doctorate in Berne. Later Thurneysen was again a link between Karl Barth and Kutter.

[23] Busch, *Karl Barth, His Life*, p. 81.

[24] Barth recorded it was this man who led him to study theology at university. See Busch, 'Autobiographical Sketches of Karl Barth', p. 158.

[25] Barth writes that with Herrmann 'my own independent interest in theology began'. See 'The Principles of Dogmatics according to Wilhelm Herrmann' in *Theology and Church*, tr. Louise Pettibone Smith (London: SCM, 1962), p. 238.

[26] On the importance of Ragaz and the Blumhardts, see Busch, *Karl Barth: His Life*, pp. 83–92. The importance of Eduard Thurneysen should not be underestimated here. He was a personal friend of the Blumhardts.

[27] *Karl Barth's Critically Realistic Dialectical Theology*, pp. 92–104.

[28] Busch, 'Autobiographical Sketches of Karl Barth', p. 157.

[29] Selinger, *Charlotte von Kirschbaum and Karl Barth*, p. 6.

[30] Ibid.

Later Barth will meet Charlotte von Kirschbaum, a companion whom he viewed as a miracle of God's grace to end his loneliness. She came to live with Nelly and himself, and she has increasingly been recognised as important for not just his emotional but his intellectual formation.

The systems of internalised significances that make up *habitus* are continually in negotiation with new experiences and encounters. The point being made here is that one speaks from out of a *habitus*, the theologian as much as anyone else. And the *habitus* is culturally constituted. In his own reflection on the difficulties of writing the biography of a Christian, particularly a Christian whose work has become so influential, Eduard Busch writes significantly about how Barth himself insisted on the distinction between the person and the theological work: 'Selbstverständlich steht für Barth auch hinter der Befolgung des Rufs zur Sache jeweils ein Mensch. Aber er steht für ihn so dahinter und muss so dahinter zurückstehen, dass zwischen Sache und Person zu unterscheiden ist und das erstere stets den Vorrang vor dem zweiten hat.' Nevertheless, Busch goes on to say, 'Mann kann nicht seine Theologie Ernst nehmen und sei bei Betrachtung seiner Person suspendieren.'[31] Illustrating his argument with examples that Barth himself acknowledged, Busch goes on to show how the person and the work are profoundly interconnected ('verfilzt') and that the person works within 'ihrer sozialpsychologischen Bedingheit und Standortgebundenheit'. In fact what freedom that person has is conditioned by 'soziale, psychologische, zeitgeschichtliche Faktoren'[32]. The corollary of this recognition of *habitus* is not the disappearance of agency. Barth still authors his massive theological tomes – and a question arises as to why he so insisted upon the distinction between a person and their work. But agency is understood as embedded in a series of social dispositions and practices. These dispositions and practices are all forms of relation – relation to others, to the meanings, values, histories and actions of others. As Charles Taylor reminds us, 'to be a living agent is to experience one's situation in terms of certain meanings';[33] meanings socially produced and negotiated. Barth's theology is not simply then an autonomous event, authored by Barth: it is also a cultural event with a public meaning. It cannot be reduced to either individual genius or a product of a certain set of sociological conditions.

[31] 'Gelebte theologische Existenz bei Karl Barth', p. 170.
[32] Ibid., p. 173.
[33] *Philosophy and the Human Sciences: Philosophical Papers 2* (Cambridge: Cambridge University Press, 1985), p. 27.

As Bourdieu explains, *habitus* as 'systems of dispositions, are effectively realized only in relation to a determinate structure of positions socially marked by the social properties of their occupants, through which they manifest themselves'.[34] As such, each agent is situated in what Bourdieu calls a 'space of social possibles'[35] that establish what it is possible to know, do, or think. This historical, material and cultural embeddedness Bourdieu examines in terms of the different fields of cultural production that compose this space of possibilities. These fields are understood as discrete and homogenous 'universe[s] of belief'.[36]

> What do I mean by 'field'? As I use the term, a field is a separate social universe having its own laws of functioning independent of those of politics or economics. The existence of a writer, as a fact and as a value, is inseparable from the existence of the literary field as an autonomous universe endowed with specific principles of evaluation of practices and works … [T]here accumulates a particular form of capital and … relations of force of a particular type are exerted … [T]his autonomous universe functions somewhat like a prism which *refracts* every external determination: demographic, economic or political events are always retranslated according to the specific logic of the field, and it is by this intermediary that they act on the logic of the development of works.[37]

To begin to understand then the place from which Barth speaks we need to examine the social structures that enabled Barth to manifest, develop and modify the dispositions constituting his *habitus*. Born and raised in Basle, in 1904 Barth began to study theology at the University of Berne. Busch notes how belonging to 'societies' such as Zofingia at the University of Berne put Barth into contact with 'an impressive array of academics or potential academics. Especially in the Basle section, he made the acquaintance of people with whom for other reasons he was to have very close connections at a later date'.[38] In 1908, when he had spent a semester at Marburg, one of his teachers, Martin Rade, asked him to join the editorial team of the journal *Die Christliche Welt*. The journal had been running for over twenty years and was 'perhaps the most influential theological journal in Germany at the time'.[39] It presented Barth with an opportunity to publish his first work. Through his socialising and educational training among his bourgeois peers, Barth was being networked; he was

---

[34] *Field of Cultural Production*, p. 71.
[35] Ibid, p. 162.
[36] Ibid., p. 164.
[37] Ibid., pp. 162–4.
[38] Busch, *Karl Barth: His Life*, p. 36.
[39] McCormack, *Karl Barth's Critically Realistic Dialectical Theology*, pp. 37–8.

participating in and establishing himself within a field of symbolic production. He was developing those practices of evaluation that would enable him to situate himself and others theologically.

But he was to be trained as a pastor. He was not trained to be a professional theologian, like Bultmann. So what then makes Barth into a professional theologian? Only to some extent was it his formal training at the Universities of Berne, Berlin, Tübingen or Marburg. He was evidently marked out as an intellectual leader in being invited to assist with the editing of *Die Christliche Welt*, and as early as 1909/10 was addressing conferences of pastors and students and publishing articles in another influential journal, *Zeitschrift für Theologie und Kirche*. But when he was appointed to the University of Göttingen in October 1922, he did not have a doctorate and continued to feel intellectually insecure on account of his lack of appropriate training.[40] That intellectual insecurity never surfaces in his prose style; there he is a man of steely decisiveness. But it surfaces in other ways, most notably the way he is threatened by the academic backgrounds of people like Bultmann and Brunner and the manner in which he responds to them – albeit by theological means. Wolfgang Schildmann points out, 'Barth, der weder Doktorarbeit noch Habilitationsschift vorweisen kann, und in akademischen Lehramt periodish mit schweren Minderwertigkeitsgefühlen zu kämpen hat, fühlt sich durch Brunner systematisiert und theologisch vereinnahmt.'[41] His doctorate was honorary and bestowed later by the University of Münster on the basis of the first edition of his *Der Römerbrief.* But once established, the education system that produced Barth as a professor of theology then disseminates him through its various networks, finally establishing through those practices of evaluation a canonical value for his work, such that today there are probably very few courses in modern Christian theology that do not require critical attention be paid to the work of Karl Barth.

To attain a position of authority, he must first demonstrate what is different about his work. What is significant in taking command of a cultural field is the degree of competition that needs to be engaged in. Bourdieu does not quite lead us to believe the social world is Hobbesian, but if cultural politics are not about survival they are about recognition.

---

[40] See Busch, 'Autobiographical Sketches of Karl Barth', p. 156 and Barth's letter to Thurneysen of 18 March 1921.
[41] *Was sind das für Zeichen?* p. 147. Schildmann examines Barth's ideal and unthreatening relationship with Thurneysen (who also had neither doctorate nor *Habilitationsschrift*) at pp. 19–36.

Barth was pugnacious from the beginning; pugnacious by temperament. In fact, he records that in his teenage years 'martial interests were at the center of my intellectual development'.[42] And of the years between 1921 and 1924, when he was establishing himself as an academic, Barth acknowledged they were difficult because 'as the champion of a new trend in theology, I had to vindicate and protect myself in the form of lectures and public discussions of every kind'.[43]

The combative element finds clear expression in the polemical style of both his editions of *Der Römerbrief* (1919 and 1922). Both volumes can be viewed as violent acts of intellectual parricide, as he marks out his distinctive theological territory with respect to teachers such as Harnack and Herrmann. The parricide is clothed in a moral and righteous indignation at what Barth felt was a betrayal of the gospel in 1914 by those teachers who openly gave their approval for the war.[44] But if the 'betrayal' had not taken place the act of parricide would still have been necessary. Barth continues to sharpen the edges of his theological distinctiveness. Using his connections with *Die Christliche Welt*, in 1923 he launched an open debate between the old and the new schools of Protestant theological thinking, focused around an exchange between Harnack and himself. Harnack opened the struggle, but then the second edition of *Der Römerbrief* is at times a sustained and explicit attack on Harnack. The result of this debate was decisive; the old school no longer maintained a dominant cultural position. In Bourdieu's terms, there was no more capital to be made from struggling with them. The 'positioning' that follows this debate proceeds by teasing out the new debates.

We can observe this 'positioning' as it takes place throughout the mid to late 1920s on three fronts. The first front is an attack on the younger representatives of liberal Protestantism – public exchanges in *Theologische Blätter* with Paul Tillich and in *Das Neue Werk* with Paul Althaus. His second front is his relationship to Roman Catholicism, following his move to the Catholic city of Münster in 1925. The third front is with respect to his dialectical colleagues. As McCormack notes with respect to one of Barth's new sparing partners: 'Barth was increasingly coming to regard Catholicism as his major opponent, rather than liberal Protestantism.'[45]

---

[42] Busch, 'Autobiographical Sketches of Karl Barth', p. 151.
[43] Ibid., p. 156.
[44] See Barth's 'Concluding Unscientific Postscript on Schleiermacher' in *Karl Barth, Theologian of Freedom: Selected Writings*, ed. Clifford Green (London: Collins, 1991), p. 70.
[45] McCormack, *Karl Barth's Critically Realistic Dialectical Theology*, p. 376.

What is at stake in the new positioning is a widening of the fields of Barth's intellectual operations, for whether attacking the old-style Protestantism or its new dialectical versions, the debates were within the Reformation tradition. With his encounter with Roman Catholicism – particularly his encounter with the Polish Jesuit, Erich Przywara, and an immersion in the work of Augustine and Aquinas – Barth is situating himself as a theologian for Western Christianity. To understand what opened this 'space of possibles' between Barth and Roman Catholicism we need to step back a little. It was not simply Barth arriving in Münster. The space had already been prepared by the state of German Catholicism after World War I. The conservatism of Catholic thinking at the time, particularly its condemnation of modernism in the 1907 encyclical *Pascendi Domini gregis*, circumscribed a position not at all antithetical to Barth's attacks on liberal Protestantism.[46] In particular Barth, like the Roman Catholics, was against historicism and progressivism and advocated a theocentrism that constituted 'le rapproche de la redécouverte du thomisme chez catholiques'.[47] In an essay published in *Hochland*, the Catholic theologian Karl Adam at Tübingen observed with respect to liberal Protestantism and the effect of crisis theology that it seemed 'a desert of dry sand over which the hot wind of provocative critique passed at top speed'.[48] In fact, German-speaking Catholic theologians had taken notice of Barth's second edition of *Der Römerbrief* from 1923 onwards.[49] The threat Barth identified in Roman Catholicism cannot be entirely separated from the new threat Roman Catholicism posed to German Protestantism, particular the weak, liberal

---

[46] See H. Vorgrimler, *Karl Rahner verstehen: Eine Einführung in sein Leben und Denken* (Freiburg: Verlag Herder, 1985), pp. 72–7 and Karl Adam, 'Die Theologie der Krisis', *Hochland*, no.23 (June 1926), 271–86. Adam explicitly draws the parallel between the role played in Protestant theology by the second edition of *Der Römerbrief* and the encyclical.

[47] Paul Corset, 'Premières rencontres de la théologie catholique avec l'oeuvre de Barth (1922–32)' in Pierre Gisel (ed.), *Karl Barth: genèse et reception de sa théologie* (Geneva: Labore Fides, 1987), pp. 151–90, p. 157.

[48] 'Die Theologie der Krisis', p. 271.

[49] It began with Przywara's essay 'Gottes in uns oder über uns? (Immanenz und Transcendenz im heutigen Geistesleben', in the Catholic theological journal *Stimmen der Zeit*, no.105 (1923), 342–62. It continued with Joseph Engert's 'Metaphysik und Historismus im Christentum', *Hochland*, no.21 (1923–4), 507–17. Przywara persisted in thinking out the Catholic differences with respect to Barth in essays published in *Stimmen der Zeit* (he was on the editorial board) between 1924 and 1934. Karl Adam also joined in the debate in 1926, with his essay 'Die Theologie der Krisis'. The focus of these rapprochements increasingly became the nature of analogy. In 1934, Barth's Catholic colleague at the University of Bonn, Gottlieb Söhngen, published two essays on the topic in *Catholica*, but it was Przywara's pupil, Hans Urs von Balthasar, who furnished the most detailed examination and critique of Barth's work, in his 1951 volume *Karl Barth. Darstellung und Deutung seiner Theologie* (Cologne: Verlag Jakob Hegner).

Protestantism. For with the establishment of the Weimar Republic, the Protestant Church lost its state protection, and there were indications of a Catholic renewal in spirituality and liturgy.[50] Barth's response was typically, and necessarily, definitive. Once the issue of *analogia entis* came to the forefront of his discussions with Przywara, then, having acquainted himself with the writing of the early Church fathers, he pronounced that, to his mind, the *analogia entis* was the invention of the Antichrist.

At the same time these debates with Catholics continued, both outside (in private correspondence) and inside the pages of *Zwischen den Zeiten*, the tensions in the school of dialectical theology were becoming more manifest. The centre of Barth's criticism against the 'pillars' of dialectical theology is here, as with Roman Catholicism, *analogia entis*, although it is not called that to begin with. It is called 'natural theology'. In the background of this theological disagreement lie the differences of being brought up within the frameworks of Lutheranism (Gogarten and Bultmann) or the Reformed Church (Barth, Brunner and Thurneysen): *habitus*, again.

It began with Barth separating himself from Friedrich Gogarten. The separation can be seen evolving in the letters Barth wrote to Thurneysen between 1924 and 1930. The relationship begins on a high note on 16 June 1920. In fact, it is following a visit from and discussions with Gogarten that Barth sees the new direction the second edition of *Der Römerbrief* must take.[51] But, significantly, in a letter dated 21 July 1924, Barth writes that Gogarten 'einen ganz andern (tragisch-aristokratisch-eschatologische-esoterischen) Begriff...von "Zw.d.Z." in Besondern hat als ich'.[52] Two years later, in a frank exchange with Eduard Thurneysen, Barth can write about both Bultmann and Gogarten 'im Einzelnen sind [Sie] mir immer merkwürdig unfasslich',[53] while, four years later, he writes to Bultmann, 'I would find it hard to deny that he is not congenial to me *kata sarka*, since he plans his essays and books in a way that would be intolerable to me and above all I find in and behind him everything that is abhorrent to me in Luther.'[54] The open debate between them focused on

---

[50] See E. Przywara, 'Neue Religiosität' in *Ringen der Gegenwart*, Band I (Ausburg: Benno Filser-Verlag, 1929), pp. 48–78 and R. Patry, *La religion dans l'Allemagne d'aujourd'hui* (Paris: Payot, 1926).

[51] See letters of 16 June and 27 October 1920 in *Karl Barth–Eduard Thurneysen Briefwechsel*. Band I, 1913–1921 (Zurich: TVZ, 1973).

[52] *Karl Barth–Eduard Thurneysen Briefwechsel*. Band II, 1921–1930 (Zurich: TVZ, 1974), p. 264.

[53] Ibid., 15 June 1926, p. 424.

[54] Letter of 12 June 1928 in *Karl Barth – Rudolph Bultmann: Letters 1922–1966*, ed. Bernd Jaspert, tr. Geoffrey W. Bromiley (Edinburgh: T&T Clark, 1982), pp. 40–3. The whole letter is a scathing attack on Gogarten.

books they had both published and erupted into the pages of *Zwischen den Zeiten* in 1929.

Barth's differences with Bultmann are much more difficult to determine. Their theological differences became increasingly apparent, first, on the publication of Bultmann's book *Jesus* (1926), which Barth did not like,[55] and then on the publication of Barth's *Die christliche Dogmatik im Entwurf, I: Die Lehre vom Worte Gottes. Prolegomena zur christlichen Dogmatik* (1927), about which Bultmann had reservations.[56] But from the beginning of their relationship an undercurrent surfaces as Bultmann persistently appeals for Barth to visit him in Marburg to talk through their differences and Barth is equally persistent in prevaricating. Perhaps of all the other 'competitors' in the field of dialectical theology that had been created, Barth recognised Bultmann as his intellectual equal. Certainly, it is difficult not to see that Barth treated Bultmann at least discourteously. Plaintively Bultmann writes on 16 February 1930, 'I . . . hope [this] is the beginning of the serious debate that we have unfortunately avoided thus far.' He adds, 'I merely ask you to do me the favor of real criticism.'[57] He even offers to organise a meeting between Barth, Brunner, Gogarten, Thurneysen and himself to discuss their differences in private, claiming that Gogarten and Brunner have 'often suggested' such a meeting.[58] But, although Barth accepts at first, through various complexities (including the fact that Gogarten cannot attend) Barth eventually withdraws. On the 2 October 1930, Bultmann pleads with Barth to come to Marburg to a conference on natural theology that Barth had accepted the invitation to speak at. But on the 3 October Barth insists he cannot come and asks Bultmann to explain this to the conference delegates.[59] It is plain that Barth is simply going his own way. In April 1927 he is already speaking to Bultmann about how he 'would rather pursue my own course as you are all doing – and Gogarten brilliantly!'.[60] The irony about Gogarten is perhaps telling – was Barth jealous of Gogarten? Certainly Wolfgang Schildmann notes how Barth employs the ironic voice whenever he is threatened by a rival.[61]

---

[55] See Bultmann's letter of 10 December 1926 in ibid., pp. 28–30.
[56] Ibid., exchange of letters 24 and 26 May and 8 and 12 June 1928, pp. 34–43.
[57] Ibid., p. 51.
[58] Ibid., p. 52.
[59] Ibid., pp. 56–7.
[60] Ibid., pp. 32–3.
[61] *Was Sind das für Zeichen?*, pp. 148–9.

These are the practices of evaluation and self-promotion that reach a climax in Barth's debate with Brunner. Again the roots of Barth's disquiet with Brunner go back to 1923[62] and surface in a review of Brunner's book *Die Mystik und das Wort* in the second edition of the journal for dialectical theology that had been established in the same year, *Zwischen den Zeiten*. Brunner had in fact been involved in the establishment of the journal. Barth begins their theological collaboration with some hesitancy. Six years later, Brunner publicly calls Barth's theology into question in a 1929 article, 'Die andere Aufgabe der Theologie'. But the famous exchange takes place in 1934, Barth having severed his connections with *Zwischen den Zeiten* in 1933. What is significant, with respect to Barth's desire to pursue his own course, is Brunner's comment near the beginning of his contribution to the debate, 'Nature and Grace': 'If I reproach Barth with anything at all it is with this, that he would like it best to carry out this guardian's duty [for the Church against heresy] alone, and that if anyone wishes to call his attention to a mistake he is not ready to believe that he, Barth, could be in error.'[63] In his reply Barth denies this desire to be the sole defender of the Church's truth, but it is the very danger that he sees in Brunner's work above all that he feels he must denounce: 'I am not wantonly branding him as a heretic, but that really is how the matter stands.'[64] Furthermore, twice in the reply Barth speaks of Brunner's success among other theologians.[65] Schildmann examines the 'komplexe Psychodrama zwischen Barth und Brunner' as a playing out by Barth of his own difficult relationships with his younger brothers Peter and Heinrich: 'Barth macht den Herrschaftsanspruch des Ältesten gegenüber Brunner.'[66] Brunner was more than three years younger than Barth and academically far more qualified. 'Für Barth als den Ältesten ist es . . . eine das ganze Leben bestimmende Erfahrung, vom Nachgeborenen "entthront" worden zu sein. Die Furcht vor dem Verlust von Macht and Würdestellung macht ihm misstrauisch und sensible für mögliche Rivalen.'[67]

So, enmeshed within the practices of a *habitus* that is cultural, theological, political, ecclesiastical and psychological, by 1930 Barth does stand

---

[62] *Karl Barth–Eduard Thurneysen Briefwechsel*, Band I, p. 145.
[63] *Natural Theology: Comprising 'Nature and Grace' by Emil Brunner and the Reply 'No!' by Karl Barth*, tr. Peter Fränkel (London: The Centenary Press, 1946), p. 20.
[64] Ibid., p. 90.
[65] Ibid., particularly p. 72.
[66] *Was Sind das für Zeichen?*, p. 147.
[67] Ibid., p. 145.

alone and as a 'champion of a new trend in theology'. He commands a distinctive position in the theological field of cultural production. As he writes to Bultmann in February of that year: 'What I heard from you ties in . . . with the basically uncongenial article on anthropology by Gogarten, and finally Brunner's eristics, to form a pattern which I might have spotted earlier . . . From my standpoint all of you . . . represent a large scale return to the fleshpots of Egypt.'[68] And it is from this point that work begins on the massive *Church Dogmatics* that preoccupies him for the rest of his life. The position he now occupies is theologian to the Church – not the Protestant or the Reformed Church, but Church in its most catholic sense. Writing from a room in Rome, looking out over the Vatican City, Barth declares he is now the spokesperson for 'the ultimate truth that must be guarded and defended in the Evangelical Church'.[69]

It is at this point (*circa* 1930) that around Barth there develops a geography of Barthianism outside Germany and Switzerland. Certain countries become prominent in the reception of Barth: Scotland, the east coast of the United States, Hungary and Holland, most particularly.[70] The establishment, and further enhancement, of a position, once it is gained, is marked by the awards his work wins, the honorary doctorates and *Festshriften* he receives, the prestigious lecture series he is asked to deliver, the number of translations made of his work, and the invitations to lecture internationally. These are fruits of the practices of evaluation that he himself employed in the production of his own work. Now they are being employed with respect to that work. A Barth industry is created. The production processes are part of the institutional practices, themselves situated with respect to other institutional practices, that produce Karl Barth, the theologian; or rather produce what Bourdieu would term the 'capital' of his work and his name.

By the term 'capital' Bourdieu identifies the character of social and cultural power, its distribution and its employment. There are four forms of such capital. There is economic capital – property, money in the bank, and various other forms of valued collateral. There is cultural capital – education, for example, with certain forms and levels of education being more valuable than others. There is social capital – influential connections

[68] *Karl Barth – Rudolph Bultmann: Letters 1922–1966*, p. 49.
[69] *Natural Theology*, p. 69.
[70] On the reception of Barth among the French see Bernard Reymond, *Théologien ou prophète? les francophones et Karl Barth avant 1945* (Lausanne: L'âge d'homme, 1985) and Pierre Gisel, 'Receptions protestantes et questions ouvertes' in *Karl Barth: genèse et reception de sa théologie*.

you have with others who may be more powerful in any related or relevant field. There is symbolic capital – the accumulation of prestige, celebrity and honour that is produced through the dialectic between knowledge (*connaissance*) and recognition (*reconnaissance*). These forms of capital are not reducible to economic terms. In fact they operate in, and are to some extent legacies of, pre-economic sociality. But Bourdieu does see a correlation between material wealth and these other forms of capital. The cultural field is composed, then, of any number of competitions for these forms of capital. Bourdieu writes that 'the principle of competition' in the social field is 'the principle of all truly social energy' and is 'productive of the agents who act'.[71] It is evident from the biographical details I have sketched that Barth's cultural power operated in, through and with social, cultural and symbolic capital so that eventually he is not the only person generating and using that capital – others do it for him.

For, having established that authority among and beyond his peers, through his peers, Tom Torrance can answer the question, 'Who is this theologian?', posed hypothetically by an English-speaking audience, with: 'Karl Barth is the greatest theological genius that has appeared on the scene for centuries. He cannot be appreciated except in the context of the greatest theologians such as Athanasius, Augustine, Anselm, Aquinas, Luther, Calvin, Schleiermacher, Kierkegaard, nor can his thinking be adequately measured except in the context of the history of theology and philosophy.'[72] Outstripping his twentieth-century context, Barth is now vying for a position in the diachronic, rather than just the synchronic, operations of the theological field. But what is important is a shift from self-production to the production of a culture and historical position by other people (who traffic in his name and share then some of his back-reflected kudos). Torrance, well placed as Professor of Christian Dogmatics in the University of Edinburgh, was marketing this man for British theology in the early 1960s.[73] He has become what Bourdieu termed a '"symbolic banker" who offers as security all the symbolic capital he [himself] has

---

[71] 'The Philosophical Establishment' in Alan Montefiore (ed.), *Philosophy in France Today* (Cambridge: Cambridge University Press, 1983), p. 2.

[72] 'Introduction' to Karl Barth, *Theology and Church: Shorter Writings 1920–1928*, tr. Louise Pettibone Smith (London: SCM, 1962), p. 7. Of course Torrance had written the important and influential book *Karl Barth: An Introduction to His Early Theology*, in 1962 and concluded this cultural dissemination of Barth's work in his 1990 volume, *Karl Barth: Biblical and Evangelical Theologian*.

[73] Barth first visited Edinburgh in the summer of 1930, having come to Scotland to receive an honorary doctorate from Glasgow University. He made a second visit in 1937. In 1956 he was given an honorary doctorate from Edinburgh University.

accumulated (which he is liable to forfeit if he backs a "loser")'.[74] The marketing continues, as the institutions produce exegetes and critics who will position themselves with respect to each other, warring between them for who has the right to speak for Barth. The cultural politics, for example, of contemporary Barthian studies is complex and career-making (or damaging). Axes of academic power exist – Princeton, Edinburgh, Aberdeen, King's London, for example – that seek to maintain a Barthian orthodoxy and an idealist approach to dogmatics over against other 'softer-bellied' appropriations and applications: those of some Yale School post-Liberals, Barthian deconstructionists or Barthian contextualists, for example. There are various organisations, journals, seminars, book series, web-pages and conferences through which this power is exercised, and its capital maintained and invested for the future. There now attaches to the very name Karl Barth a public meaning that need not necessarily be supported by any reading of his work. Carl Zuckmayer testifies to this when, having been sent a letter by a now retired Karl Barth in 1967, he replies: 'It would be a scandal for a writer like myself not to know and respect you. For a long time your work and activity and position have been of particular significance to me so far as I have read about them or had experience of them. To be sure, I have not read your *Church Dogmatics* and I am theologically unsophisticated.'[75] Barth is read about rather than read. It is a 'scandal' for a literary figure of Zuckmayer's own status not to 'know and respect' the man. The name Karl Barth has become public property. It is attached to a figure who has surpassed the field in which he worked, and the institutions that structure that field, to become a cultural icon in the post-War Swiss and German intellectual scenes.

It is at this point that another transformation in the reception of Barth's work and the production of an international theologian takes place. As Barth becomes commodified and traded as an icon of Protestant orthodoxy so his life becomes edited in accord with the imagined *persona*. We can see this taking place in an early publication by Thurneysen of the correspondence throughout their years in the parish. In the Introduction Thurneysen describes how Barth drew strong lines of distinction between his theology and that of the religious socialists Leon Ragaz and Hermann Kutter. He then adds: 'Traces of these [lines of distinction] are to be found in the letters, but because of the sharpness in them that belonged to that time they

---

[74] *Field of Cultural Production*, p. 77.
[75] *A Late Friendship: The Letters of Karl Barth and Carl Zuckmayer*, tr. Geoffrey Bromiley (Michigan: Eerdmans, 1982), p. 5.

are not suitable for publication.'[76] Of course they are all published now and the 'sharpness' is very evident, but it is the cultural politics of the censorship and forgetting that is significant. The most obvious form this takes is with respect to Barth's relationship with Charlotte von Kirschbaum – as both Renata Köbler and Susan Selinger point out. Although Busch in private conversations spoke about Barth and von Kirschbaum, in his own biography of Barth nothing of the scandal of the relationship, Barth's struggles with his wife Nelly or her refusal to grant him a divorce surfaces. The same censorship continues in Bruce McCormack's in-depth study of Barth's theological formation up to 1930 – where there is no mention of Charlotte, though a rhapsodic account of Barth's meeting with Nelly Hoffmann. Once the reputation of 'Barth' is created, it generates its own protective mechanisms. Or, more accurately, Barth's 'symbolic bankers' reproduce the competitiveness, the pugnacious polemics and protective mechanisms that set Barth apart from others.

The work

From the start his writing set out to shock and be polemical,[77] but what, of course, launched Barth on the trajectory of a glowing academic career was that inaugural famous/infamous book, *Der Römerbrief.* This book first made his name public within certain German, Protestant theological circles. Had he not written the book he would not have been invited to leave his pastoral role in Safenwil. But why did he write it? And to whom was it addressed? And was it bought by those to whom it was addressed? The answers to all these questions are complex. Barth himself – and this returns us to the importance of those inherited and nurtured dispositions – spoke of writing the book as a perverse act of revenge for the intellectual neglect suffered by his father (who had lectured on Paul's writings and, though ignored by [the historico-critical exegetes] 'had been just as learned as they (only from a different point of view)'.[78] Were the addressees therefore not the very exegetes he had studied under at Berne and Berlin? On the other hand, in a letter to Martin Nil in 1930, Barth himself suspected 'dass der Schroffe Gerichston seines "Römerbriefes" auch einfach

---

[76] *Revolutionary Theology in the Making: Barth–Thurneysen Correspondence, 1914–1925,* tr. James D. Smart (London: Epworth Press, 1964), p. 16.

[77] See McCormack's comments on his first published essay of 1907, *Karl Barth's Critically Realistic Dialectical Theology,* p. 70.

[78] *Karl Barth, Theologian of Freedom,* ed. Clifford Green, p. 72.

in "Zusammenhung" mit einer persönlichen, schuldhaft empfundenen Lebenskrise stand, mit dem durch ein väterliches Verbot erzwungenen Abbruch einer intensiven Liebesgeschichte'.[79] Whatever the answers to the questions, the dissemination of that book was categorical for Barth's future. It was published in Switzerland, having been turned down by a number of other publishing houses, by what we would call a vanity press. Without the financial backing of Barth's friend, the industrialist Rudolf Pestalozzi – a Christian socialist connection of Barth's friend Thurneysen – *Der Römerbrief* might never have been published at all but remained the private commentary notes of a Reformed pastor (which is how it began). It sold only 300 copies. The breakthrough came when, after Barth's famous lecture at Tambach – having been invited only because a more famous Christian socialist, Ragaz, was unable to accept the invitation – he was introduced to Georg Metz, the Lutheran pastor and theological adviser to the publishing house Christian Kaiser Verlag owned by to Albert Lempp. These became Barth's main publishers until their closure in 1943. Metz took up the remaining 700 unsold volumes and promoted the work in Germany. These sold quickly. It was the cultural conditions prevailing in Germany (but not in Switzerland) that facilitated a theological 'best-seller'. The sales figures called forth the more famous *Second Edition*. With these successes, Metz went on to set up the journal *Zwischen und Zeiten*.

What is significant here is that the meeting between Barth and Metz was not simply personal. It was the meeting of two institutions, the academy (related closely to the ecclesial because of Barth's insistence that all theology was Christian preaching) and commercial media; two different fields of work and production. The meeting fashioned the pastor into the theologian, giving him a public voice on a far wider stage by publishing, promoting and disseminating his theological ideas.[80] But the association of theologian and publisher is even more complex – for the publishing house mediates relations between ideas and other fields of cultural operation: the university and church, for example. It forges the association between the writer and the public – and the stronger the association the better the sales and the more well known the author. This public was forming and changing throughout Barth's career. In these earliest stages the

---

[79] Quoted by Busch in 'Gelebte theologische Existenz bei Karl Barth', p. 170.
[80] It was Metz who later introduced Barth to Charlotte von Kirschbaum, who without doubt made possible the *Church Dogmatics* as we have them. Metz regretted this introduction for the rest of his life, because of the scandal it caused among evangelical theologians. See Köbler, *Schattenarbeit: Charlotte von Kirschbaum*, pp. 38–9 and Selinger, *Charlotte von Kirschbaum and Karl Barth*, p. 14.

public had to be found, identified and constituted. Books are published all the time, and more drop beneath cultural attention than are given it. Publication is no guarantee of wide reception, and so the question arises why this book became so famous/infamous that Barth earned a name for himself as a theologian. Why were people persuaded? Torrance falls back on the Romantic account of the genius, but this too easily skates over the process of the production of belief. At any given time in any given field there is what Bourdieu calls a 'space of possibles'. This space orients research, defines the problems, the methods for tackling them, the references, intellectual benchmarks, and important concepts. It is the 'space of possibles' that situates and dates any cultural producer both socially and economically with respect to those who will receive or consume the work produced.[81] In order for a work to gain attention it has to be situated with respect to interests that are being served and others that are being thwarted: it negotiates 'belief' in its theses, rendering them credible. If this negotiation fails then the work cannot fulfil its function as an event of communication. The polemical tone of Barth's two editions of *Der Römerbrief* court controversy, but do not in themselves explain why they provoked controversy. Important in the early reception of his work are the kinds of people who review it, even if they are critical about it. Jülicher and Harnack both condemned the book's apparent flouting or rejection of accepted academic standards. But to be reviewed by Jülicher, Harnack, Bultmann and the Berlin New Testament scholar Karl Ludwig Schmidt set the author among a certain group of thinkers. Others were also drawn into conversation and even a public exchange, notably the Tübingen theologian Gerhard Kittel.[82] The author is situated among those who consider themselves to be the author's peers and although still a pastor he is now being placed in an academic context. The offer of an academic post was the next step in this cultural logic.

From *habitus*, institutional training, to commercial promotion and dissemination we have now to turn to the multilayered relationship between various symbolic fields of cultural production. The object produced has to be consumed by those who are competent to understand either its significance or insignificance. To a large extent the skills acquired for this competence demonstrate communities of shared knowledge and

---

[81] *Field of Cultural Production*, pp. 176–7.
[82] Throughout Barth also maintained contact, through a long exchange of letters, with Martin Rade. See *Karl Barth – Martin Rade: Ein Briefwechsel* (Gutersloh: Verlagshaus Gerd Mohn, 1981) and the 'Einleitung' by Christoph Schwöbel.

experience. That is, those competent have been trained in situations analogous to Barth's own, and are aware, as Barth is, of current scholarship on Paul's *Der Römerbrief*, for example, so that they can recognise the importance of exegesis and know something about the tools honed for such exegesis. The work has to enter fields contending for public authority and legitimacy. As Bourdieu notes:

> The public meaning of a work in relation to which the author must define himself originates in the process of circulation and consumption dominated by the objective relations between the institutions and the agents implicated in the process. The social relations which produce this public meaning are determined by the relative position these agents occupy in the structure of the field of restricted production. These relations, e.g. between author and publisher, publisher and critic, author and critic, are revealed as the ensemble of relations attendant on the 'publication' of the work, that is, its becoming a public object.[83]

Within this field the work as a public object has to become representative of cultural trends that move it beyond any single field into relations with other fields. Barth recognised that other Protestant theologians were saying similar things, but he and his work were becoming 'representative of a new theological trend'.[84] Busch notes that by 1923 'this "theology of the Word" was also felt to be a new school. As such it attracted many lively minds from that lively time – even including Martin Buber'.[85] Barth's thinking now begins to transgress the boundaries of its field of production and begins to compete or ally itself with other cultural products and forces; it either resonates or clashes with the greater cultural *Zeitgeist*.

Several scholars have commented upon the strong resonance between *Der Römerbrief*, Expressionism and Weimar culture generally, comparing the work to paintings by Max Beckmann, the manifestos of the Dadaists and futurists, and the iconoclasm of Brecht's early work.[86] Barth's writing is attuned to the violent reaction against a bourgeois cultural optimism. His prophetic and apocalyptic voice is attuned to a wider cultural iconoclasm. Kurt Nowak has argued persuasively that Barth's return to a concept of revelation that was transhistorical has to be placed in the context of the collapse, following the First World War, of German idealism, with

---

[83] Ibid., p. 119.
[84] Busch, *Karl Barth: His Life*, p. 138.
[85] Ibid., p. 144.
[86] See Stephen H. Webb, *Re-figuring Theology: The Rhetoric of Karl Barth* (Albany, N.Y.: State University of New York Press, 1991); Richard H. Roberts, *A Theology on its Way: Essays on Karl Barth* (Edinburgh: T&T Clark, 1992), pp. 164–200; McCormack, *Karl Barth's Critically Realistic Dialectical Theology*, Gorringe, *Karl Barth: Against Hegemony*, pp. 74–82, 116–18.

its conception of a historical process moving towards a totality.[87] Later, when the Protestant Church was still reeling from the events of Nazi Germany, and its own collusion with them, Barth's strong 'authoritarian' voice[88] offered a confidence in the continuing relevance of both the Church and theology. One wonders to what extent still this trading on his name is an attempt to be convinced that theology can continue to speak with a big voice in a world that deems it marginal. Whether this is so or not, with the recognition that any form of cultural production establishes itself (or fails to establish itself) within a wider matrix of forces, knowledges and productions, we are returned to *habitus* – not the effects thereof, but its production. As Althusser has taught us, social relations (as pastor, as father, as son, as husband, as teacher, as professor, as writer, etc.) are lived out through complex ideologies that, in part, constitute a cultural imaginary.

We will have more to say about the nature of this cultural imaginary in the third section of this essay. For the moment, having established the density of operations that produce the 'theologian' and make it impossible – without radical reduction – to view the agency of the theologian as above or outside culture, let us proceed to examine the nature of theology itself and analyse again the relationship of the text to the world, theological discourse to public truth.

APOLOGETICS AND THE PRODUCTION OF CHRISTIAN THEOLOGY

One of Michel de Certeau's most important contributions to historiography lies in the analysis of what he termed 'The Historiographical Operation' – in an essay with that title. The aim of his analysis is 'to show that the historical operation refers to a combination of a social place, a "scientific" practice, and writing. Such an analysis of its preconditions that its discourse does not take up will allow us to specify the silent laws which organize the space produced as text.'[89] History, he insists, is a

[87] 'Die antihistorische Revolution: Symptome und Folgen der Krise historischen Weltorientierung nach dem ersten Weltkrieg in Deutschland' in H. Renz and F.W. Graft (eds), *Umstrittene Moderne: Die Zukunft der Neuzeit im Urteil der Epoche Ernst Troeltsch* (Gutersloh: Verlagshaus Gerd Mohn, 1987), p. 133.
[88] This is the adjective Dietrich Ritschl used in describing Barth's seminars at Basle. See his 'How to Be Most Grateful to Karl Barth Without Remaining a Barthian' in Kim (ed.), *How Karl Barth Changed my Mind*, pp. 86–93. In the same volume T.H.L. Parker speaks of how he 'was drawn by a theology that was expressed in strong, clear, masculine language' early in 1939 (p. 80).
[89] *The Writing of History*, tr. Tom Conley (New York: Columbia University Press, 1988), p. 57.

production. It is a practice of writing from a particular place,[90] a practice extended through time: hence his use of the word 'operation'. In this section I wish to examine the theological operation in a similar manner: that is, examine in order to specify some of the 'silent laws' that are operative in the very production of a theological text.

Barth's theological writing is particularly good for such an examination, because he explicitly wished to isolate the discursive practices of theology from contamination by any other secular discourses. A theology that negotiated its place with respect to the discursive practices of its cultural context was apologetic. And there was as much room for apologetics as for natural theology in Barth's thinking. Like his teacher Wilhelm Hermann, he demanded a radical separation between theology and any other science, particularly metaphysics.[91] Barth dramatically opposes dogmatics as the study of God's self-revelation in the service of the Church to the *Kulturprotestantismus* of apologetics, and alerts the Christian theologian to the dangers of such a project. But his dialectical method performs his own wrestling with the relation between the Word of God and the words and works of the world, as we will see.[92] And the wrestling raises a question about the idealism of dogmatic theology; a question, furthermore, that suggests the lines drawn between dogmatic, practical, moral and pastoral theology is *in practice* always compromised. What emerges from an examination of Barth's polemics against apologetics is how profoundly reliant he is upon those other discursive practices he wishes to erase the traces of in theology. The 'silent laws' that produce the space from which theology speaks announce an inevitable and productive syncretism. Theology can no more refine itself of such syncretism than chemists can arrive at pure substances.

'[A]s long as he [*sic*] is an apologist the theologian must renounce his theological function,' Barth writes in one of his perceptive analyses of

---

[90] I am aware that de Certeau distinguished between place (*lieu*) and space (*espace*). 'Place' was definable, limited and enclosed, whereas 'space' is what is continually being produced by the practices of everyday life. One's own spacing then may transgress the boundaries marked out in cities and on maps. I am working between de Certeau's understanding of these two words. The place from which theology speaks is specific in some respects (an institutional position, for example), but the possibilities for the discourse are socially and culturally organised by a matrix of operational factors whose boundaries are imprecise and permeable.

[91] See McCormack, *Karl Barth's Critically Realistic Dialectical Theology*, pp. 49–68.

[92] I am aware in giving emphasis to the Church as the body of Christ and the role of the sacraments in creating, sustaining and fostering the growth of that body that these are more Catholic elements than Barth would have espoused. But I am not trying to reproduce Barth's theology in this essay; rather, I wish to engage it in developing a theological project with respect to the Christian faith today. The Church is not today where Barth once stood.

Schleiermacher.[93] He believed Schleiermacher had failed as a theologian to the extent that he compromised theology on exactly this score. As his own twofold introduction to the *Church Dogmatics* – 'The Task of Dogmatics' and 'The Task of Prolegomena to Dogmatics' – makes plain, theology may be exegetical, dogmatic or practical, but since its task is to examine 'the agreement of the Church's distinctive talk about God with the being of the Church' it has no role to play *vis-à-vis* the 'secular or pagan'.[94] Theology so conceived speaks from faith to faith. Where it involves itself with unbelief, it is not 'pure unbelief',[95] but those forms of unbelief within the Church itself, within interpretations of the faith, among heresies. But the seriousness within which unbelief has to be taken when it lies outside the Church or interpretations of the faith means that, first, it cannot take the theological task itself 'with full seriousness',[96] and, second, it can only proceed on the assumption that the dogmatic task of faith coming to an understanding of itself is completed. The theologian, therefore, compromises himself or herself when 'He [*sic*] must present himself to [the educated among the despisers of religion] in a part which is provided for in their categories.'[97] Where the task of theology accomplishes a genuine apologetics, it does so only as a by-product of its exegetical, dogmatic and practical tasks. This genuine apologetics is recognised by its effectiveness. That is, it produces an event of faith that is otherwise beyond all human polemical endeavours; the work of theology is 'empowered and blessed by God as the witness of faith'.[98] This effect cannot be prescribed or planned for in advance. The unbeliever overhears an intra-faith conversation through which occurs the speaking of God's Word, a revelation that 'itself creates of itself the necessary point of contact'.[99]

---

[93] *Protestant Theology in the Nineteenth Century*, trs. Brian Cozens and John Bowden (London: SCM, 2001), p. 428. It needs to be pointed out that, on the basis of his exposure to and researches in nineteenth-century German theology and his in-depth analysis of Schleiermacher's work during his Göttingen employment, Barth conflates 'apologetics' with *Kulturprotestantismus*. For an understanding of theologically driven apologetics see Mark Edwards, Martin Goodman and Simon Price (eds), *Apologetics in the Roman Empire: Pagans, Jews, and Christians* (Oxford: Oxford University Press, 1999).

[94] *Church Dogmatics* I.1, pp. 4–5.

[95] Ibid., p. 32.

[96] Ibid., p. 30.

[97] *Protestant Theology*, p. 428.

[98] *Church Dogmatics* I.1, p. 31.

[99] Ibid., p. 29. The reference to a 'point of contact' returns us to the rivalry with Brunner, who spoke of the necessity for there to be some formal *Anknüpfungspunktes* for there to be theological discourse at all.

As Gorringe observes, ' "dialectical theology" was from the start a way of dynamiting the concordat between culture and theology'.[100] But the kind of polemic Barth was engaged in against *Kulturprotestantismus* has to be understood against the background of the German understanding of *Kultur*. This is important because Barth is not polemical against theology's relationship to its social context, as the work done on his radical politics, referred to above, demonstrates. Barth's daily routine included working through the newspaper and his appreciation of Schiller, Dostoievsky and Mozart would militate against any reduction of Barth's thinking to a bald, asocial, ahistorical reading of his ideas. A more complex process of cultural negotiation is both suggested and serviced through his intellectual labours. Barth himself, when discussing a theologian like Schleiermacher, deemed it significant to relate that theologian's thinking to biographical details concerning his upbringing, his involvement with Eleanor Grunau and the context of nascent Romanticism.[101] But the word *Kultur* has a much more specific resonance than the English 'culture'. It is related to *Bildung* (which, in turn, is related to the Ancient Greek notion of *paideia*). As words like *Kulturvoll* indicate, *Kultur* is a self-education of the spirit in which the very best of what is human is cultivated. And such cultivation is to be approved.[102] To be cultured was not only to be trained in taste and able to appreciate the highest achievements of human creativity; to be cultured was to have been formed by those achievements such that their ideals were internalised. Much of Barth's polemic then against *Kulturprotestantismus* has to be understood in the context of the trenchant German and Austrian critique of bourgeois mores that had various religious veneers – Jewish, Catholic and Lutheran. This critique can be found in Nietzsche, as much as in Franz Overbeck, Arthur Schnitzler, Thomas Mann and Bertoldt Brecht.

Barth's theological polemic against culture, and the task of Christian apologetics, are, then, produced in the context of the idealism, aestheticism and pedagogy of *Kultur* – according to whose ideology 'religion' was one of its finest fruits. Nevertheless, the polemic, uncontrolled, slides easily

[100] *Karl Barth: Against Hegemony*, p. 57. Barth's polemic has to be viewed alongside theologians like Paul Tillich who were beginning to champion the correlation of theology and culture by turning to existential philosophy (particularly Heidegger) to provide a metaphysical depth to *Kulturprotestantismus*.
[101] See his early essay 'Schleiermacher's Celebration of Christmas' in *Theology and Church*, pp. 136–58.
[102] I am indebted to Michael Hölzl for drawing my attention to these persistent resonances of *Kultur* in contemporary Germany. See here George Steiner's attack upon such an understanding of *Kultur* in his essay, 'To Civilize our Gentlemen' in *Language and Silence* (London: Faber and Faber, 1967), pp. 75–89.

towards a more radical condemnation of social fallenness. Annexed to Kierkegaard's 'infinite qualitative difference' between God's Word and human words, even in his edition of *Der Römerbrief* (1919) Barth exhorted, 'That you as Christians are to have nothing to do [*nichts zu tun habt*] with monarchism, capitalism, militarism, patriotism and liberalism is so obvious that I need not say anything.'[103] Proclaiming the new world in Christ, and God's counter-cultural NO, Barth's eschatological fervour was reactive, and addressed explicitly to the Protestant theologians he felt had betrayed the *evangelium* through their accommodation of the gospel to *Kultur*. But it is exactly at the point of what Christians are to do or not do that a theological analysis aware of its own cultural embeddedness has to begin. For Barth's sentiment in the first edition of *Der Römerbrief* is naïve, but the grounds upon which it is naïve need to be made explicit. It is the very fact that Christians *do* act (*zu tun*) in the world, even if their actions are graced and therefore eschatologically informed, that means they cannot be inoculated against an involvement in 'monarchism, capitalism, militarism, patriotism and liberalism'. Barth's radical separatism, at this point in his work, betrays, in fact, an inadequate mode of dialectical thinking.[104] Inadequate because it is unable to think through the relationship of this God of cultural judgement to Barth's equal insistence, against Harnack among others, that Christians are not neutral subjects in the events of the world; they cannot remain indifferent to the social, political and economic circumstances in which they live. We have observed above how encultured Barth's theological thinking is. Marquardt might have over-stretched the radicalism of Barth's early work by suggesting its affinities with the writings of Lenin, but nevertheless he, and more recently Tim Gorringe (who has compared Barth's thinking to Gramsci's), have shown how contextual Barth's theology is.[105] This early dialectical thinking, then, does not adequately account for what Christians *do* do (*zu tun*), while too quickly prescribing what they should not do.

The relationship between Barth's dialectical theology and the negotiations in his work, explicit and implicit, with his cultural context will be the key to recognising the wrestling to keep out and police what theology needs in order to proceed: the words and works of the world. Barth's approach to dialectics in that first edition of *Der Römerbrief* – whilst emphasising *Krisis*

---

[103] *Der Römerbrief*, 1st edn (Zurich: EVZ-Verlag, 1963), p. 381.
[104] I am saying nothing here that Barth did not admit, almost forty years later, in his 1956 address 'The Humanity of God'. See *The Humanity of God* (London: Collins, 1961), pp. 37–65.
[105] See Marquardt, *Theologie und Sozialismus* and Tim Gorringe, *Karl Barth: Against Hegemony*.

and *Diakrisis* – is much more Hegelian. Michael Beintker observes Barth's concern with dynamics, growth, movement and process in the earlier text and his emphasis on thinking as always in flight. He concludes: 'Damit ist die Dialektik von Romer I als bewegungsmassiges Denken derjenigen Hegelscher Philosophie sehr nahe.'[106] The clearer statement of the 'infinite qualitative difference' appears in the second edition of *Der Römerbrief.* Here, the deepening emphasis upon what Michael Beintker calls the 'widerspruchsvollen Komplexität profaner Weltlichkeit' means that 'Der Theologie kann allerdings die Komplexität profaner Weltlichkeit nicht von der Beziehung zwischen Gott und Mensch isolieren.'[107] Dialectical theology (Barth's *Realdialektik*) as 'total contradication' (*widerspruchvollen*) baptises incommensurability as theological mystery, and weds theological mystery to a highly voluntarist notion of God. The inadequacy of the earlier dialectics, then, arises because Barth needs to give more nuanced accounts of history, agency and power such that he can reflect more upon the method of his own discourse. He needs to think through the relationship between dialectic as *Denkform* and the noetic and 'ontological connexion between Christ and creation'[108] – the dialectics of salvation. He needs to negotiate dialectic as *widerspruchvollen Komplexität* with dialectic as process. He needs to wrestle not only with Kierkegaard, but with Hegel – and simultaneously.[109] Beintker, with respect to examining Barth's dialectic in the second edition

---

[106] *Die Dialektik in der 'dialektischen Theologie' Karl Barths* (Munich: Ch. Kaiser Verlag, 1987), p. 113.

[107] Ibid., pp. 58–9. Beintker distinguishes this form of dialectic from the form in the first edition of *Der Römerbrief* by differentiating between the employment of 'complementary' and 'supplementary' paradoxes. In the complementary *Paradoxdialektik* an asymmetrical relationship holds between the thesis and the antithesis, but (to use the Hegelian term) the thesis can sublate the antithesis and hence move forward. With the supplementary employment of paradox no movement is possible because the two terms are radically antithetical to each other.

[108] *Church Dogmatics* III.1, p. 51.

[109] As several commentators have pointed out (including Barth himself), beyond appreciating the theological importance of concepts such as paradox, either/or, the moment, difference, and fear and trembling Barth never really undertook a thorough study and analysis of dialectic. See Beintker, *Dialektik*, pp. 230–8. It is surprising that, to my knowledge, only in the chapter on Hegel in *Protestant Theology in the Nineteenth Century* does Barth really engage with Hegel's thinking. The early distinction he makes between Hegel's *Dialektik* and Kierkegaard's *Realdialektik* in *The Göttingen Dogmatics* goes unelaborated (*The Göttingen Dogmatics: Instruction in the Christian Religion*, I, tr. Geoffrey W. Bromiley (Grand Rapids: William B. Eerdmans, 1990), p. 77). Later, in the *Church Dogmatics*, considering Hegel's dominance in German thinking with respect to construals of history, reconciliation and community, he appears mainly as a name in a list of other names. There is neither refutation nor quotation of Hegel in the section almost screaming for comparative and penetrating analysis – III.1, 'Creation, History and Creation History'. We will come to the reference in IV.3, 'The Holy Spirit and the Sending of the Christian Community', later.

of *Der Römerbrief* and noting the 'not uncomplicated relationship between Barth and Hegel', points to 'eine Strukturverwandtschaft zwischen Hegel und Barth im Blick auf das Synthetische als Ur- and Zieldatum'.[110] But this 'structural resemblance' cannot be developed until Barth reconsiders the time and eternity paradox in terms of a lesson Overbeck taught him concerning the operation of *Urgeschichte*. For as Robert E. Hood observed, for Overbeck the '*Urgeschichte* is the *telos* toward which all history is moving; yet, it is not an abstraction from history'.[111] Barth will only be able to begin this reconsideration when he develops his doctrines of the Trinitarian God, creation and reconciliation. As we will see, this will lead to a critical interplay between the dialectical strategy in the first edition of *Der Römerbrief* and the dialectical strategy in the second.

By the time we come to the Introduction to the *Church Dogmatics*, a more adequate dialectic is evident. Here Barth's sharp certainties and clear-cut distinctions are always intentionally compromised by his recognition of the impossibility and yet necessity of the theological task itself. He proceeds by identifying clear loci – the Church, on the one hand, unbelief, paganism, heathenism, on the other. But then he qualifies the Church by speaking of the Roman Catholic, Evangelical and Protestant Modernist struggles *to be* the Church: 'the Church must wrestle with heresy in such a way that it may be itself the Church. And heresy must attack the Church because it is not sufficiently or truly Church.'[112] Faith and the Church are located within this paradoxical struggle that constitutes Barth's dialectical method. They are not then objects as such, nor can they therefore be identified as such. They are positions under constant negotiation; positions articulated only having embarked on the way of the theological enquiry, and, even then, 'We have to state quite definitely that our own under-standing of the being of the Church is in no sense the only one.'[113] Those little words 'quite definitely' betray much: a polemic conducted with respect to both Roman Catholicism and Protestant Modernism in which Barth is 'quite definite' with respect to both his dogmatic certainties (about apologetics) and his uncertainties (the 'intractability of faith' whereby 'divine certainty cannot become human security'[114]).

---

[110] Beintker, *Dialektik*, p. 72.
[111] *Contemporary Political Order and Christ: Karl Barth's Christology and Political Praxis* (Allison Park: Pickwick Publications, 1985), p. 10.
[112] *Church Dogmatics* I.1, p. 33.
[113] Ibid., p. 32.
[114] Ibid., p. 12.

The same dual strategy is evident with respect to his other, determinative, locus – unbelief. His claim that Christian dogmatics 'speak in the antithesis of faith to unbelief'[115] marks a precise border between belief in God and godlessness. It is a border separating theology as a science from the other secular sciences; a border maintained through the lack of any 'ground of common presuppositions'[116] – hence the impossibility of apologetics. But then there are degrees of this unbelief, since there are other accounts of the faith 'in which we hear unbelief express itself',[117] and Barth ends the opening section on 'The Task of Dogmatics' by claiming any success for this work is only possible 'on the basis of divine correspondence to this human attitude: "Lord, I believe; help thou my unbelief."'[118] So when does unbelief become 'pure unbelief'? And since the negotiations to understand the faith constitute an ongoing *agon*, then when is faith ever without unbelief?

So what then of Barth's understanding of apologetics if the criteria governing that understanding are both identified and qualified, and stated quite definitely with respect to both their identification and qualification? Who identifies the presuppositions that radically distinguish the grounds of difference between the task of theology and the tasks of other sciences? Who judges when the event of faith has taken place? Does this event of faith proffer a 'pure faith' unmixed with unbelief? How are the degrees of faith and unbelief calibrated? Who discerns when theological discourse has been 'empowered and blessed by God'? The Church? Which Church? The contested and contestable Church?

We can confront the problem here from another direction. We can ask why it is that though theology is human words answering to and working within the operation of the Word of God, in attaining the knowledge of God, there is no 'human security'. Why must theology therefore always be procedural, or 'on this way'? Why is it that 'We always seem to be handling this intractable object with inadequate means?'[119] For Barth, there are four aspects implicated in any answer to these questions. The first two are theological aspects, and the second two are anthropological aspects. First, there is the nature of the difference and the divide between the gracious addresses of God in Jesus Christ and human beings. Second, there is the

---

[115] Ibid., p. 30.
[116] Ibid., p. 31.
[117] Ibid.
[118] Ibid., p. 24.
[119] Ibid., p. 23.

operation of 'the free grace of God which may at any time be given or refused';[120] a freedom whose logic lies in the depth of God's self. Third, there is, from the human perspective, the need to speak in and from faith: 'the presupposition of an anthropological *prius* of faith'.[121] The reception and operation of this faith are manifestly associated with the two theological aspects treated above. But, even so, this mimetic activity of human beings, the 'Christian utterance', the 'humanly speaking' which constitutes 'the work of human knowledge',[122] is an 'act of human appropriation'. And this appropriation of the Word in human words is constantly in question because it 'is by nature fallible and therefore stands in need of criticism, or correction, of critical amendment and repetition'.[123] This fallibility in appropriation and representation – for there do seem two acts for Barth, human speaking and the act of appropriation – is related to the fallen, sinful nature of being human. This fallenness is the fourth of the aspects implicated in any answer to questions concerning theology's self-reflexive process on, inadequate access to, and partial delivery of, truth.

What these aspects assume about dogmatic theology is threefold. First, that there is a pure, transhistorical truth – associated with the Word – that is being pursued through the contingencies and vicissitudes of historical Christian living and thinking. Secondly, that there are better (and therefore worse) appropriations of this truth, the measurement of which is again transhistorical: Anselm is a high point, also Calvin; Aquinas is a lower point, also Schleiermacher. Thirdly, that obedience to the Word, if followed through by all Christians, would lead to a consensus and agreement on all matters of doctrine – would lead, that is, to a Church dogmatics that all Christians could subscribe to whatever their time, place, race or gender.

Putting to one side the voluntarist account of God as the agent of grace, which renders all events of grace arbitrary interruptions into creaturely existence;[124] and putting aside the way in which this characterisation of

---

[120] Ibid., p. 18.
[121] Ibid., p. 39.
[122] Ibid., p. 15.
[123] Ibid., p. 14.
[124] There is a question here as to whether the events of God's grace are arbitrary and interruptive only from the human perspective. That is, is there a continuum of activity as far as God is concerned with respect to creation such that the veiling and unveiling of God's self is what human beings in their darkened and unredeemed state discern? Or is creation so wholly other from God, not only in its fallenness – which can only be contingent with respect to the determination of divine salvation – but in its essence, such that any divine activity with respect to creation enters it from an ontologically distinct and prior exteriority? When Barth is developing his doctrine of creation, based upon his *analogia relationis*, he is emphatic that time and creation are not in contradiction to the eternal Godhead, but 'in Him'.

both God and God's agency constructs another clear-cut and categorical distinction between God and godlessness, God's self-presence and God's utter absence in creation; putting aside, then, two major theological reservations about this account of God *vis-à-vis* the world, Barth is emphatic that the realm in which theological enquiry is either blessed or idle speculation is discursive. It boils down to 'Christian speech [that] must be tested by its conformity to Christ. This conformity is never clear and unambiguous.'[125] So that which dogmatics investigates is nothing other than 'Christian utterance'.[126]

Barth points out that this attention paid to Christian utterance by dogmatics renders theological enquiry a 'self-enclosed circle' of concern,[127] and it is the self-enclosed nature of this concern which means that theology takes itself, rather than *extra ecclesia* concerns, seriously. Dogmatics cannot be other than unintentionally apologetic because of the self-enclosure of Christian utterance. The moment it steps out of this enclosure to speak to those without faith it adopts alien categories. 'Apologetics is an attempt to show by means of thought and speech that the determining principles of philosophy and of historical and natural research at some given point in time certainly do not preclude, even if they do not directly require, the tenets of theology.'[128] But it is at this point that a critical intervention can be made. Discourse is fundamental. It defines the faithfulness of dogmatics and the unfaithfulness of apologetics, while betraying the incomplete and fallible nature of all dogmatic enquiry. But who can police the boundaries of any discourse, Christian or otherwise? Put more precisely, who can ensure the self-enclosure when the constitution of that enclosure is a question of language and representation? Does the belief in the self-

---

[125] Ibid., p. 13.
[126] Ibid., p. 12. Of course this idea of the dogmatic task as investigating what Christians say and do developed into post-liberalism's distinction between first- and second-order discourses. The assumed role of the dogmatician is then both diagnostic (with respect to its investigation into Christian utterance) and regulative (with respect to bringing that utterance into a better understanding of its relation to the Word). It is not only doubtful that such a distinction can be made between practice and theory, it is not only questionable whether the distinction should be made (which privileges academic theologians, or at least sets them as a class apart from others by reinforcing a dualism between practical and dogmatic theology), it is manifest from Barth's own writings how little actual Christian utterances (apart from those of other academic theologians) are taken into consideration. We gain little insight into the actual everyday living of this church with respect to whom and for whom Barth is writing his dogmatics. The question of authority – for whom is this task being undertaken, with what jurisdiction and to whom is it addressed? – hollows Barth's text. We have to turn to Bonhoeffer to correct this theological idealism.
[127] Ibid., p. 42.
[128] *Protestant Theology*, pp. 425–6.

enclosure of certain linguistic practices not presuppose the distinct separation of different discourses and forms of reason? Barth points to as much when he declares: 'There has never been a *philosophia christiana*, for if it was *philosophia* it was not *christiana*, and if it was *christiana* it was not *philosophia*.'[129] The theological discourse or Christian thinking is rendered utterly distinct from philosophical discourse, or historical discourse or scientific discourses of various kinds. But who defines and maintains the autonomy of discourses? Doesn't Barth's description of research conducted on the basis of 'determining principles' sound like the academic rationale for distinct and jealously guarded faculty boundaries in a post-Berlin university? For, and this is the main point I wish to make here, if discourses are not bounded, if discourses exceed institutional, contested and contestable framings, then an apologetics can proceed without the theologian *necessarily* renouncing his or her 'theological function'. Theological discourse can be understood as already participating in wider cultural negotiations and politics. Recently, Kathryn Tanner, in a critical discussion of post-liberalism's Barthian account of the autonomy of discrete language-games (of which Christianity would be one), has observed that contemporary cultural anthropology argues strongly against the corollary of this thesis which suggests 'Christians have a self-sustaining society and culture of their own, which can be marked off rather sharply from others.'[130] Christian utterance then is constructed out of the cultural materials at hand. It is not homogenous but always hybrid, improvised, syncretistic and implicated in networks of association that exceed various forms of institutional, individual or sectarian policing. Furthermore, since Christians are also members of other associations, networks and institutions, what is both internal and external to Christian identity (and its continuing formation) is fluid.

What is significant for my thesis is that *in the very performance of his dialectic*, the very process of the realisation of his thoughts, Barth rethinks and qualifies his dogmatically asserted ideas in a manner that suggests there is a negotiation with the other discourses he has already banned. And this complex form of dialectic is neither Hegelian or Kierkegaardian, but both. For, while Barth suggests Christianity is self-defining and must be so in order to protect itself from the

---

[129] *Church Dogmatics* I.1, p. 6.
[130] *Theories of Culture: A New Agenda for Theology* (Minneapolis: Fortress Press, 1997), p. 96. Interestingly, while the critique of post-liberalism is unabated, all Tanner's references to Barth – the theological spinal chord of post-liberalism – are affirmative.

corrupting external influences of secular society, he himself reveals how interdependent Christian utterance is upon the discourses of other disciplines. His own writing demonstrates how vocabularies and categories are not discrete and how Christianity always defines itself in terms of that which it allies itself to or distinguishes itself from. In defining the dogmatic task he employs categories like 'knowledge', 'consciousness', 'conception', 'understanding', 'formal' and 'ontological-ontic'; he refers continually (though admittedly not depending upon their investigations) to Plato, Aristotle, Descartes, Kant and Heidegger; he situates his task with respect to the older Protestant orthodoxy, to 'historical development of at least the last two or three hundred years'[131] and to the Mediaeval writings of Anselm, Bonaventura and Aquinas; he speaks of 'other sciences' social and natural. Barth's discourse can only proceed to define his particular form of Protestant sectarianism, then, upon the basis of shared vocabularies, categories and reference points that stand 'outside' and other. The very German he writes, while translating these other discourses into his own Christian thesis, is working across other languages like Greek and Latin. His is not a 'self-enclosed' discursive reflection; and neither *can* Christian theology or Christian living be self-enclosed. As the dialectic issues from an understanding of the ongoing and yet to be perfected Word and work of God in the act of reconciling the world to Himself, so Christian theology can neither be completely systematised nor, *a priori*, stake out the limits of what is in and what is outside Christ. Theology *is* a cultural activity; the dialectic it is implicated in is, simultaneously, transhistorical, historical, and material. And here Barth reengages the Hegel in the first edition of *Der Römerbrief* with respect to the Kierkegaard of the second edition.

For it is, I suggest, Hegel more than Schleiermacher who lies behind Barth's categorical assertion that 'There has never been a *philosophia christiana*, for if it was *philosophia* it was not *christiana*, and if it was *christiana* it was not *philosophia*.' For it is Hegel who poses the challenge of the relationship between philosophy and theology, by conflating the dialectic of reason with Trinitarian procession, and rendering all discourse subject to the master discourse of the Absolute Spirit. Thus it followed that 'everything that seems to give theology its particular splendour and special dignity appears to be looked after and honoured by this philosophy in a way comparably better than that achieved by the theologians

---

[131] *Church Dogmatics* I, p. 9.

themselves'.[132] The language of appearance is telling here – Barth (and a number of Hegel scholars before and after him) is not quite certain where Hegel the orthodox Lutheran falls into heterodoxy. But Barth wishes nevertheless to point out that Hegel's work consummates the Prometheanism of human confidence in the act of thinking, in the Enlightenment categories of mind, idea, concept and reason, which he, Barth, views as inimical to both dogmatics and the dialectical encounter with the Word of God which is the contents of dogmatics. It is Hegel then who proclaims the possibility of a *philosophia christiana* – and Aquinas, whom Barth consistently brackets with Hegel. His reading of Aquinas is wrong and his persistent reading of Hegel's dialectical method as 'thesis, antithesis and synthesis', with an emphasis upon consummation of the absolute, owes more to left-wing Hegelians after Hegel (Strauss and Marx, in particular) than to Hegel himself.[133] Nevertheless, his observation that for Hegel 'God is only God in his divine action, revelation, creation, reconciliation, redemption; as an absolute act, *actus purus*'[134] demonstrates how close Hegel (and Aquinas) is to Barth. And, characteristically, in Barth's short but excellent analysis of Hegel in *Protestant Theology in the Nineteenth Century*, the condemnation of the univocity of *Geist* and reason, which reveals Hegel's inability to take seriously either sin or God's freedom with respect to confronting human beings in their sin, is offset by a recognition of unfulfilled and 'great promise'[135] in Hegel's work. 'Doubtless, theology could and can learn something from Hegel as well. It looks as if theology had neglected something here, and certainly it has no

---

[132] *Protestant Theology*, p. 382. This repeats his conclusion about Hegel's speculative trinity in *The Göttingen Dogmatics*, where he observes Hegel's 'replacement of the Christian Trinity by a logical and metaphysical Trinity and by the relegation of the Christian Trinity to the sphere of naïve, symbolical, and inadequate conceptions' (p. 105). But nothing positive about Hegel's thinking is said in this earlier work. By the time the last form of the lectures on the history of nineteenth-century Protestant theology was given (winter 1932–3), Barth is much more appreciative of Hegel's potential.

[133] Elsewhere Barth makes evident that he interpreted the relationship in Hegel's thought between *Sittlichkeit* and *Staat* as the deification of German nationalism that courted the hubris leading to the betrayals by the theological establishment in the First World War. This too is a wrong reading of Hegel's *Elements of the Philosophy of Right*. See Allen Wood, 'Introduction' to H.B. Nisbet's translation (Cambridge: Cambridge University Press, 1991); Paul Lakeland, *The Politics of Salvation: The Hegelian Idea of the State* (Albany: SUNY Press, 1982); Andrew Shanks, *Hegel's Political Theology* (Cambridge: Cambridge University Press, 1991); and my *Cities of God* (London: Routledge, 2001), pp. 137–46. Hegel would in fact concur with Barth's own judgement (albeit with a different doctrine of the Trinity): 'the State as such belongs originally and ultimately to Jesus Christ' ('Church and State' in *Community, State and Church*, trs. A.M. Hall et al. (Gloucester, Mass.: Peter Smith, 1968), p. 118).

[134] *Protestant Theology*, p. 385.

[135] Ibid., p. 407.

occasion to assume an attitude of alarm and hostility to any renaissance of Hegel that might come about.'[136]

When we examine what it is that remains promising for Barth in Hegel it is in fact the Trinitarian-informed reflexivity of his dialectic. Though Barth chides him for his unsatisfactory doctrine of the Trinity, he applauds Hegel's reminder 'of the possibility that the truth might be history' and that theology's knowledge 'was only possible in the form of a strict obedience to the self-movement of truth, and therefore as a knowledge which was itself moved'.[137] Furthermore, in Hegel's commitment to theology as a material practice participating in the unfolding of a history of God's own self-unveiling, theology is reminded 'of the contradictory nature of its own knowledge'. For 'Hegel, with his concept of mind, must wittingly or unwittingly have been thinking of the Creator of heaven and earth, the Lord over nature and spirit, precisely by virtue of the unity and opposition of *dictum* and *contra-dictum*, in which Hegel had the spirit conceiving itself and being real.'[138]

There are three things, then, that Barth recognises of theological value in Hegel: history as a material process informed by God; theology as a discursive practice participating in what he will elsewhere conceive as '[t]he covenant of grace [a]s *the* theme of history';[139] and the need for theology to be reflexive about that practice because the words and works of human beings can never be identical to the unveiling of God.

The question remains concerning the extent to which Barth integrated these insights into his own theological thinking – certainly not when the lecture on Hegel was given in the early 1930s. But there is a hint of what Barth will develop as he and the Christian Church stood watching the world turn dark on the eve of the Second World War. For in what appears almost to be an aside in the Introduction to the *Church Dogmatics*, he observes: 'The separate existence of theology signifies the emergency measure on which the Church has had to resolve in view of the actual refusal of the other sciences in this respect.'[140] The observation points not to a pragmatism, but to the temporal specificity about theology. Its 'separate existence' is a response to a culture and a historical moment when the

---

[136] Ibid., p. 403.
[137] Ibid, pp. 401–2.
[138] Ibid., p. 402.
[139] *Church Dogmatics*, III.1, p. 60.
[140] Ibid., I.1, p. 7.

theological is despised.[141] As with his view of discrete discourses for discrete disciplines, what this implies is that the dogmatic in opposition to the apologetic task of theology becomes a cultural production (and a cultural producer in its own right); one that *necessarily*, on Barth's own axioms, 'stands in need of criticism, or correction, of critical amendment and repetition'. The necessity comes about when Christian theology and therefore the task of the Christian theologian is elsewhere 'implicated in what the Church has had to resolve in view of the actual refusal of the other sciences in this respect'.[142] The necessity comes about when Christian theology and therefore the task of the Christian theologian are implicated in a different kind of cultural productivity. This theology was already being written elsewhere, had Barth been able to transcend his own German and evangelical mind-set.[143] Other people were already writing Christian theology within cultural contexts not dominated by a perceived hostility to Christian utterance. The necessity to interrupt also comes about because, for all his dogmatic tone and categorical assertions, Barth's Christian utterance is also, as we have seen, human, fallible and fallen.

By the end of the Second World War – when Barth was completing the opening volume of his doctrine of creation – we fund him commenting on 'history, the theological practice of participating in that history and the need to consider more carefully that biblical witnesses speak as men, and not as angels or gods'.[144] This sentiment articulates a different reflection and a new kind of dialectic.

Thus we have to reckon on their part with all kinds of human factors, with their individual and general capacities of perception and expression, with their personal views and style, as determined by age and environment, and of course with the limitations and deficiencies of these conditioning factors – in this case the limitations of their imagination. [145]

---

[141] In his study *Christ and Culture*, H. Richard Niebuhr points out the association between the Christian response to the cultural and the cultural response to Christianity. He does not develop this insight in any depth, but, significantly, the first of his five models for the 'enduring problem' of Christian theology with respect to its cultural context, Christ against culture, first arises because of the persecution of the Church. This defines the Church as a new creation in Christ totally separate from what Barth called 'world-occurrences', and a Christology emphasising Christ as King, Lord, and Lawgiver. See *Christ and Culture* (New York: Harper & Row, 1951), pp. 45–115.

[142] *Church Dogmatics*, I.1, p. 7.

[143] In his own cultural context we have already witnessed how the debates between Barth, Bultmann, Przywara, Ritschl, Tillich and Brunner made his own theology possible. If we go further afield we find the development of *nouvelle théologie* among certain French Jesuits and Dominicans. Von Balthasar bridges the two theological worlds.

[144] *Church Dogmatics*, III.1, p. 93.

[145] Ibid.

Barth is specifically examining the creation stories as the Word of God, but in his development of the category of 'saga' and his recognition of the different genres of Biblical writing, he speaks more generally of Biblical witness. The commitment to a God who does not transcend history but informs it at every point, to an account of eternity as the origin and telos of the history, not its erasure, leads to an understanding of Biblical discourse as culturally and psychologically 'determined'. I am not going to follow the psychological trajectory of Barth's thinking as such, only comment that 'personal views', expression and style – and, some would even say, individual levels and direction of perception – cannot be divorced from the 'conditioning factors' of 'age and environment'. But in my concern to assess the possibility for apologetics that begin from a Christian theological standpoint, this recognition of the cultural embeddedness of Biblical discourse is an important move towards seeing that theological discourse cannot be simply self-referring and 'overheard' by other publics. Biblical witness borrows materials and forms of representation, and refigures them for its own purposes. The accounts it furnishes of things prehistorical or historical involve cultural negotiations, 'textual relationships'[146] and human knowing that 'is not exhausted by the ability to perceive and comprehend'.[147] Barth even employs Schleiermacher's hermeneutical category of 'divination' to speak of the way the writer has to discern the vision of the true historical emergence (the operation of God in creation) that preceded the 'historical' events so cherished by professional historians and historicism. The questions of 'depiction and narration' issue not from discussing the abstractions of time and eternity, but the covenant of grace that *is* the theme of God's history. Time is in God, and so though the truth of God's Word is eternal, it is also highly specific. 'Creation is not a timeless truth … there are no timeless truths; truth has a concretely temporal character.'[148]

Of course, Barth's attention here is to Biblical witness and Biblical writing. But since this witness and writing must be the source and prototype for all Christian witness and writing, then, although Barth says little about the cultural and historical embeddedness of his own discourse, this must follow. In fact, again almost as an aside, he writes: '[C]oncerning the ground and being of man and his world, we are referred to our own metaphysical and scientific genius, or to our own powers in the

[146] Ibid., p. 87.
[147] Ibid., p. 91.
[148] Ibid., p. 60.

construction of myth or saga.'[149] Christian theology tells God's story in the place where any theologian finds himself or herself situated. Such story-telling cannot but rehearse and refigure the language, ideologies, cultural assumptions, fears, guilts and dreams of its times. These are de Certeau's 'silent laws' that organise the space for its production. The theologian attempts to read the signs of those times in terms of the continuing covenant of grace, but in reading those signs cultural negotiations are set in operation such that the theologian's discourse is itself a sign of the times. Theological discourse is necessarily involved in the wider cultural dissemin-ation and exchange of signs. Other people will be telling the story of what is from where they are and possibly using some of the same materials and reference points. And while Christian theology (like the Biblical witnesses) speaks of the 'genuinely historical'[150] relationship between God and human beings – such that cultural relativism is not a question raised – Christian theology cannot transcend the historical and cultural determination and conditions. If it cannot transcend them then it equally cannot distil for itself some pure dogmatic discourse.

Christian theology is, then, implicated in cultural negotiations, and to that extent is always already engaged in an ongoing apologetics. Barth, it seems, moves towards an integration of what Beintker (after Henning Schroer) termed the 'complementary' and 'supplementary' of paradox. Barth forges a theological method that brings together, in a creative tension, the synchronic dialectic of Kierkegaard's 'infinite qualitative difference' with the diachronic dialectic of Hegel's 'possibility that the truth might be history' and that theology's knowledge 'was only possible in the form of a strict obedience to the self-movement of truth, and therefore as a knowledge which was itself moved'. The synchronic and the diachronic can supplement each other in the work of the theologian with respect to the world.

Allow me now to pursue this further by referring back to the third of Barth's affirmations about Hegel's project: the need for theology to be reflexive about that practice because the words and works of human beings can never be identical to the unveiling of God. Beintker characterises the 'complementary' use of paradox as involving an asymmetrical relationship between thesis and antithesis, such that the reconciliation or sublation proceeds through the absorption of the latter by the former. This parallels the asymmetrical relation in Hegel's thinking between the in-itself and the

---

[149] Ibid., p. 61.
[150] Ibid., p. 66.

for-itself such that, in the dialectical process of being with oneself in an other, then the other is integrated into one's own projects. In this way the other fulfils and perfects the same; it becomes part of the free activity of the subject. Barth's description of the dialectic of sexual difference bears something of this Hegelian model.[151] But since theology moves between Christ's Word and a cultural situation in which '[t]here are no forms, events or relationships . . . unmistakeably confused by man in which the goodness of what God has created is not also effective and visible, the only question being how this is so'[152] – then it has no unqualified access to that asymmetrical relationship. And, if this is so, it may not so easily take up the 'complementary' use of paradox that judges the other only to have value with respect to the same. It cannot judge and subjugate the world to its own discourse. For theology cannot leave out the possibility that in this cultural other God is at work, and engagement with this other may mean it is not subordinated but allowed to challenge radically the theological project. Cultural negotiation must run such a risk – the risk of being disrupted. The 'supplementary' use of paradox allows for what George Hunsinger has recently termed 'disruptive grace'.[153] But the 'supplementary' use of paradox is also asymmetrical, and it is at this point that the theologian needs to cultivate a healthy agnosticism with respect to what he or she knows. Space must be allowed, on the basis of what theology understands about itself and the God with whom it has to do, for the other to speak. This enables the cultural engagement of Christian apologetics to be a negotiated engagement. But the product of this negotiated engagement will inevitably be syncretistic.

The last reference to Hegel, whose dialectic I am suggesting opens Barth's theology to the possibility of apologetics as Christian cultural negotiation, comes in *Church Dogmatics* IV.3/2 and the development of his doctrine of reconciliation. Here Barth's dialectical structure is firmly in place in a discussion of the interface between *Hominum confusione et Dei providentia* in the call of Christ to all humanity. But he seeks a third way beyond the antithesis, and this is where he introduces Hegel. Again it is the Hegel of the thesis–antithesis–synthesis – Hegel reduced to a formula that can then be haughtily dismissed. What Barth wishes to avoid is a *tertium quid.* So what he offers 'the Christian community as *it is required* to go

---

[151] See my *Cities of God*, pp. 183–202.
[152] *Church Dogmatics* VI.3, p. 698.
[153] *Disruptive Grace: Studies in the Theology of Karl Barth* (Grand Rapids: William B. Eerdmans, 2000).

beyond that twofold view' (emphasis mine) is the 'reality and truth of the grace of God addressed to the world in Jesus Christ'.[154] What this amounts to is that the Christian community is enjoined to speak to the world about Jesus Christ while recognising that, on the one hand, Jesus Christ 'is not a concept which man can think out for himself, which he can define with more or less precision, and with the help of which he can then display his mastery over . . . the problem of this antithesis',[155] and, on the other, that '[w]e think and speak like poor heathen, no matter how earnestly we may imagine that we think and speak of it [the grace of God addressed to the world in Jesus Christ].'[156] Which leaves us where exactly? With the knowledge of the *diastasis*, concerning which there is no 'real synthesis', and yet . . . the fallible Christian community as the bearer of and the witness to a better hope testifies to the work and Work of God as a 'new thing in relation to that contradiction'.[157] It not only testifies, but in testifying seeks to participate in the unfolding of that new world; and so it attempts to perform and produce that 'new thing'.

To take this idea further, the Christian community's practices of transformative hope, executed in the name of Christ, are disseminated through the world because the living community of the Church is implicated in other 'communities' and practices. Those characterised as the community of the Church participate in the operations of other desires that are not *prima facie* theological, only *de jure* theological because Jesus Christ is both the 'loftiest, most luminous transcendence' and 'heard in the deepest, darkest immanence'.[158] These members of the community of the Church are also members of other forms of fellowship, other bodies – industrial, commercial, agricultural, political, sporting, domestic. We recall that Barth too was a member of a political party. To return to a moment mentioned earlier in the first edition of *Die Römerbrief*, it is because Christians *are* involved in 'monarchism, capitalism, militarism, patriotism and liberalism', among other things (things working against the hegemony of such ideologies), that the work and words of the living community extend out into the 'deepest, darkest immanence' in their testimony to and performance of a 'new thing'. This movement in, through and beyond the Church, in through and beyond the Church's endless cultural negotiations,

---

[154] *Church Dogmatics* IV.3/2, p. 706.
[155] Ibid.
[156] Ibid., p. 707.
[157] Ibid., p. 708.
[158] 'The Humanity of God', p. 46.

is not a dialectic of progress or growth, because it moves between mysteries and confusion, but it is nevertheless teleologically driven. It is, then, a positive dialectic tracing and performing what Hegel called 'the march of God in the world'.[159] We may not like Hegel's metaphor, but I suggest upon this basis an apologetics, no longer saddled with defining itself against *Kulturprotestantismus*, can proceed: reading and producing the signs of the times, and negotiating a role in defining public truth; taking its own historical and cultural embeddedness with all theological seriousness. Theology, like de Certeau's account of history, is something 'made'; it is a cultural operation, where both the 'cultural' and the 'operation' are understood as transits of grace.

But just on the edge of finding Barth and the development and reception of his theological project all disappearing into the cultural politics of his time and ours, we need to reintroduce that transcultural and transhistorical position from where theology proceeds. For the Christian theologian, who we can now take not simply as the professional dogmatician, but anyone living in Christ, is first a follower, a disciple, and in being a disciple acts and speaks from both a commission and a command: 'Go forth [*poreuthentes*] therefore and make [*matheteusate*] all nations my disciples; baptise [*baptizontes*] them everywhere in the name of the Father and the Son and the Holy Spirit, and teach [*didaskontes*] them to observe all that I have commanded [*eneteilamen*] you. And behold I am [*ego . . . eimi*] with you always' (Matthew 28.19–20). These are imperatives issued in the name of God the I AM. They are not only stirring and challenging words, they are dangerous words – as a continuing history of colonialism, zealotry, hatred, prejudice and violence, in various forms from various faiths (sacred and secular), testifies. And yet we cannot explain away either this imperatival commission or the Christian theological vision that informs it. By that I mean, and with this return to an early essay by Barth on the relationship between theology and culture, 'culture is the promise originally given to man [*sic*] of what he is to become'.[160] In this essay, from 1926, there is a recognition that '[n]o Christian theologian (alas!) with his preaching and scholarship will ever visibly walk this earth as "Angelic Doctor" (*doctor angelicus*) free, for example, of *all* human philosophy. There is no Christian love which cannot be justly labelled as sublimated, highly refined eroticism. No Christian temporal prophecy

---

[159] *Elements of the Philosophy of Right*, tr. H.B. Nisbet (Cambridge: Cambridge University Press, 1991), p. 279.
[160] 'Church and Culture' in *Theology and the Church*, p. 341.

can keep itself from measuring by the actual political and economic standards of its own age. Throughout its whole course, the Church swims along in the stream of culture.'[161] Nevertheless, there is also a twofold understanding of theology's relationship to culture. On the one hand, it is critical because the cultural is an expression and a development of the fallen, the foundry in which so many idols and fetishes are cast to keep human beings from coming to terms with the violence, anger and alienation being perpetrated. On the other, it is the only place in which the human creature can come to a recognition of a more glorious possibility. 'The term *culture* connotes exactly that promise to man: fulfilment, unity, wholeness within his sphere as creature, as man, exactly as God in his sphere in fullness, wholeness, Lord over nature and spirit, Creator of heaven *and* earth.'[162] As that eschatologically informed sphere, theology speaks to and in and through the cultural of a promised and operative reconciliation; a resurrection life not just beyond this world in some *post-mortem* realm but in this world as this world's concealed [*mysterion*] reality. The speaking of such a transfiguring hope, which issues from an equally fundamental judgement, is a speaking in the name of, a working in and out of faith to faith. It is this working that locks the theologian into the operation of the eternal in the temporal, which is at the eschatological heart of participation in Christ.

CONCLUSION

From our analysis of the discursive practices of Karl Barth what then can we say about the place from which theology speaks? Four theological points are foundational for our further investigation:

(1) Christians can speak theologically at all only on the basis of the revelation of God in Jesus Christ. If there is more to our folly than a Romantic façade it can only have to do with that which has been revealed through Christ to the Church. Our human words, as testimony to that which we have received, are coming to understand, and hold to be true, must issue from a relationship to the Word of God. If they do not issue from such a relationship, if they are not, in the testimony they give, both doxological and obedient to the call to speak, then they are vain, dangerous and seductive simulacra. But as all our knowledge is culturally mediated,

---

[161] Ibid., p. 351.
[162] Ibid., p. 343.

then the question will always remain as to how we ever know the extent of our words' affinity to the Logos incarnate.

(2) The Scriptures, in witnessing to the revelation of Jesus Christ, participate in that relationship which is both doxological and vocational. Their witness presents the revelation as founding the Church, but it also presents the scope of God's desire as exceeding that foundation. God became incarnate that the world might be saved, not that the Church might be founded. The Church is a means for the dissemination of the revelation and the ongoing cultivation of those who will be the disseminators. But the question always remains open, as Augustine knew, concerning who are the citizens of the city of God, how they are identified and thus who constitutes the Church.

(3) The incarnation testifies to a subsumption of the human by the divine; a subsumption that could only come about because of an affinity between the uncreated creator and human creatures. There must be that in God which makes the incarnation of the Son possible, rather than arbitrary. For to be made in the image of God is to exist as that image in the mind of God. Creation itself, while not God, is an expression of the creative power, goodness and imagination of the Godhead. But, within the created orders, the affinity between human beings and God is only known analogically by faith, and the extent of that knowledge is in proportion to a certain anagogical disciplining of the soul. There is an ascent toward, or an intensification with respect to, wisdom; though each person so anagogically disciplined loses (proportionally) the knowledge of such ascent or intensification. It is simply a matter of becoming smaller.

(4) 'Speaking in the name of' is related to being made 'in the image of' God. That is, our speaking is only possible at all insofar as we are made in the image of God. I will develop this more in the next section of the essay when I discuss the hermeneutical nature of being human. Here it is important to emphasise the theological and anthropological bases for that hermeneutical activity: we are, as human creatures, made to be mediators and made to be reflectors upon not only that which we mediate (knowledge of God), but that which constitutes our mediations.

So conceived, the answer to the question 'From where does theology speak?' is: from Christ. From Christ and of Christ and in Christ theology speaks *to* the cultural of that which the cultural displaces for the most part, even while simultaneously haunted by the absence it engenders and maintains. The Freudian term for this cultural activity is *Verdrängung*[163] or

---

[163] See Sigmund Freud, *Die Traumdeutung*. Stidenausgabe. Band II (Frankfurt am Main: Fischer Verlag, 2001).

'denial' – it expressively denies that about which the soul dreams: redemption. In a sense what theology then aspires to facilitate (though not on the basis of its own powers and integrities, but only on the basis of prayer and obedience[164]), is an interpretation by Christ of culture's own dreaming. Theology's task with respect to culture is to allow for that searching by Christ, in Christ, of the cultural imaginary. This is a reading of the signs of the times not just for the Church (that it might position itself better in its imperatival commission to preach, make, baptise and teach) but for the times themselves, so that the culture itself might begin to understand its own aspirations and limitations, the hope for which it longs and the depths of fallenness into which it continually commits itself.

In the work in and out and towards faith theology must be rooted in the Church, but at its open western door – on the threshold between the world and the east-facing altar; as ready to serve in one direction as in the other. The Christian theologian stands at that place between the breaking of the bread and its distribution throughout the world. As the Christian theologian looks back into the church, the order of life is presented there – the baptism font, the chancel steps where confirmation, marriage and burial rites are spoken, the altar where the mass is celebrated and shared. As the Christian theologian looks out into the world, the serried ranks of city life are presented there – so many high points and squalid allies, neon-lights, plasma-screens, crowded tenements, seductions, excitements and destitutions. This place is 'between' and as such we would have to challenge two alternative understandings of the Christian theologian currently conceived. The first is that of Jean-Luc Marion, in his book *God Without Being*, where the theologian *par excellence* is the bishop.[165] The second is that model presented by certain post-liberals and Protestant neo-orthodox where the theologian is a figure in the church who provides a second-order examination of the grammar of the faith with respect to that church. I have dealt with the latter in footnote 126. We can recognise from the 'between' that theology cannot speak simply from within the church (as Marion suggests). This place 'between' is the place of prayer; prayer as simultaneously worship and intercession, confession and petition, doxology and yearning for the coming of the Kingdom. This yearning has depth – of experience, of knowledge, of passion – only in so far as it engages with the possibility of

---

[164] That is, on a certain *Gelassenheit* or 'letting-go' such that an education (*ex-ducere*) can proceed from a reception actively desired and earnestly sought.

[165] *God Without Being: Hors-Texte*, tr. Thomas Carlson (Chicago: University of Chicago Press, 1991), pp. 139–58.

the impossible. The relational activity experienced in the 'between' is prayer. The place of prayer is the place where the material and the spiritual inform each other, the place where the universal cannot be separated from the particular, where the eternal economics of divine givenness operate within history – as providence, as grace. Prayer is the realisation of a place in Christ. Only in Christ is it prayer. And prayer is not a safe place, in the sense that it is not a stable place. Prayer requires a surrender of control. This is not necessarily a surrender of reason, as it is not a surrender of consciousness. It is a surrender, perhaps more precisely a releasing of the body, to the jurisdiction of the soul. Not that the soul is separate from the body, it is the body's inner form as Aristotle and Aquinas both understood. But prayer is where the labour(ing) begins. This is the kitchen, the work-place, for the theologian's cultural negotiation. For prayer is the place where relation is known. And relation, as we will see in the next section of this essay, is key to the question which now offers itself: if theology speaks from a place that is profoundly encultured, if the practice of theology is always then apologetic, then what are the processes by which cultures and, thereby, the public perceptions of reality change such that the discursive and encultured practices of theology effect these transformations?

CHAPTER 2

The governing question II: how do cultures change?

Having demonstrated in the last section how profoundly embedded theological discourse is in its cultural context, in this second section I wish to examine what the processes are by which cultures and, thereby, the public perception of reality change. If, with Marx and against him, the Christian vision is not simply to interpret the world but to work for its transformation, then how are the major knowledges of any particular time and place produced and what causes them to change? Why is it, for example, that the belief in angels was widely held in Mediaeval Christendom, widely rejected in Enlightenment's modernity, and currently regaining ground in what, as shorthand, we might term postmodernity? Another question lurks behind my initial one: how does the theological project (Christian, in this instance) become a transformative public practice with respect to the cultures that contextualise it? In *Cities of God*, I drew upon the critical reflections of anthropologists like Clifford Geertz, Sherry Ortner, James W. Fernandez, Victor Turner and Homi Bhabha in order to develop a theological approach to reading the signs of the times.[1] But here what I wish to provide is not tools for the description of a culture or the recognition of an important cultural axis. Rather, I wish to examine the relationship between the critical interpretation, production and the transformation of cultures. To some extent, such an examination would be just another way of looking at the operations and productions in which Barth's work was and still is situated. This section, therefore, supplements the analysis of the last section, but it focuses on the poetics, that is, the systems and structures through and by which critical interpretation takes place, and the resulting cultural *poiesis*, that is, the modifications that subsequently occur.

---

[1] *Cities of God*, pp. 22–3.

CULTURAL HERMENEUTICS AND PHILOSOPHICAL
HERMENEUTICS

A distinction has often been drawn between hermeneutics, on the one hand, and critical theory, on the other, such that Foucault can spurn any interest in hermeneutics in developing his mode of archaeological and genealogical critique.[2] The central concerns of critical theory are power, domination, ideology and the production of illusion; whereas the central concerns of hermeneutics are reference, sense and meaning. In the past I have reiterated such a distinction.[3] But the critical moment is only made possible on the basis of a prior act of interpretation. There can be no critical intervention with respect to a discursive practice without first an evaluation of what is being communicated, inferred, presupposed, etc., in that practice. These evaluations embody modes of interpretation – they practise a hermeneutics even if they do not go on to systematise those modes of interpretation and so develop a theory of interpretation. To insist upon a radical separation between hermeneutics and critical theory – as Foucault does – can make the critical intervention appear to be a dogmatic truth-claim, a truth-claim that cannot itself be negotiated, criticised, refined, denied. The very fact that critique can foster a range of further critical responses is founded upon the interpretative act that necessarily precedes the critical one.

It seems to me, in order to undertake the cultural analysis I propose I need to combine a procedural, interpretative task (hermeneutics) with a critical, reflexive task (critique). That is, to approach interpretation as a political engagement that will affect the myriad symbolic exchanges that take place within, constitute and modify cultures. As a political engagement interpretation is a move in a cultural power-game concerned with making judgements about what is true, what is believable, and what cannot be credited. What this double task underlines is that one never simply *begins with* a cultural hermeneutics (reading the signs of the times) without already being *implicated in* a cultural production. Being *implicated in* recognises that there is no position outside of cultural production. Interpretation does not begin *in vacuo*. Furthermore, the mode of the interpretation will be governed by what modes of interpretation are (a) available and (b) recognised as legitimate. The very way we interpret

---

[2] See for, example, his remarks in the Preface to *Birth of the Clinic: An Archaeology of Medical Perception*, tr. A.M. Sheridan Smith (New York: Vintage, 1975), pp. xvi–xvii.
[3] See the Introduction to my *Theology and Contemporary Critical Theory*, 2nd edn (Basingstoke: Macmillan, 2000), pp. ix–xx.

is, then, part of the cultural situation in which the production takes place. In fact, I will suggest that the micro-modifications that take place in any culture, causing it to shift in time, are the results of the endless relays of interpretative acts. Cultural change proceeds via cultural hermeneutics. Critique operates within these micro-modifications. Critique is consti- tuted in the interpretative act. Although there are degrees of critique (degrees of how critical for a given position the critique is – up to the complete undermining of that position), any critique is an internal reflec- tion within an ongoing process of transformation that issues from/in reading, citing, reciting and interpreting various cultural activities. The end product of cultural interpretation is not then 'meaning' in any abstract, dogmatic sense. Rather, the end product is twofold. First, semantically, there is the continuation of the production of beliefs, concepts and values constituting a culture; a cultural inflection or modification occurring through the various processes of engagement. And second, socially, there is formation – the formation of persons and their self-understanding and self-evaluation.

Cultural production, then, involves the formation of both knowledges and subjectivities. It implicates both the interpreter – the complexity of whose position will become evident shortly – and that which is being interpreted. Avoiding the language of subject and object, the modifications occur with respect to both 'positions' and the hundred and one other 'positions' that constitute the depth of each of these 'positions'.[4] Furthermore, since there is no place from which one could assess all possible modifications that can occur within any culture, the interpretative event is open-ended and critical. Here I concur with Gadamer's notion of the moving horizons, although Gadamer is less concerned than I with the critical engagement between horizons – less concerned, that is, with cultural politics or the power-brokering involved in making interpretative

[4] The establishment of the dichotomy between subject and object presupposes a world of discrete and autonomous phenomena. This leads to a view of relation as both arbitrary and extrinsic. It leads to the hyper-individualism needed to support the metaphysics of empiricism and monopoly capitalism. The world-view of cultural hermeneutics would hold such an account of the individual person and an account of knowing based upon the input of sense perception as incoherent. The language of 'positions' and 'position-takings' [*prises de position*] owes much to Bourdieu's understanding of how a 'position' is a space for creative work, for agency. The field of cultural production is therefore a dynamic one: '[A] field of possible forces presents itself to each agent as a *space of possibles* which is defined in the relationship between the structure of average chances of access to different positions ... and the dispositions of each agent' (*The Field of Cultural Production*, p. 64). We examined this relationship between establishing oneself in a field of intellectual enquiry and the disposition of the agent, or the *habitus*, in the first part of the last section.

judgements. This is because the universal operation of hermeneutics that his work announces deals with the interpretation of history and literature, not material practices.[5] He works within a tradition of Romantic philosophical hermeneutics from Schleiermacher to Dilthey to Husserl that is orientated towards examining consciousness and is bound to a certain metaphysics of subjectivity.[6] His project of philosophical hermeneutics investigated the movement of truth through historical traditions as they operated over time, but it never critically engaged the idealism and ideology of the tradition upon which it reflected. However, as Richard Bernstein has pointed out in pressing Gadamer's work beyond philosophic hermeneutics, Gadamer's appeal to Aristotle and recognition that there are three elements involved in hermeneutics (understanding, interpretation and application) demonstrate that '[p]hilosophic hermeneutics is the heir to th[e] tradition of practical philosophy.'[7] Practical philosophy, as Aristotle understood and practised it, was concerned with ethics, politics, *poiesis*, rhetoric and cosmology as well as metaphysics. In a letter to Richard Bernstein Gadamer concedes 'how much I am caught up, one might say, in the tradition of German Romantic and post-Romantic philosophy. I live, as it were, in a closed horizon of problems and lines of questioning, which still understands itself to be philosophical, and which recognizes neither a social-scientific nor a sceptical question of philosophy itself.'[8] Nevertheless, the hermeneutics central to what he terms the 'analysis of effective-historical consciousness' – the analysis of traditions and their transmission – exceeds a narrowly philosophical remit. In the same letter to Richard Bernstein, then, we find that Gadamer also concedes, 'Our experience of things, indeed even of everyday life, of the modes of production, and yes,

---

[5] The practice of writing history and the practice of writing literature *can* be examined materially – as Bourdieu and Michel de Certeau demonstrate. But Gadamer's work does not undertake such an examination.

[6] I would not include Heidegger in this tradition of Romantic hermeneutics. *Dasein* is not reducible to subjectivity, and his phenomenological analysis of the way *Dasein* comes upon itself in the midst of its historical being – *Dasein* as a 'thrown-projection' – is the extent to which Heidegger rejects Marburg neo-Kantianism and the transcendental ego. This ontological analysis is deepened in Heidegger's later work with respect to his examination of the 'thing', the clearing and *Ereignis*. In fact, Bourdieu's concept of *habitus* could be interestingly compared to Heidegger's account in his early work of *Dasein*'s 'disposition' (*Befindlichkeit*). (He has in fact written a book on Heidegger: *The Political Ontology of Martin Heidegger* (Oxford: Polity Press, 1991).) Nevertheless it remains true that Gadamer is both profoundly influenced by Heidegger – to the extent that some have viewed his hermeneutical project as an adaptation of Heidegger's thinking – while yet remaining bound to concepts of 'consciousness', rather than embodiment.

[7] *Beyond Objectivism and Relativism* (Oxford: Blackwell, 1983), p. 40.

[8] Ibid., p. 262.

also of the sphere of our vital concerns, are one and all hermeneutic [*ist eine hermeneutische*].'[9] Cultural hermeneutics is related to practical philosophy. Ontological and epistemological categories are understood to emerge from and issue into various forms of action, wedding practical wisdom (*phronesis*) with the learned skill of handling language (*techne*) and habits of everyday living (*praxis*). The activity of interpretation is conducted alongside and with respect to other people and the many cultural forms that are the products of the interaction between people (institutions, tools, art-forms). I am agreeing here with some remarks critiquing idealism by Dietrich Bonhoeffer: 'Concrete personal being arises from the concrete situation... On the epistemological and metaphysical path one never reaches the reality of the other.'[10] Cultural hermeneutics is concerned with the concrete reality of others. The ethical nature of such a project – in contradistinction to idealism – becomes evident when we recall another statement by Bonhoeffer: 'From the ethical standpoint man is not "immediately" mind by and in himself, but only in responsibility to "another".'[11] Recognising that relations to others are not the properties of individual people, but ontologically prior to all understanding of individuality, cultural hermeneutics examines that relational responsibility to another. It is in this way that the practice of cultural hermeneutics announces a cultural ethics; and I will be developing such a notion in the final section of this essay. Responsibility requires (as Hegel understood) skills in reflection and self-reflection, and so remains indebted to idealism. But to be responsible is more that just a mental activity. It is also, simultaneously, a somatic activity in which something is received and experienced as something of import (in the various connotations of that word). As Charles Taylor has demonstrated, 'our feelings incorporate a certain articulation of our situation, that is, they presuppose that we characterize our situation in certain terms'.[12] In the reception, then, there is also a specific appropriation that is dependent upon the linguistic context in which the recipient is situated. The mental acts of reflection and self-reflection themselves, as again Hegel showed us, are localised achievements. This linguistic context is constituted in and through other such achievements, the practices they embody and forms of *habitus* they create. There is, then, an economy of 'response' that crosses over and integrates in any such

---

[9] Ibid., p. 263.
[10] *Sanctorum Communio*, tr. R. Gregor Smith (London: Collins, 1963), pp. 31–5.
[11] Ibid., p. 32.
[12] *Human Agency and Language: Philosophical Papers*. Part I (Cambridge: Cambridge University Press, 1985), pp. 63–4.

appropriation the different domains of the epistemological, the ontological, the linguistic, the cultural, the political and the ethical. Operating at the borders of embodied and visceral self-reflection, embodied and visceral communication between self and other, self, other and all the narratives that situate that self and that other, economies of response render infinitely complex the subject–object dichotomy of philosophical hermeneutics (as Gadamer conceives it). As such, cultural hermeneutics views the subject – object dichotomy as false and reductive.[13] But cultural hermeneutics does not lie 'beyond' philosophical hermeneutics, rather it deconstructs (in both a positive and critical sense of that term) and extends such a hermeneutical project (and the dialogical anthropology that supports it) into the mode of production concerned with the practices of our everyday life. Furthermore, in hanging much more loosely to Gadamer's language of ontology and the emphasis upon recognition, conversation, dialogue and mutual respect that facilitates the event of understanding that it is the purpose of a philosophical hermeneutics to elucidate – then cultural hermeneutics can pay attention not to the fusion of, but the critical engagement between, horizons. We can retain something of Gadamer's understanding of 'horizons', which he expressly relates to 'situations', standpoints that limit the possibility of vision and vantage points.[14] In fact, as will become evident shortly, providing thicker accounts of what constitute both a 'situation' and a 'standpoint' is important for the development of cultural hermeneutics. I will also retain something of Gadamer's account (after Hegel's) of recognition (*Anerkennung*[15]), developing it with respect to those 'economies of response'. But there remains, in Gadamer, not only too little

---

[13] The movement (with all that movement involves of modification, transformation and transferral) that is touch – and desire is inseparable from touch – perhaps provides the best analogy for what is involved in any economy of response. For the fundamental role touch plays in relational knowledge and the economy of response, see the theological discussions of touch in Aristotle and Aquinas in 'Truth and Touch' in John Milbank and Catherine Pickstock, *Truth in Aquinas* (London: Routledge, 2001), pp. 60–87 and Graham Ward, 'Eros and the Church' and 'The Schizoid Christ' in his *Christ and Culture* (Oxford: Blackwell, 2005).

[14] *Truth and Method*, trs Garret Barden and William G. Dörpel (London: Sheed and Ward, 1975), p. 269.

[15] The German word is highly suggestive. It is not *Erkennung* – which can also be translated 'recognition' – but *Anerkennung*. For Hegel it is a positive evaluation of a position, but the prefix *an-* , as the celebrated *Wörterbuch* (Leipzig: Verlag von S. Hirzel, 1854) of Jakob and Wilhelm Grimm reminds us, suggests proximity to, a nearness which still implies a distance. There is, then, something of apperception (glimpsing a knowledge of what is valuable rather than grasping that knowledge as a possession) about the contents of what is recognised. An agnosticism persists, a lack of precise identification – and I will demonstrate towards the end of this section how this structural 'lack' is fundamental to the ongoing process of any pro-ject and key to the transformation of what I term the cultural imaginary.

analysis of the power of certain situations, standpoints and traditions with respect to other situations, standpoints and positions,[16] but also too little appreciation that the fusion of horizons involves a certain passivity of the text, history or tradition such that there can be an 'appropriation'. In brief, Gadamer not only fails to examine the operations of power with respect to an engagement between horizons, he fails to recognise a power involved in the moment of 'appropriation' that is central to his philosophical account of interpretative understanding. Cultural hermeneutics, then, makes more of the engagement, even contestation, between horizons. As Bourdieu's work has enabled us to recognise, the different cultural discourses, and therefore the different forms of interpretative reasoning, are not situated upon a level playing field and they have on deposit various forms and different amounts of capital. But then, it is the claim of cultural hermeneutics that this engagement (which is as inescapably political as it is interpretative) lies at the heart of the transformative processes within cultures. Furthermore, no one can predict or police the directions the critique is to take or the responses to it that are, themselves, further acts of cultural interpretation.

If the argument above holds then certain corollaries follow. To begin with, cultural hermeneutics can never be an exact science, and although certain general statements can be made on the basis of local analyses, what is general about the statements will be found to be the *manner* in which such statements are made. That is: the way in which they are announced makes them general. They are not normative. They are not general on the basis of the law or principle they tender. For the most part general observations will be found to be only further instances of what Donna Haraway calls 'situated knowledges'. Nietzsche is vindicated: '[T]he *permanent* exists only thanks to our coarse organs which reduce and lead things to shared premises of vulgarity, whereas nothing exists *in this form*. A tree is a new thing at every instant: we affirm the *form* because we do not seize the subtlety of the absolute moment.'[17] Putting aside Nietzsche's irony of the contingent moment being 'absolute', general observations possess a rhetorical form that may suggest they are articulating the grammar of what can be known, but a statement is a production and the 'knowledge' asserted is a product. Even the investigation into the

---

[16] Bernstein, *Beyond Objectivism and Relativism*, p. 156.
[17] Quoted in Roland Barthes, *The Pleasure of the Text*, tr. Richard Miller (Oxford: Blackwell, 1990), p. 61.

distinction between universal form and particular expression is itself a product of (and therefore also a producer within) the local reflection.

To deem all knowledges as situational, and all productions of knowledges as exercises in rhetoric that makes beliefs believable, does not necessarily imply that social construction goes all the way down. Nor does it commit us to a linguistic idealism. Language certainly makes our worlds. Charles Taylor, whose thinking I am indebted to in my understanding of cultural hermeneutics, draws attention to 'the artificiality of the distinction between social reality and the language of description of that social reality. The language is constitutive of the reality, is essential to its being the kind of reality it is.'[18] But there remains that which we can call mediations of the real. There remain events, eventualities and experiences. In Nietzsche's observation a tree remains throughout all the perceptions through time that there are of it. There are certain constancies the effects of which constitute various situated knowledges. For example, in Christian theology the event of Christ has generated and generates many different situated interpretations; interpretations not only of that event (in the past) but of the meaning of Christian practice in the present with respect to that event in the past. And while the Christian knowledge of that Christ event remains a specific and situated one, nevertheless over the history of such interpretations traditions are constituted, community decisions taken as to what characterises a strong or a weak interpretation of that event, and criteria agreed upon by these communities about the bases upon which a strong or weak interpretation of that event can be evaluated. Constancies emerge in and through the history of interpretative engagement. In fact, one might measure the importance of an event by the strength of the hermeneutical activity it generates, and by the traditions of hermeneutical activity that accrue because of it.

Furthermore, constancies can become sedimented into specific vocabularies, formulae and sets of ideas that invoke universals. A particular event might be interpreted in terms of its goodness, its truth, its beauty, or its justice. That is, appeal is made to a transcendental vocabulary with a long philosophical tradition. Nevertheless, that appeal is always a situated one. That citation or recitation of the universal issues in this particular situation, constituting a knowledge that again is situational. The claim made with respect to that event will be a rhetorical one accepted by those who share the beliefs and values associated with that vocabulary and its tradition.

---

[18] 'Interpretation and the Sciences of Man' in *Philosophy and the Human Sciences*, p. 34.

In this way the situatedness of knowledge does not deny that general observations are made, likewise appeals to creeds, confessions, normative laws and universals. But every general observation is a knowledge-claim made on the basis of an interpretation of the particular. Interpretations cannot explain; they point to shared, intersubjective meanings and beliefs about what is true, what is real. Interpretations can assert *that* belief *as* true, *as* what is real, but that assertion is a mode of the interpretative expression, as explanation is a mode of interpretation.[19] Sandra Harding, treating the objects of scientific investigations, points out:

Trees, rocks, planetary orbits, and electrons always appear to natural scientists only as they are already socially constituted in the same ways that humans and their social groups are already socially constituted for the social scientist. Such objects are already effectively removed from pure nature into social life – they are social objects – by, first of all, the contemporary general cultural meanings that these objects have for everyone, including the scientific community.[20]

The event or text for which explanation is being sought is transformed by the very act of engagement, and both event and interpretative engagement with it are affected because both participate in wider cultural transformations.

This radically hermeneutical situation might seem at first glance to be antithetical to any theological investigation, but in fact the situatedness of knowledge need not be of concern to Christian theology. This hermeneutics would imply that all things are given in the moment and in the situation in which they are given. The universal truth that is in God and is God is given in every particular in every moment. No law can determine the freedom of its gift or explain its appearance. Such a nonfoundationalism would develop a Christian theology of the gift, of the triune God in relation to creation, of time as the image of eternity – such that the singular uniqueness of every particular was sacred and, therefore, though not itself universal, nevertheless participating in that which governed all universality. Such a theology would articulate around the sacrality of the contingent or what Henri de Lubac termed 'real gratuitousness'.[21] Creation is constantly given 'or rather continues constantly to give me, to myself'.[22]

---

[19] The German *Auslegung* (used by Schleiermacher) means both interpretation and explication and Schleiermacher understood explication as inseparable from interpretation.
[20] 'Rethinking Standpoint Epistemology' in Linda Alcoff and Elizabeth Potter (eds.), *Feminist Epistemologies* (London: Routledge, 1993), p. 64.
[21] *The Mystery of the Supernatural*, tr. Rosemary Sheed (New York: Herder and Herder, 1967), pp. 68–96.
[22] Ibid., p. 100.

Furthermore, accepting what Gianni Vattimo would call a hermeneutic ontology[23] does not necessarily mean interpretative relativism. Later I will develop a distinction between two or more interpretative positions being 'related to' – or rather 'in relation to' – each other, and relativism as such. For the moment let me clarify the grounds upon which we can affirm that there are stronger and weaker forms of interpretation. A strong interpretation would be one in which more of the details and nuances of the text were treated; where a wider range of possible meanings was not dealt with cursorily or simply displaced; where the value of previous investigations was assessed. Of course, there is a politics involved in the production and judgement of a strong or a weak reading. There is a politics whereby some judgements receive greater validation in accordance with publicly available criteria. The academy as a community of scholars and researchers, who produce, disseminate, maintain and evaluate such criteria, is not without its divisions and differences. Nevertheless, interpretation is not just a matter of personal opinion. There are benchmarks whereby the standard or quality of the interpretation can be measured so that this interpretation of a text or performance or work is 'thicker' (to adopt Clifford Geertz's term, taken from Gilbert Ryle) than that.[24] This does not mean there cannot be a conflict of interpretations or even incommensurate interpretations. The judgement among certain liberal Christian theologians that the incarnation is a metaphor and the judgement among orthodox Christian theologians that the incarnation is a historical event in which God became human in Jesus of Nazareth are incommensurate. But both sides can measure the quality of the thinking and interpretation behind the judgement. The judgement will not be validated by both sides, and this presents us with an important question. Each 'school' (liberal/orthodox) has developed criteria for evaluation through the process of their internal enquiring. These, I suggest, function as the grammars of interpretative practice. I employ the word 'grammar' because each of these practices is discursive. According to these grammars *this* interpretation in *this* school or tradition of practice is stronger than that. Judgements are more or less well founded. What is incommensurate is not the quality of the interpretation but the traditions and practices of enquiry that evaluate the quality of the

---

[23] See *The End of Modernity*, tr. Jon R. Snyder (Cambridge: Polity Press, 1991), pp. 113–81.

[24] The examination system is founded upon such a principle. When, as a teacher, I examine and mark such readings of, say, Barth's doctrine of the Trinity or Coleridge's 'Kubla Khan' I grade according to the quality of the reading given. That quality is inseparable from the level of attentiveness to the texts themselves and the ideas they generate. As there are inadequate and better readings of texts so there are inadequate and better readings of a cultural event or phenomenon.

interpretation. Interpretations are rooted in grammars of critical practice that may and do conflict with each other, but nevertheless demonstrate there is no democracy of interpretation. Democracy in terms of levelling the playing field is always attempting to make politics disappear; the sharing of power is the erasure of power. Acts of interpretation are always implicated in hierarchies and therefore political struggles in which knowledge and power are profoundly interrelated. Because of being implicated in hierarchies, acts of interpretation are never relative. It is because of this that there can be a critical practice of interpretation at all. We *do* argue, we *do* agree, disagree and attempt to clarify the grounds for why we agree or disagree – *because* all acts of interpretation are not equal. An interpretive ontology continually denies the possibility of interpretive relativism.[25] The liberal concern for the *laissez-faire* of opinion is profoundly nihilistic and depoliticising because it promotes a secular *apatheia* – a radical and dangerous disengagement. But it is also counterfactual; for to interpret *is* to engage.

The final corollary of radical hermeneutics is that there is, *pace* Schleiermacher, no general hermeneutics with specialised branches (law, literature, Biblical studies). As there is no isolatable text, action or object so there is no isolatable interpreter or isolatable act of interpretation. There is only a critical hermeneutics, a cultural hermeneutics. But this critical/cultural hermeneutics does not render futile any investigation into interpreters and acts of interpretation. What it does is to render cultural/critical hermeneutics a situational practice, specific to the cultural contexts in which it operates. Schleiermacher's general hermeneutics themselves become an articulation that is historically and culturally specific.[26] Cultural hermeneutics is a story we tell ourselves about where we are.

---

[25] There is a philosophical anthropology *in nuce* here – *homo hermeneuticus* – that endorses what the Chinese novelist and Nobel prize winner, Gao Xingjian, observes with respect to totalitarian ideologies: 'If you wanted only to tell the truth, then there was no point in living.' *One Man's Bible*, tr. Mabel Lee (London: Flamingo, 2003), p. 142.

[26] Schleiermacher's hermeneutics have been put together from various hand-written texts and lectures, given over a number of years. Given this fact, what is the 'then' in which he stood? I am also aware that the standard interpretation of Schleiermacher's philosophy of interpretation (that given by Gadamer in *Truth and Method*) has been challenged first in Germany (see Manfred Frank, *Das individuelle Allgemeine. Textstrukturierung und Interpretation nach Schleiermacher* (Frankfurt am Main: Suhrkamp 1977) and his introduction to Schleiermacher's *Hermeneutik und Kritik* (Frankfurt am Main: Suhrkamp, 1997)) and in the English-speaking world (see Andrew Bowie's Introduction to his new translation of *Hermeneutics and Criticism* (Cambridge: Cambridge University Press, 1998), pp. vii–xxxi). This new understanding of Schleiermacher's theories emphasises the nonfoundationalism and incompleteness of the hermeneutical process and makes connections between Schleiermacher and more contemporary radical forms of hermeneutics. I shall not engage in the debate at this point.

It is the manufacture of an event of meaning in a situation; a discursive event and a discursive meaning. Cultural hermeneutics is an expression of our need to examine and make sense of where we are. Its function is to take up, rehearse and transform that which has been culturally produced. It is an engaged reflection within and upon that cultural production itself. It is a critical, and political, act – not innocent (that is, unbiased or pretending a privileged access to truth), not objective in the sense given that term by certain philosophies of science.

A legitimate question arises here with respect to what Geertz terms 'local knowledges'. How local is local? If there are no discrete language-games or discursive practices – as I demonstrated in section 1 of this essay – then to what extent can the interpretations that arise from situational practices produce only local knowledges? A geographical metaphor is being employed with 'local' in order to convey the point that acts of judgement are embedded within sets of conditions that operate in *this* particular language, *this* cultural tradition, *these* practices as they are embodied in *these* people. Thus the critical interpretation always remains material, but it is not *de facto* opposed to universalism, globalism, or the attempt to argue for certain operational, translocal norms. The hermeneutical engagement would only enjoin that inductive reflection must always return to the specificities of the material. It is these sets of conditions that operate in, produce and organise particularities that compose what I would call a 'situation'. As such 'situation' bears an analogy to the dialectical relation between *habitus* and 'field' in Bourdieu's thinking.

STANDPOINT EPISTEMOLOGY

We engage from a situated standpoint, as Gadamer recognised.[27] This is the second of several important distinctions between cultural hermeneutics and philosophical hermeneutics following in the wake of Schleiermacher. One of the most important contributions to contemporary discussions on epistemology has come through the development of standpoint theory by a number of feminists. Several of these feminists are involved in the critical examination of practices in the natural sciences, in particular with

---

[27] Early in *Truth and Method* 'standpoint' is associated with 'standpoint of taste' in Kantian aesthetics, which is marked by an account of the isolated subject that Gadamer is critiquing throughout. It is not surprising therefore that Gadamer fails to think through the allusion he makes later to situations and standpoints within traditions, choosing instead to develop the spatial metaphor of 'this moving horizon out of which human life always lives, and which determines it as tradition' (p. 271).

subjecting the notion of induction to a critique altogether different from Hume's. I will return to this in a moment. The source of the thinking on standpoint, by Sandra Harding and Nancy Hartstock, for example, is Hegel's master–slave dialectic and the adoption of the standpoint of the proletariat in Marx, Engels and Lukacs. This is significant because although the feminists I have named – and others such as Patricia Hill Collins, Donna Haraway, Lorraine Code, Bat-Ami Bar On and Lynn Hankinson Nelson – develop an epistemology with respect to seeing things from the perspective of women's lives,[28] their fundamental claim concerns the production of beliefs from specific locations and the challenges those beliefs pose to a culture's dominant, naturalised and unquestioned accounts of truth. Alison M. Jaggar observes the metaphysics uncovered and emphasised when she states, 'The standpoint of women generates an ontology of relations and of continual process.'[29] Wherever there is epistemic privilege there is epistemic marginalisation. The forms of this marginalisation are many. Hegel's master and slave dialectic, Marx's, Engels' and Lukacs' bourgeois and proletariat dialectic all dealt with class, rather than race or gender. But Edward Said has examined standpoint theory with respect to colonialism and subaltern studies, and Patricia Hill Collins in terms of 'African-American women, African-American men, Latina lesbians, Asian-American women, Puerto Rican men'.[30] All of these standpoint studies, in an effort to avoid essentialism, are committed to an investigation into cultural exchanges.[31] They employ a broadly historical materialist approach to social reality. Furthermore, as regards Western cultures that are organised around what Harding calls 'intellectual

---

[28] '[I]t is not the experiences or the speech that provides the ground for feminist claims; it is rather the subsequently articulated observations of and the theory about the rest of nature and social relations – observations and theory that start out from, and look at the world from the perspective of, women's lives,' Sandra Harding, *Whose Science? Whose Knowledge?*, p. 124.

[29] *Feminist Politics and Human Nature* (Brighton: Harvester Press, 1983), p. 376.

[30] For Edward Said see his Foreword to *Selected Subaltern Studies*, ed. Ranajit Guha and Gayatri Chakravorty Spivak (New York: Oxford University Press, 1988), p. viii. For Patricia Hill Collins, see her *Black Feminist Thought: Knowledge, Consciousness, and the Politics of Empowerment*, 2nd edn (London: Routledge, 2000), p. 270

[31] It is interesting to observe how Adorno similarly avoids essentialism with respect to Jewish ethnicity by emphasising how social learning is associated with 'imitative action'. So there are not endemic racial character traits but rather 'that inclinations, skills, anxieties which have long lost their real meaning leave their mark on the faces and behaviours of later generations', 'Research Project on Anti-Semitism' in Stephen Crook (ed.), *The Stars Down to Earth* (London: Routledge, 1994), p. 209. Adorno's is a much more Aristotelian analysis, emphasising 'mimesis' rather than epistemology. My own thinking is much more in line with this approach.

participatory democracy',[32] these change through the contestations between positions of epistemic privilege and marginalisation.

This is somewhat akin to Bourdieu's understanding of cultural production in a field of positions. But Bourdieu's work supplements standpoint epistemology on two counts, it seems to me. First, it recognises a whole range of positions that compose the spectrum between the marginalised and the privileged – there are therefore degrees of marginalisation and degrees of domination specific to each field of symbolic production and across the various productive fields operating at any one given time. Secondly, his work demonstrates how, in order for the marginal to take a position (*prise de position*) in the field of cultural production, it has to work with what is possible. In other words, the marginal standpoint, in order to be situated in the field at all, can no longer speak as entirely marginal. Those who take up such a standpoint must therefore constantly reflect upon its instability. As Haraway emphasises: 'The standpoints of the subjugated are not "innocent" positions.'[33]

We will return to this because it highlights areas in need of clarification where the epistemological project and the moral project are confused.[34] For the moment it is important to appreciate that not only is standpoint epistemology able to examine questions about power, politics and public truth, but its examination is itself a negotiation for the redistribution of power and its cultural productions. It provides tools for a cultural negotiation aimed at social transformation. Hartstock writes that 'a standpoint is a technical theoretical device that can allow for the creation of better (more objective, more emancipatory) accounts of the world. Thus, I make no claim about the actual consciousness of existing women, but rather I am arguing about the theoretical conditions of possibility for creating alternatives.'[35] By 'theoretical' here, Hartstock is not accepting the dualism of

---

[32] Harding, *Whose Science? Whose Knowledge*, p. 151.

[33] 'Situated Knowledges' in *Simians, Cyborgs, and Women* (London: Free Association Books, 1991), p. 191. More recently, Grace Jantzen has drawn attention to the dangers in standpoint epistemology of polarising the marginal to the dominant, and privileging the standpoint of the marginal, in her book *Becoming Divine* (Manchester: Manchester University Press, 1998). For such privileging can involve the development of counter-positions that 'merely reinforce the ground rather than change it' (p. 217). Furthermore, such privileging can valorise victimage (p. 215). Bourdieu's work helps both to situate the cultural negotiations between standpoints in wider fields in which the circulation of power and knowledge take, maintain and contest 'positions' and to problematise the operations involved in cultural positioning itself.

[34] This is not to say that the epistemological project and the moral project can be strictly separated: knowledge, its production and acquisition, is not value-free. But there have to be criteria for evaluating the moral values of the knowledge produced, disseminated and acquired. For these criteria to emerge a distinction needs to be drawn between epistemology and ethics.

[35] *The Feminist Standpoint Revisited and Other Essays* (Boulder: Westview Press, 1998), p. 236.

theory and practice, and, to some extent, one wonders whether the use of the word 'theory' at all, with respect to standpoint epistemology, reflects the extent to which the project has exorcised some of the older metaphysical ghosts of the empirical sciences. For this 'theoretical' work is engaged and culturally embedded. It is a labour (Gramsci is an important source for Hartstock's thinking); it is therefore much closer to the combination of hermeneutics and praxis advocated and delineated by Richard Bernstein. By 'theoretical' Hartstock seems to intend a level of generalisation such as is achieved through inductive thinking. Nevertheless, what is provided for her in this 'technical theoretical device' is a point for examining how cultures transform, how situated beliefs become both believable and discredited. 'The standpoint theories . . . take their problematic from shifts in the kinds of beliefs being generated.'[36] And it is that operation with respect to theological discourse that I am wishing to examine more closely. Harding suggests that attention to standpoint 'must be accompanied at every point by richer conceptualisations and analyses of the interlocking relationships between sexism, racism, heterosexism and class oppression'.[37] But I would wish to take this further, encouraging the production of these 'richer conceptualisations' by adding the oppression, by silencing or privatisation, of faith-commitments in liberal 'intellectual participatory democracy'. I want to suggest that Christianity constitutes a standpoint. In fact, any theological commitment constitutes a standpoint with respect to the epistemic dominance of secular, material and immanent world-views. The theological commitment cannot be erased in these 'secular accounts' of standpoint because for many people the questions of gender, race and class are inseparable from their theological beliefs.

To develop this idea of the theological standpoint we need to understand what is meant by a standpoint with respect to epistemology. For a standpoint is not a subject-position. Although a number of feminist epistemologists use the language of perspective, it is not perspectivalism that is being embraced. The question of relativism we will treat again later, but for the moment we need to see how standpoint is antithetical to what Lynn Hankinson Nelson terms 'epistemological individualism'.[38] The experience of the solitary knower is not a standpoint, for a standpoint, as the quotation above from Harding suggests, arises from a tradition of

---

[36] Harding, *Whose Science? Whose Knowledge?*, p. 171.
[37] Ibid., p. 178.
[38] *Know Knows: from Quine to a Feminist Epistemology* (Philadelphia: Temple University Press, 1990), p. 291.

reflection and articulation; from what I earlier termed the grammar of critical enquiry. Hartstock, in her delineation of the five claims evident in a standpoint, emphasises that a standpoint 'is achieved rather than obvious, a mediated rather than immediate understanding'.[39] This understanding of 'achievement' (indebted to Hegel) returns us to my earlier remarks concerning the economy of response. A 'characteristic pattern of beliefs'[40] has to emerge out of the myriad personal experiences to constitute a view, an 'objective location'.[41] The word 'objective' is a key and controversial term in feminist epistemology as we shall see – and, I suggest, is one more metaphysical ghost, or trace of Popper, that standpoint epistemology can do without. But what is paramount is that a standpoint is a shared knowledge; an understanding of the world that, in being articulated, is recognised and held to be a better account of the world than others available (by patriarchal structures, for example, with respect to women). Lynn Hankinson Nelson takes this further by showing that there is no such thing as a solitary knower. Knowledge requires belonging to a sociolinguistic community and so to develop epistemologically we need intersubjective experience. '[W]e do not, individually or collectively, observe or experience the world from outside the theories our species and our particular communities have developed *to date* [my emphasis].'[42] This consideration of language is also an important supplement to what appears at times among those trained as researchers in science to be an emphasis still on specular accounts of knowledge.

Those two words 'to date' are significant, because the emergence of a standpoint is concerned with time and historical unfolding. Just as Engels pointed out that there could be no reflection upon the proletariat until the proletariat had not only fully emerged but also begun to organise itself as such, so feminist standpoint theory can only issue from the traditions of feminist reflection and action that have constituted a community of those who find that the tenets of feminism articulate their experience of the world. A grammar of critical enquiry has to emerge – and emerge from modifications to already existing grammars. There is a moment of conversion, therefore, of *metanoia* as change of mind or self-recognition, and this is what Hartstock seems to be hinting at when she speaks of a standpoint being achieved. If we play this idea in a Christian theological key we might

[39] Hartstock, *Feminist Standpoint Revisited*, p. 110.
[40] Harding, *Whose Science? Whose Knowledge?*, p. 137.
[41] Ibid., p. 123.
[42] *Know Knows*, p. 290.

say that Christianity as a standpoint could not emerge during Christendom, or even the Reformation. The standpoint can only emerge within a deeper cultural atheism and the advance of the secular world-view.

A standpoint is not then a subject-position. But I wish to take this further, further than most feminist epistemologists have taken it – although the work of Lorraine Code certainly does inform my thinking in this development. For while there is a recognition that any standpoint will address itself to other standpoints and maybe combine, say, a concern with race with a concern with gender or sexual orientation or faith-commitment, there is still an ambivalence as to the constitution of a standpoint. There is a lack of clarity between individual experiences, reflected and articulated, and the establishment, in history, of an 'objective location'. What do the 'characteristic patterns of belief' consist of that emerge from the tradition of praxis and enquiry and constitute the standpoint? How are they arrived at? Who arrives at them? Who legitimates that *this* is a 'characteristic' and *that* now forms a 'pattern'? For the discernment of 'pattern' is the recognition of a grammar of being. I think closer examination of the difference between subject-position and standpoint can help to clarify the operations that take place both in this cultural production (of a standpoint) and in the simultaneous negotiation of that standpoint with other standpoints.[43] It will also help to clarify why being a Christian constitutes a specific cultural standpoint.

A subject-position can be delineated through a set of identifications. Of course a 'subject-position' viewed as a productive site of interpretation is frighteningly abstract. I raised this with respect to Karl Barth in section 1. The materiality of individual bodies seems to vaporise. 'Persons' become processes. The question that arises, therefore, concerns the relationship between 'person' and 'subject-position'. I would wish to defend the idea that personhood is irreducible to subject-position, but that is not enough. 'Irreducible' still needs to be elaborated. Person is inseparable from individuating embodiment. That is fundamental. But the moment we begin to think through that embodiment with respect to any individual human being then we have already embarked on a series of interpretations and assumed certain ideas about what it is to be human. For example, the I who

---

[43] There are occasions in Hartstock's work, for example, when the standpoint is first arrived at and only then can subsequently begin its cultural negotiation with hegemony. But attention to Hegel would show that the set of identifying characteristics and patterns composing a standpoint is constantly emerging and forming alongside and within the hegemonic itself. A standpoint does not emerge externally. Even marginalisation is an internal product of hegemony. A greater appreciation of this would facilitate the recognition that 'standpoints' are mobile, and are as unfinished as the knowledges they produce.

writes here and speaks is a white European male in his mid-forties, living in England, from a working-class background although now earning a professional salary and holding a tenured position. These identifications could be extended – enjoys pasta, cannot drink malt whisky too late at night, swims as often as he can, etc. Each identification, if further elaborated, would involve some form of autobiographical narration. Each identification is also time-bound: I may not always live in England and I may in time come to dislike pasta. But from a certain place in time I can make specific identification claims about myself that distinguish me. I am not a woman. I am not Asian. I am not homeless, etc. Sets of identifications enable us to have a sense of ourselves, and I would argue that we have 'sense of ourselves' rather than identities. There is a theological argument for our having definitive identities based upon the uniqueness of our creation and calling. The Book of Revelation, taking up an idea in Deuteronomy, states: '[T]o him that overcomes . . . I will give a white stone, and in the stone a new name written, which no man knoweth saving he that receiveth it' (Revelation 2.17). But this identity or new name is an achievement wrought over time, a formation that may be discerned on occasions, but the understanding of which is finally eschatological. Definitive identities are not available to us *in medias res*. We work with sets of identifications some of whose terms are more embedded and more enduring than others. Though they cannot be entirely separated from the social and cultural contexts in which they were established or learned, each identification term refers back to me, and though others may also claim a similar identification, the wider set of identifications distinguishes me from anyone else. In referring back to me, it is not the case that only my claim of them makes them valid. Identifications are affirmed by the observations of others – 'he really can't drink malt whisky after nine in the evening' – the presence of others (family, friends, colleagues, passers-by) and the existence external to me of the institutions to which I belong. These external factors restrain not the stories I can tell about myself but the validity of the stories I can tell about myself. By 'valid' I mean that the truth contents of the story can be defended against any objections to the contrary. An alteration in these constraining external factors may affect what I can believe about myself and the way I have interpreted my experience; may demand a change to make my story more credible. Nevertheless, I am the protagonist of the narratives interlinking these sets of identifications and which generate my sense of what I hold to be true about my distinguishing tastes and myself.

This set of identifications in this moment in time constitutes a subject-position, but at every point these identifications have been socially constituted and cultivated. That is, they have arisen through that economy of response that I sketched earlier. My recognition and understanding of – my identification with – what it is to be a white male academic in his mid-forties is only possible through the million channels of experience and communication, given and received, with respect to other social agents. Wittgenstein famously composed a commentary on the opening line of John's Gospel when he said 'In the beginning is the Act.' But the 'act' – which is the smallest unit in what will constitute an event – is only possible because first there is relation. The ministrations of complex networks of relation make possible sets of identifications. Because I am in-relation, which is another way of saying that I am immersed in economies of response, I act (where even being passive is understood as an act of reception). I act as a subject with some sense of myself as the one who acts – though, in acting, that sense may undergo modification.

This is significant for I would argue that there is no major leap taken between subject-position and standpoint. Subject-position and standpoint do not stand in dialectical opposition with each other as individual to group, personal autonomy to collective. With standpoint we are concerned with specific sets of identification that have arisen in the same way – through social interaction. No subject-position is autonomous. As Lorraine Code observes: '[E]very cognitive act takes place at a point of intersection of innumerable relations, events, circumstances, and histories that make the knower and the known what they are, at that time.'[44] I would take issue with only one word here – 'cognitive'. For this again reduces action to mental events whereas I would argue that action is interrelational – it takes place in and between sentient and intelligent bodies, not just minds. Standpoints arise from identifications made in the social construction of situated knowledge. This does not mean the subject-position's sense of self is completely determined, because it does not mean that the individual disappears or simply becomes a nodal point or transistor in a network of forceful relations. The subject-as-agent is reflective in the economies of response. He or she has to evaluate and interpret experience and come to understand his or her own desires.[45] This follows from what I outlined earlier about human beings as hermeneutical beings. In this

[44] *What Can She Know? Feminist Theory and the Construction of Knowledge* (Ithaca: Cornell University Press, 1991), p. 269.
[45] For the role of desire in human agency see Charles Taylor, 'What is Human Agency?' in *Human Agency and Language*, pp. 15–44. For a critique of the way feminist epistemology has given little attention to the role of desire see Pamela Sue Anderson, *Towards a Feminist Philosophy of Religion* (Oxford: Blackwell, 1998), pp. 66–97.

evaluation certain identifications become more important than others; certain identifications are recognised as being more fundamental than others. It is in and through this reflective process of evaluation and interpretation of one's experience of and in the world and of one's desires with respect to this being in the world that standpoint identifications are both recognised and forged. To return to a point I made earlier – if the relation is more primary than the act, then desire (which is the animator of the will to act) is directed within relation. Desire leads to self-determination.

We will see the difference between and the significance of recognition and forging if I sketch the kind of identifications I mean. For what constitutes a standpoint comes from and refers back to wider cultural traditions, horizons and practices; various interpretive communities (to use a Stanley Fish term[46]) that intersect with but cannot be reduced to the biographical and idiosyncratic. We showed this in section 1 with Barth. These traditions, horizons, practices and communities are not themselves stable entities; they are constantly undergoing new reorientations towards future states as reflective negotiations with the past occur within the present. For example, important biographical elements would include my English nationality, my professional role as an educator, my standing as a priest in the Church of England, and my commitment to socialism. Each of these positions is composed of sets of identifications, which establish cultural relations and association, and are irreducible and complex. In the process of defining and redefining, they absorb, they reject, they modify and they syncretise. It is not that these identifiers such as Anglican priest and socialist mean nothing – I could give some account of what constitutes my identification with socialism. In fact, it is exactly the opposite – they signify too much; signify above and beyond my grasp, my own account.

Now it is evident that the identification involved in my being English differs from the identification involved in being a priest or a socialist. Both identifications belong to traditions of thought and practice; both belong to specific collective associations. But the belonging involved in being a priest and/or a socialist issues from active choice. I am English as an accident of being born in England. It is not inevitable that I would evaluate more highly things concerned with those identifications that have involved my agency. I could decide to actively engage in my English identity – become a member of the National Front, for example. In fact, my being a priest in

---

[46] *Is There a Text in This Class? The Authority of Interpretive Communities* (Cambridge, Mass.: Harvard University Press, 1980).

the Church of England is itself an active engagement in that set of identifications associated with being English. But two things become clearer. First, with respect to the identifications of a subject-position, the sets of identifications with being English or a priest or a socialist are irreducible. Secondly, the difference between a recognised set of identification and a forged one is engagement. To be engaged is to be implicated in all the exchanges and cultural negotiations that make a belief believable. For I have been persuaded of the importance of belonging, and identifying myself with, certain associations rather than others. My desire and agency, my evaluations and interpretations of being in the world, have been forged in a certain politics of belief and believing.

We are now in a position to understand more clearly what is meant by the 'characteristic patterns of belief' as they emerge from the tradition of praxis and enquiry and constitute a standpoint. We are now in a position to give some answer to those questions, how are standpoints arrived at, who arrives at them, and who legitimates that this is a 'characteristic' and that now forms a 'pattern'? Standpoints are constituted through identifications and engagements with reflective practices that have a history and certain organised centres of association. One can speak of 'becoming' a feminist, a priest, a socialist. Being born female does not imply one is a feminist and similarly being a Christian does not imply one is a priest and being political does not imply one is a socialist. In Christian theology, of course, there is the 'priesthood of all believers' spoken of in the Letter to the Hebrews, and thinking this statement through in this context will help to clarify further the nature of standpoint. For by 'priest' I am referring to a social and cultural role that is publicly identifiable as such. I drew attention above to the recognition by feminist standpoint theorists that such a reflection is only possible because there already exists a history of feminist reflective practice and a community of those who find that the tenets of feminism articulate their experience of and hope for the world. A standpoint can only issue on the basis of a tradition of public visibility and an association, recognised publicly,[47] of those who identify themselves as continuing that tradition. As the Letter to the Hebrews recognises, the 'priesthood of all believers' has to be understood Christologically: that is, by virtue of all Christians being *en Christo*, all participate in a priestly ministry. One might say that those who are socially and culturally confirmed as priests are public

---

[47] The identification of belonging to the association (of those who function socially and culturally as priests, for example) may be contested both internally and more generally, but such contestation only affirms the existence of the association itself.

representatives of this position in Christ. With respect then to the question of how standpoints are arrived at and who arrives at them we can see that they arrive through what Gadamer would call the movement of 'effective historical consciousness'. They are arrived at by those within a specific tradition of reflective practice who identify themselves with sets of beliefs, having become persuaded of the validity of their truth-claims, in the ongoing cultural negotiation of that tradition with other traditions and newly formed associations. They are arrived at through acts of evaluation, interpretation and determination in economies of response that seek to identify continuities, common ground or developments with their tradition and discontinuities, differences and potential threats to their tradition. The legitimation of 'characteristics' as belonging to the 'patterns of belief' as they emerge, change and are contested is negotiated internally by that tradition, though that negotiation may well take into consideration observations made and comments passed by other traditions of reflective practice. For just as there are no autonomous subject-positions, so there are no autonomous traditions. Tradition-based associations, from which standpoints issue, are not monadic and homogenous. No one can effectively police the narrative boundaries of a tradition or association. This will become important in the analysis of the relationship between standpoints and wider cultural transformations.

The point I wish to make here is that subject-positions are established within standpoints, standpoints provide subject-positions with sets of identifications some of which are recognised and some of which are forged. If we return to that brief delineation I gave of my own subject-position, we can see how certain identifications I made there – being white, male and middle-class – already operate at the edge of standpoints. Any of them could be taken (and in the past were taken) as conscious positions with which to negotiate the world and evaluate one's response and experience within it. As such, subject-positions enunciate particular sets of intersecting cultural traditions and horizons that will inevitably be incomplete apprehensions of any culture or even those traditions and horizons themselves.[48] To this extent, the enunciations from these subject-positions will be unable to apprehend all the assumptions that make that position possible; and so

---

[48] Schleiermacher understood this: 'every individual is only a location in which the language appears' (*Hermeneutics and Criticism*, p. 9). This translation makes Schleiermacher into a Lacan before his time, nevertheless to some extent I am developing the corollaries of such an idea. But I suggest this is rendered more complex by recognising that people are located in several different discourses, or language-games. The cultures they inhabit are plural, and this is increasingly so in our multiracial, multilingual societies.

stand in need of being interrupted by the enunciations of other subject-positions. There may indeed be conflicts between various identifications within any one subject-position; and that conflict may or may not be self-recognised. Nevertheless what 'I' am transcends biographical and physiological loci, and strives to attain coherence or a mode of being-in-the-world in which these various intersections are lived 'comfortably' or with integrity.[49] Furthermore, any subject-position may embrace several standpoints, for several traditions of reflective practice may converge, overlap or stand in tension. A feminist can be a member of a religious community and have decided political affiliations. Speaking and acting from any single standpoint will be affected by the relations between that standpoint and the other standpoints and subject identifications. This set of relations will bring to each standpoint something distinctive and particular about that subject. Just as personal hierarchies emerge between evaluations and interpretations with respect to the extent to which they determine subsequent actions, so a hierarchy may structure the relations between various standpoint identifications for any one subject. This may be particularly so if one of the standpoints has transcendent significance. A commitment to a religious practice might (though not necessarily) be considered more significant and determine the character of the interpretation of and engagement in other standpoints – being a socialist, for example. This evaluation of one standpoint with respect to others may be enjoined by the traditions of that standpoint. So the commitment to the heavenly city is deemed more important than commitment to the earthly city, in certain traditions of Christianity. But the evaluation of the subject-position emerges from practices in which there have been reflections upon the tradition with respect to other experiences of life and the determinations of desire.

Traditions can be authoritatively stronger or weaker, more authoritarian or less. The authoritative strength or weakness of any tradition is governed by a number of factors such as the length of its history, its geographical distribution, its ideological content, the organisational structure that has given and continues to give that tradition its current public recognition, the character of that public recognition (whether the tradition is seen as significant, useful, good in any number of senses in which those term might be interpreted), and the *charisma* of the figures who gave or give it public prominence. This authority, then, maps only to some extent on the

---

[49] My anthropological assumption here is that human beings do not will their own confusion, and that even radical forms of schizophrenia are attempts to accommodate fissures and fractures of traumatised personhood that threaten to engulf the self with a radical dis-order.

tradition's symbolic capital, for it is an authority that is stronger or weaker with respect to its power to discipline the desires (and therefore the bodies) of those committed to and situated within it. Because of this complex range of factors governing the authoritative strength or weakness of any tradition, and because every tradition is irreducible, then there is no necessary alignment (maybe no *possible* alignment) between the set of identifications that compose a subject-position and the set of identifications that compose a standpoint. But we must observe, with respect to this examination of the emergence of standpoints and the authoritative strength or weakness of the traditions they perform, that the language of 'epistemic privilege' with respect to being marginalised (important to a number of feminist stand-point theorists) is once more qualified. I drew attention earlier, via Bourdieu, to the degrees of marginalisation in any given symbolic field and between any given set of symbolic fields. But we can take this further now. In wishing to move beyond the problem of the valorisation of vict-image that can occur through giving privilege to the marginalised, Grace Jantzen argues that we need to develop credible 'counter-positions, lest . . . we merely reinforce the ground rather than change it'.[50] In order for cultural transformation to be possible there needs to be a developed basis for contestation. The degree to which such a development has already taken place, such that a standpoint can assert a public presence and a specific disciplining of desire (initiating acts of self-determination) and engage effectively in critical hermeneutics, requires that it contests vict-image and marginalisation. It cannot claim the 'privilege' of these positions without recognising the highly ambivalent nature of such marginalisation. Its marginalisation has to be reckoned alongside the high evaluation given to its standpoint, such that there is a continuing tradition of reflective practice that is able to persuade others to identify themselves with it, and situate their own knowledge about the world within it.

It is in this forging of links between traditions of reflective practice and subject-positions, in the politics of belief and believing, that agency is exercised through evaluation, interpretation and self-determination. The hermeneutical process is as continuous throughout these micro-negotiations as it is between the macro-negotiations between standpoints in the establishment of public accounts of what is true. We can then talk about 'my standpoint', only having recognised that this 'my' has none of the clear precision of the Cartesian 'ego cogito', and is thrown more radically than

---

[50] *Becoming Divine*, p. 217.

the Heideggerian understanding of *Dasein.* It must be admitted though that much care needs to be taken when shifting grammatically from that first person singular to the first person plural. Although a standpoint issues from a tradition of reflection and specific organisations sustaining that ongoing reflection, we-saying, while pointing towards wider applications, is much more local. As there is no one feminism and so no one feminist standpoint,[51] so there is no one socialism or socialist standpoint or no one Christianity or Christian standpoint. There is, as Lorraine Code emphasises, 'a politics of we-saying'[52] that demands responsibility and understanding from those who need to speak of 'we'. Of course by raising these examples a difference between the character and operation of a cultural engagement from a Christian standpoint does become evident. Put briefly, for I will develop this further below when treating projection, though culturally there are diverse forms of Christianity and therefore multiple inflexions of the Christian standpoint, theologically there remains the belief in one Church and one baptism; a conformity with Christ that indicates there is formally (in Christ) only one Christianity, though what is understood as 'Christ' and being 'in Christ' may vary considerably. We will take this further because it goes to the heart of what is at stake in negotiations with culture from a Christian standpoint.

PRO-JECTION AND INTENTION

The task of interpreting and changing our cultures begins then from somewhere even if that somewhere is always *in medias res.* It begins with an 'I', an agent, who is also identified with a 'we'. But having begun r to where are 'we' moving and who or what determines that movement? Gadamer's recognition that any hermeneutical engagement operates with respect to horizons as visions suggests that such engagement inevitably yields a relationship between standpoints and goals. But what determines the utopian and teleological moment that is constitutive of cultural engagement? If a teleology is inescapable what characterises the specific nature and objects of that teleology? Feminists like Sandra Harding, Bat-Ami Bar On, Donna Harraway, Nancy Hartstock, Lynn Hankinson Nelson, Helen Longino and Lorraine Code all agree that we need to define the situation in which we are embedded – in order to critique the myth of a view from nowhere (closely associated with the patriarchal perspective). They agree

---

[51] Jaggar, *Feminist Politics and Human Nature,* pp. 385–6.
[52] *What Can She Know?,* p. 309. See also Nelson, *Know Knows,* pp. 277–8.

about how standpoint is not claimed but achieved – that is, the product of a specific learning and formation in a critical enquiry. But they disagree about the goal. For Harding, Hartstock and Bar On it is maximal or strong objectivity. '[F]eminist standpoint theory can direct the production of less partial and less distorted beliefs,' Harding writes.[53] Code, while accepting that feminists should be involved with epistemological issues, does not view the establishment of a 'feminist epistemology' as either desirable or feasible. Instead, she advocates that feminist analysis 'will aim to engage differences that strengthen community and to develop political strategies sufficiently contextualized to address diverse experiences of dominance and subjugation'.[54]

I need to enter into this debate because it raises questions about the orientation of standpoints, their position in time and their investment in the future. The question posed to feminist epistemology as a philosophical project is how, within an acceptance of the social construction of know-ledge and the recognition that all knowledge is culturally situated, to understand a term that many feminists believe to be at the heart of male-stream epistemology: objectivity.[55] Harding, in her more recent work (that responds to previous criticism) wishes to speak of objectivity as a 'compe-tency concept'.[56] Those in the margins see the systemic blindnesses and ideologies of the centre-parties more clearly, and experience also the repercussions of such blindness and ideologies. Hence to engage from a standpoint is to add to the evaluation of knowledge by bringing about less partiality and less systemic distortion. This is what Harding means by a 'strong objectivity', as opposed to a 'weak objectivity' (which is modern-ity's malestream positivist appraisal of objectivism). Objectivity, as such, functions as a regulative ideal as we transcend the limitations (even privil-eged, marginal limitations) of our standpoints through the endless cultural negotiations (intentional and unintentional) we are involved in and which make up our everyday living. Putting this account of objectivity into more Kantian terms assists in clarifying that this is not then an appeal to the myth of the given and the natural. '[A] positivist epistemology is fundamentally incompatible with the historical materialist method,'[57] Jaggar observes,

---

[53] *Whose Science? Whose Knowledge?*, p. 138.
[54] *What Can She Know?*, p. 307.
[55] See Alison Wylie, 'The Philosophy of Ambivalence: Sandra Harding on *The Science Question in Feminism*' in Marsha Hanen and Kai Nelson (eds.), *Science, Morality and Feminist Theory* (Calgary: University of Calgary Press, 1987), pp. 59–74.
[56] Ibid., pp. 75–86.
[57] *Feminist Politics and Human Nature*, p. 379.

critically. But the empirical and positivist residuum of employing such vocabulary remains. Observe Lynn Hankinson Nelson who tries to develop a scientific account of knowledge through feminist epistemology and W.V. Quine's antifoundational emphasis on the acquisition of language and knowledge as fundamentally social: ' "Knowledge" is socially constructed through and through – but the construction is constrained by the evidence . . . constrained by their consistency with our experiences of the world.'[58] Words like 'evidence' and 'consistency with our experiences' seem to fall outside of social construction. What counts as evidence? Who is counting it? What does not count and why? Similar problems occur with Jaggar's appeal for 'an adequate representation of the world from the standpoint of women'[59] and 'a more comprehensive representation of reality than the standpoint of men'.[60] This language of adequation has a history of association with nominalism and correspondence theories of language very close to the positivist and empiricist positions she wishes to critique. But there is no need intrinsically to reinstall the language of objectivity – even as a utopic horizon – for two reasons. First, philosophically, regulative ideals are formalist notions, they are empty of content, quasi-transcendentals that mask their own indeterminacy. That is, we may argue that the thinking of each subject moves transcendentally towards them (as Kant did) but the movement is illusory for the regulative ideals are only endless retreating horizons (which 'move' as the subject 'moves'). The second reason for rejecting the language of objectivity is hermeneutical. We may from a given standpoint be expanded in the process of accommodation and transformation, but since the whole story can never be told, since we can never escape our cultural and historical specificity, then the language of objectivity has no hold. 'Objectivity' is an aspect of a language-game (with an accompanying metaphysics and an implicit, albeit secularised, theology) belonging to a cultural order in which there are clear and precise subjects and objects, and a discourse which can mediate transparently between them, or which does not distort either the seeking or the finding involved in the process. This is a language-game that feminist epistemologists reject. Objectivity requires a world of inert objects, transparent subjects and the belief in a God's-eye perspective. 'Objectivity' to be 'strong objectivity' has to undergo such a semantic shift that the two uses of the word 'objectivity' become equivocal. And this is what one senses occurring

[58] *Know Knows*, p. 295.
[59] *Feminist Politics and Human Nature*, p. 384.
[60] Ibid., p. 385.

when Harding adds the qualifiers 'weak' and 'strong' and distinguishes between two fundamentally different forms of objectivity.

Code, as I have pointed out, does not view the development of a feminist epistemology as either desirable (on the grounds that it whitewashes over concrete differences between the situations of various women) or viable.[61] She argues for multiple epistemologies and a 'mitigated relativism' fostering recognition of, and therefore a politics of, difference. But what is significant for this investigation into the relationship between standpoints and goals is the common commitment of both Harding and her critics to a purposiveness. In a way it goes back to Hegel's account of the process of self-reflection: any standpoint involves a work. It is 'achieved'. There is, then, to the hermeneutical and critical task, an inerasable teleology. But the utopianism implicit within this teleology is not some idealistic *a priori* external to activity but a historical and material condition of intentional action. In a sense, 'objectivity' functions in some feminist epistemologies as the naming of a direction; it provides a rationality for a certain set of feminist beliefs about the task they are undertaking. Because without a direction, without the pedagogical hope of 'achieving', then critique is doomed to an arbitrary kicking against the dominant pricks.

Let us take this naming of the direction further, and ask whence comes this naming, what determines its specificity. What the entry into the debates over feminist epistemology demonstrates is that if, for some, feminist standpoints are held to be capable of moving towards these maximal or strong objectivities that is because the specific cultural logic constituting those standpoints posits and then necessitates such a goal. The goal is not intrinsic to either the feminist standpoint or feminist epistemology as such – as Jaggar and Code demonstrate. It is no coincidence that Sandra Harding, Nancy Hartstock, Lynn Hankinson Nelson and Elizabeth Potter all have backgrounds in science, for it is from here that the language of objectivity issues. But their naming the direction of their work in the language of objectivity and scientific method allows us to understand that standpoints furnish not only positions-from but positions-to. Standpoints furnish 'pro-jects'.[62]

---

[61] *What Can She Know?*, pp. 314–24.

[62] One can observe here a fundamental difference between the pro-jects of feminist epistemology (which is concerned to uphold the acquisition of knowledge) and cultural hermeneutics (which subordinates knowledge to understanding, seeking to offer an account of how we come to that understanding such that we believe we know something). I would suggest cultural hermeneutics is a prior negotiation to the acquisition of knowledge. I think this is what Lorraine Code is pointing to in her work – that the feminist epistemological pro-ject has to be situated within much wider processes of hermeneutical activity.

By pro-jects I mean that beginning somewhere a critical engagement furnishes a direction, a pro-jection. For Harding it is a feminist pro-ject with respect to the scientific establishment. For Code it is a more general philosophical pro-ject with respect to the recognition of both difference and community. Pro-jects are governed by a utopic moment associated with 'recognition'. We must explore here the economy of this recognition. Code, as far as I am aware, does not examine this crucial category, but at the centre of the question of recognition (as Plato understood) is knowledge. How do we come to know and name difference and affinity, or, in Code's terms, difference and community? Recognition is fundamental to the processes whereby one comes to affirm and be defined by the tradition of a standpoint and also, concurrently, to reject other possibilities for identification.

Hegel treats the question of recognition in terms of a social ontology – in *Phenomenology of Spirit* and *Philosophy of Right*, recognition is both the subject's recognition of itself in and through its social engagement with the other (master and slave, for example), and the recognition of one's own existence by others (as a person and an owner of property, for example). The heart of the operation of recognition, then, is social transformation that comes about by the positive evaluation of another position with respect to one's own.[63] Gadamer treats the question of the operation of recognition, and the constitution of knowledge, with respect to mimesis and aesthetics more generally – the illumination, even revelation, that proceeds through an engagement with 'the play of art'.[64] Code proceeds as if the recognition of difference and community were transparent. Hegel and Gadamer remind us that it is not – it is implicated in a hermeneutical, political, epistemological and ontological activity. Let us put aside the question, arising from the univocity of *Geist* in Hegel, of whether there is a genuine other and, therefore, whether there can be recognition of genuine difference. For both Hegel and Gadamer representation, mediation, is ineradicable. Representation is a mode of being and recognition comes to know a participation in

---

[63] There have been two important works on 'recognition' that I am indebted to. The first is the thorough analysis by Axel Honneth, *The Struggle for Recognition: The Moral Grammar of Social Conflicts*, tr. Joel Anderson (Cambridge: Polity Press, 1995). The second is Charles Taylor's essay 'The Politics of Recognition' and the series of astute commentaries it gave rise to, in Amy Gutmann (ed.) *Multiculturalism and 'The Politics of Recognition'* (Princeton: Princeton University Press, 1992). There is also an interesting essay by Nancy Fraser, 'From Redistribution to Recognition', in her collection *Justice Interruptus: Critical Reflections on the 'Postsocialist' Condition* (London: Routledge, 1997), pp. 11–40.

[64] *Truth and Method*, p. 103.

that which exceeds the contingencies of context. Recognition is a hermeneutical activity and a hermeneutical experience in which a critical knowledge of what is considered important is both communicated and constituted. This critical knowledge is, then, dialectical; inseparable from the processes of self-reflection; inseparable, in my terminology, from the economies of response. It is knowledge of difference or strangeness, knowledge of affinity or familiarity, and knowledge of the degrees of both with respect to each other. It is this dual edge that makes the knowledge critical – rather than dogmatic. Recognition always installs, then, a questioning; and the experience of recognition is an experience of being questioned. Therefore Code's recognition of difference and community needs to be developed more fully, become both more fully reflexive and more fully embodied. Knowledge is not an acquisition and recognition is not simply a mental act – as Thomas Nagel suggests in his *The Possibility of Altruism* (an account of recognition and understanding that Code critiques in her essay 'Persons, Others' in her *Rhetorical Spaces: Essays on Gendered Locations*). Recognition and knowledge are embodied operations implicated in the complex economies of responding to the world as sensate, material, intersubjective and cognitive beings. Cultural hermeneutics would emphasise that this critical knowledge of difference and affinity was not a possession, but, as Hegel saw, an achievement through practices of learning in which these things are always being received again non-identically, while still in question and arriving. The utopian moment in recognition arises from understanding that the whole is not yet – the recognition is never absolute. Nevertheless, there is here a work in progress, a work sustained by the hope of personal and social transformation, governed by what Honneth calls 'a state of communicatively lived freedom'.[65]

The economy of recognition bears the project towards its future, though the nature of the utopian telos (how 'lived freedom' is understood and imagined could exist) emerges from one of the cultural axes or truth-

---

[65] *The Struggle for Recognition*, p. 5. This is the point I would take issue with the too neat alignment of 'recognition' with 'identity politics' in Fraser's work. It would suggest that identity is itself a project in the economy of 'recognition'. Identity is not fixed but always moving beyond its own grasp of itself because of its encounter with the other. Fraser seems to view it the other way round: there is recognition because there is an established and authentic identity. She holds to what Taylor calls 'the ideal of authenticity' ('The Politics of Recognition', p. 36). The subtle Hegelian concept of *Anerkennung* is debased because rendered non-dialectical. For an historical account of this notion of 'identity' see Charles Taylor, 'The Politics of Recognition', pp. 28–34 and *Source of the Self* (Cambridge, Mass.: Harvard University Press, 1989), ch. 15.

claims[66] which form the standpoint. These axes or truth-claims provide the criteria that frame the engagement, producing notions of goals, progressions and movements in a specific direction. A project is constituted in and through a double epistemic privileging. The first epistemic privileging is external, that is, the standpoint itself with respect to other standpoints that are seen to dominate what is publicly accepted as true. For both feminism and Christianity, I would argue, there is a necessary privileging of their tradition-based knowledge with respect to a cultural hegemony that perceives that 'tradition' as marginal or subservient. The second epistemic privileging is internal, that is, an axis understood as essential to the pro-ject as such – epistemology of science, in Harding's case, the recognition of difference in Code's.

I will say more about the necessity of this privileging in a moment. But, at this point, I wish to revisit a traditional philosophical category associated with subjectivity: intentionality. Cultural hermeneutics as critical enquiry proceeds not just from a standpoint but from an intentional standpoint, and it is in this way that pro-jects are associated with intentions. I am limiting intention here neither to acts of individual willing nor to the property of certain mental states, though neither am I denying that there are individual intentions to act and what Searle calls the presentation of Intentional content in action.[67] Phenomenological investigation into seeing *as*, and the recent turn in philosophical attention to the operations of desire, have rendered accounts of intentionality complex. Searle does not take account of these other philosophical trends, nevertheless his work is highly significant for drawing out important structural elements in what I will

---

[66] I need to clarify here any difference that might lie between a cultural axis as a truth-claim and 'sets of identifications'. My standpoint as a Christian theologian engaged in the project of analysing contemporary culture would entail an acceptance of the truth-claims made by orthodox Christianity – the shorthand for which might be one of the Creeds. I would identify with the kind of person, a Christian, who accepted these truth-claims, I would not be identifying with the claims themselves. The claims and the practices they enjoin – belief in them, an attempt to understand the implications of them for the Church and for myself – mould the set of identifications. One could say the sets of identifications emerge from speaking the grammar of the faith.

[67] In *Intentionality: An Essay in the Philosophy of Mind* (Cambridge: Cambridge University Press, 1983) John R. Searle examines intention with respect to properties of specified states of mind and the actions of an individual. Nevertheless, rather than exaggerate the differences between my account and Searle's it is important to point out how Searle, while offering no account of emotions (and somatic experience), does associate intentional states with beliefs and desires and views the mind in terms of biological operations of the brain. Searle is no Cartesian dualist. Furthermore, he recognises that Intentional states, and the possibilities for translating those states into Intentional actions, require situating them in Networks of other Intentional states and against a Background of 'practices and preintentional assumptions' (p. 19).

term the economy of intention.[68] Intention, as Searle points out, cannot be reduced to belief and/or desire, because of the relations between intention and causality – I can only intend what I believe I can cause. I may desire that it rain, but I cannot intend it to rain. I may have conflicting desires, but not conflicting intentions to act. Nevertheless, intention performs both belief and desire. Intention requires the belief in a set of conditions that can satisfy the acted-upon intention. As such belief and desire are coordinates in the economy of intention as it moves towards making present the conditions for its satisfaction.[69]

Of course Searle is also correct in observing that many of our actions are spontaneous and so may lack an intentionality prior to the action itself. Like changing from first to second gear when accelerating, we perform certain intentional acts out of a disciplined habit; i.e., on the basis of being schooled to act in certain intentional ways. Furthermore, Searle distinguishes between 'the Intentional content of the intention in action and the experience of acting' because 'the experience of acting is a conscious experience with an Intentional content, and the intention in action just is the Intentional component'.[70] One may act intentionally then without being conscious of experiencing such an intentional action. But if we examine both this lack of consciousness prior to the intention to act and this lack of a conscious experience of acting intentionally, then we discover that intention, like the belief and desire that are inseparable from intention, is a melded formation; i.e., brought about by the disciplinary praxeis that constitute both habit and *habitus*. As beliefs are learnt and believing is endemic to intending, as desire is disciplined (such that we learn or are persuaded about what, for our happiness and well-being, short-term and long-term, is more or less desirable) and inherent in the presentation of intentional content in intentional act, so intention cannot be divorced from the operations and productions of cultures. In this sense, intention approximates to motivation – it is the dynamism that galvanises and maintains pro-jects. In the final section of this essay I will examine, following Paul Ricoeur, how intentionality is governed by imagination.

---

[68] The 'economy of intention' is inseparable from what I have called the 'economies of response' and what we might call 'economies of recognition'.

[69] The economy of intention according to Searle, and I see no reason to disagree given that he is not attempting to divorce mental acts from physical acts, is composed of some, if not all, of the following: 'prior intention, the intention in action, the bodily movement, and the action' (*Intentionality*, p. 92).

[70] Ibid., pp. 91–2.

As such, and Searle acknowledges this in his attention to the Networks and Backgrounds, intentionality is not simply located in rational subjects, transparent to themselves. It would appear that 'This holist conception [of intentionality] involves a denial of . . . atomistic assumptions' and would be contrary to any Cartesianism.[71] But although no Cartesian, Searle does remain committed to, as the analytical tradition of the philosophy of mind remains committed to, unreflective construals of the subject. This is the point where we would differ. I am arguing for the constitution or form-ation of personhood or the sense of self as agent within traditions and practices of traditions of knowledge, within communities (even if those communities turn out to be imaginary or neo-tribal voluntary societies). Searle's attention is upon the individual. The subject already occupies a position in the world and with respect to that world that Searle takes for granted. The subject is self-identical, a given. If not always or even rarely self-transparent, the subject is not hermeneutical in its being such that he or she continually lives with the question of what he or she is as such, 'always already in some interpretation [and] constituted as human by this fact'.[72] The subject is constituted prior to the social for Searle. It has an identity qua subject outside of the networks of relation which, for me, constitute the subject's knowledge of itself as subject. Certain 'atomistic assumptions' remain in Searle's examination, I suggest. It is not that the subject, in my thinking, is itself constituted within social and cultural matrices so much as that the subject's knowledge of itself as a subject is constituted in such matrices. We will return to this because it demonstrates quite clearly the assumptions (here anthropological) of my own position – the operations, even in talking about the logics of standpoints, pro-jects and intentions, of my own standpoint, pro-ject and intention.

Intentionality is, then, in-formed to the degree that belief and desire are in-formed. But it does not follow that all action is culturally deter-mined, for responsibility lies in the way the economies of intention, response and recognition intersect in the will-to-act. One may inhabit a standpoint and that standpoint will furnish a project with respect to the world, but an agency remains such that any subject-position can disen-gage itself or orientate itself towards private satisfactions. I will speak more of this with respect to power and ethics later. For the moment what is important is that not only does the move from 'I will do A' to 'I am doing A' involve a cultural negotiation with respect to sets of

---

identifications composing a standpoint, but that that 'willing' and that 'doing' are themselves informed by and inform cultural negotiations that are necessarily project-focused. That is, they believe in and desire the conditions for their satisfaction and such beliefs and desire orientate them towards a goal. Intentional states and intentional acts are situated within and informed by larger pro-jects. And it would follow from the necessity of this coinherence of intentionality and telos that the relativism of any given starting point cannot readily announce itself. An operative pragmatism, then, foils the simple judgement that any pro-ject is arbitrary. The operative pragmatism, rooted in the standpoint's pro-jection and the intentional states and actions it disciplines, is intrinsically necessary for the performance of claims held by the standpoint: one acts from a standpoint because one believes it is best and therefore right to do so – where 'right' is a ethical claim.

Let me be specific here in order to develop the basis for a new Christian apologetics or Christian *Kulturkritik*.[73] A Christian of a certain tradition is enjoined by the founding texts of the Christian faith (as espoused and evaluated by that particular tradition) to read the signs of the times. Hence the subsequent reading or cultural engagement becomes a pro-ject because it is governed by a purpose rooted in one of the dominant axes of a particular standpoint – to seek to understand the activity of God in the world with respect to present grace and future salvation, or to present grace as an intimation of an eternal salvation. When the instruction is given in the Gospels – particularly in Matthew's Gospel where Jesus rhetorically enquires of the Pharisees and Sadducees 'Can you not discern the signs of the times?' (Matthew 16.3) – the Greek word 'to discern', *diakrinein*, is also 'to judge'. Discernment is the constitution and passing of a judgement. The judgement is arrived at through the comparative relations established

---

[73] This term was central to the work of Horkheimer and Adorno where it means 'cultural criticism'. Two essays have become classical statements of what is involved in such criticism: Horkheimer's 'Tradition and Critical Theory' (1937) and Adorono's 'Cultural Criticism and Society' (1949). Adorno views the basis for *Kulturkritik* as intellectual freedom. It becomes necessary because of the way in which the public sphere is saturated with cultural values, even with the fetishisation of 'culture' itself. Its task is to rail against the fetishism, forms of cultural reification and mythologising, superficiality, excess and loss of substance. While denying any possible transcendent horizon within which this critical operation is conducted, it is nevertheless interesting to find him drawn to religious metaphors to describe the job of *Kulturkritik*: 'Whenever cultural criticism [*Kulturkritik*] complains of "materialism", it furthers the belief that the sin lies in man's desire for consumer goods, and not in the organization of the whole which withholds these goods from him: for the cultural critic, the sin is satiety, not hunger.' *Prisms*, tr. Samuel M. Weber (Cambridge, Mass.: MIT Press, 1983), pp. 24–5. One could say Christian *Kulturkritik* simply returns the rhetoric of this task back to its traditional roots.

between the claims and beliefs of the traditions that have formed a way of seeing the world and the 'signs of the times' or the way the world presents itself. The signs of the times may affirm that the state of universal salvation as detailed in the traditions (through those different representations of the redeemed condition found throughout the Scriptures, for example, in the last three verses of the Book of Amos) is being realised. The signs of the times may also open a radical disjunction between the claims of the tradition and the present cultural situation. We saw this in the last section with Barth's second edition of *Der Römerbrief.* Either way, reading the signs of the times requires acts of cultural engagement and interpretation such that a critical judgement can be made. As such, discernment is an act of prophecy, an eschatological task in Christian theology. In the context of a discipleship learning how to discern, Jesus tells them to beware the leaven, interpreted later as the teaching, of the Pharisees and Sadducees. This teaching, while demanding signs from heaven, is unable to discern what signs are already evident; evident, that is, to those who have been or are being taught differently. I do not wish to develop, at this point, the complex question of what makes something into a sign; the other side of which is what allows other things to be rendered insignificant – and who decides which is which. I have tried to treat this question with respect to root metaphors and key symbols in the methodo-logical Introduction to *Cities of God*.[74] What is uppermost here is that the eschatological nature of the interpretative task or discernment – associated elsewhere in Matthew with watching and preparing – is inseparable from a theological account of history or providence and the building and/or coming of the Kingdom. Acts of discernment with respect to the cultural milieu are orientated towards the future and so are intentional.[75] While they are rooted in local acts of personal and communal willing and desiring – for some enjoy the cinema while others prefer involvement in sporting activities or com-munity action groups – they are not reduced to these acts. For the Christian traditions informing the negotiation place these acts of discernment and understanding within a pneumatology central to an understanding of God-with-us. This is central to construals of

---

[74] See pp. 22–3.

[75] It is curious that Searle makes no mention or use of Elizabeth Anscombe's famous study *Intention* in which she draws attention to the temporality operative within intentional actions; their commitment to a future.

incarnation and the Trinity. By such acts of interpretation and discernment the world is brought to an understanding of itself and each member of the Christian community participates in the unfolding of a redemptive operation through time. As such all intentional activity from the Christian standpoint articulates something of the grammar of eschatological hope and participates in the dialectical tension of *parousia*.[76] The Christian interpretative pro-ject, then, has a telos intrinsic to the cultural axis or truth-claim of its particular standpoint. It is a necessary axis that, in this pro-ject (for I engage in many others[77]), orders the other elements of the standpoint and constitutes an intentional project. It produces the self-understanding of Christian agency: the Christian is one who is involved in this kind of cultural activity. The Christian is then not only defined but also formed by acting out the cultural axes of the standpoint.

Let me develop this notion of a cultural axis, and, in doing so, give a more nuanced account of the operation of intention that will make the operational pragmatism of any pro-ject more evident.[78] For what I wish to argue is that cultural transformation takes place on the basis of these operational pragmatics that are brought into play with any intentional pro-ject. For a cultural axis or truth-claim can never be recognised in a pure state. Its isolation for this or any other analysis therefore needs qualifying. To be specific, if in the Christian pro-ject I am describing I am drawing attention to the operation of faith as it seeks to understand itself in the

---

[76] I owe the distinction between eschatology and *parousia* with respect to hope to conversations with Michel Hölzl. We (that is, those who identify themselves with the Christian standpoint) might take this observation about the relation of hope to the intentional action of any pro-ject further by suggesting that all intentional action articulates a grammar of hope – whether the standpoint be Christian, feminist, socialist, ethnic, etc. Action would then always announce a utopian moment although the contexts for defining the kind of action may determine that moment as (a) a divine or transcendent movement, (b) evidence of an *a priori* condition, (c) a regulative ideal or (d) a secular transcendental.

[77] I suggested earlier that there may be a hierarchy of standpoints within any one person's activity; the same would go for pro-jects – some pro-jects take priority over, and are given a higher value than, others. What characterises those pro-jects that take priority is probably the breadth of significance they embrace. For example, a religious pro-ject may have priority over a political or professional one because it is associated with a more totalising vision of existence. Its world-view may be understood as encompassing far more than the contingencies of any political or professional situation. In fact, its world-view may be understood as ordering modes of behaviour with respect to all other pro-jects. Thus a Christian may be involved in certain political and professional pro-jects only because of his or her Christian commitment.

[78] I am aware that, in emphasising the operational pragmatism, I am pointing up the *contingency* involved in any pro-ject whilst attempting to give an account of a *necessity* implicated in the constitution of the pro-ject itself. This paradox needs further thought than I have given it at the moment.

contemporary world, I also have to recognise the operation of other local desires and intentions – of class, gender and ethnic origin, for example – that will be embedded in that same operation. I said above, while not limited to personal acts of willing and desiring, these are part of the way I perform my standpoint activity. These factors will colour the way the cultural axis of a standpoint is enacted and understood; they will colour the 'achievement' of the standpoint and the 'recognition' called for. Furthermore, the theological categories drawn upon in engaging the standpoint have been learnt in specific cultural grammars. We saw this in the first section of this essay with Karl Barth. His understanding of the task of theology and the role of the theologian was in part determined by his *habitus* and the cultural fields of symbolic production at the time. The tradition may hand down key words – like 'faith' or even 'God' – but we have had to learn how to inflect those words, and it is with the heritage of these past understandings that we begin our present interpretation.

It is not only that the cultural axis of any standpoint is never pure, but it is always under negotiation itself at any time at which the standpoint is engaged. As we have learnt from Kierkegaard acts themselves are never pure, such that it is impossible to perform in any final and unambivalent manner any standpoint claim. In other words pro-jects are unfinished; more work remains to be done, more of the telos demands to be realised than is realised. There always remains a difference between what is sought for and what is achieved. The pro-jects of the feminist standpoints, as those of the Christian (and there is no reason why one cannot be committed to both standpoints), seek forms of societal change that no state of affairs could ever perfectly embody in a way that would satisfy all those identified with those standpoints. Furthermore, there always remain consequences of intentional actions on behalf of a standpoint that exceed the pro-jections of the standpoint, in fact may run counter to what was intended. No one can police the consequences of any single action.

CULTURAL PRAGMATICS AND THE QUESTION OF RELATIVISM

It is at this point that we have to treat cultural pragmatics. By this I mean that all acts of cultural engagement, cultural interpretation and cultural negotiation (and here engagement, interpretation and negotiation are inseparable) are local strategies with respect to myriad other local strategies that constitute the historical field of possibles at any one time in any particular situation. It does not follow from the locatedness of the strategy that a more generally applicable observation is impossible, for, as we have seen, situated knowers are not bound by their situations, they belong and relate to several other situations. Neither does it follow from the located-ness of the strategy that the cultural engagement is arbitrary. As we observed above, no standpoint and therefore no pro-ject can admit to its being arbitrary. It cannot admit to it because: first, its starting point is a set of identifications with the axes or truth-claims of that standpoint and therefore of that pro-ject (identifications which have been 'achieved' and embedded through discipline and practice); and, secondly, because the very project itself prescribes a teleology. Cultural pragmatics then do not admit to being arbitrary, but what is the association between being arbi-trary and being relative? For certainly, the locatedness of the cultural engagement does recognise that elsewhere things are done differently and understood differently. The consciousness of a specific time and context for the cultural engagement must also accept the open-endedness of its own conclusions; judgements can only be provisional.

Feminist standpoint epistemologists have also had to face this question of relativism (what Bernstein calls the 'Cartesian anxiety') because the use of a word like 'epistemology' and 'objectivity' is associated with unequi-vocal knowledge, and 'standpoint' from such an epistemological point of view can only mean 'perspectivalism'. But they have observed an argu-ment made by Gadamer (not with reference to Gadamer as far as I know), that relativism is the necessary product of objectivism and as such is fraught with inner contradictions: 'That the thesis of scepticism or relativism refutes itself to the extent that it claims to be true is an irrefutable argument.'[79] In Donna Haraway's more clipped idiom, rela-tivism is a 'way of being nowhere while claiming to be everywhere equally'.[80] The only possible place from which one could be a relativist is God's. But recognising that interpretation is always *relative to* a situ-ation, a standpoint, and the various agents in the situation and working from the standpoint, what is the relation between the relativism of Bernstein's 'Cartesian anxiety' and located knowledges? Lorraine Code claims: '[I]t is wrong to assume that any notion of relative truth has to be parasitic upon absolute, universal truth.'[81] This is part of her defence of a 'mitigated relativism' as opposed to 'the "anything goes" characterization of relativism,'

---

[79] Gadamer, *Truth and Method*, p. 308–9.
[80] *Simians, Cyborgs, and Women*, p. 186.
[81] *Rhetorical Spaces: Essays in Gendered Locations* (London: Routledge, 1995), p. 198.

according to which there is, for a relativist, no way of choosing among rival, conflicting knowledge claims. Every claim has as strong a presumption of truth as any other; there can be no basis for adjudication. In consequence, the argument goes, sexist, racist, or homophobic utterances would all carry a claim to rational assent and toleration that would be just as valid as any evidence adduced to counter them.[82]

What mitigates this extreme relativism – which demands, like universalism, a view from nowhere – is the specificity of being always somewhere. This somewhere, in which the convictions of standpoints are culturally negotiated, defines both the limits and the scope of the judgements made. Rather than relative, one might say the judgements, arguments and claims of standpoints are always relational. A pro-ject is therefore always a hermeneutical strategy with respect to the way it 'works with construction *of*, *out of*, or *from*, interpretation *of*, truths *about*'.[83] In this way engagements are not simply performances of the standpoint tradition but improvisations based upon the grammar of that tradition's claims. They can never transcend the cultural pragmatics through which they operate and reproduce themselves in a non-identical manner.

Cultural pragmatism, whilst admitting of relational judgement rather than the relativism of all judgement, remains involved, then, in local interpretative strategies that, through the intentional pro-jects of standpoints, take on more general claims to being true. But as such there is something unfinished and unsatisfactory about these strategies. In fact, the truth of the vision underlying the project is not only never realised fully, it is continually contested by other standpoints or having to understand its own claims with respect to other standpoints. The Christian has to reckon with the atheist, the Jew, the Muslim, the Sikh, etc.... The Christian not only has to work towards an understanding of his or her standpoint with respect to these other strongly held allegiances, he or she may have to acknowledge that some of the cultural axes of the Christian standpoint seem to find better performances elsewhere – the treatment of the poor, say, or the disciplines of prayer and fasting. But it is the very unfinished nature of intentional pro-jects from cultural standpoints that fosters the ongoing negotiations. The teleology of the pro-ject lies in dialectic tension with the pro-ject's actual execution. A certain lack or incompleteness opens between expectations and

---

[82] Ibid., pp. 192–3.
[83] Ibid., p. 196.

executions which maintains the need for further engagement, interpretation, negotiation. Put in Christian theological terms, faith, while
believing and hoping to achieve its understanding, never finishes the
pro-ject of trying to understand. To put this in more Leninist terms,
the cultural revolution then becomes a permanent one. I will have
more to say about the logic and the operation of this 'lack' and the
way it is intrinsic to transforming the cultural imaginary and therefore accounts of what constitutes public narratives of what is true in
the next section of the essay with respect to the work of desire. For
the moment we need to appreciate one further consequence of this
cultural pragmatism that will return us to the question of relativism,
and the need to define more closely how this profoundly relational
account of cultural operations promotes neither relativism, scepticism
nor perspectivalism. The account is nonfoundational, but it is not
nihilistic.

    Let us proceed by examining the fate of ethics with respect to
cultural hermeneutics engaged from standpoints. For the most controversial consequence of the argument I am making is the lack of any
site in such hermeneutics for judging the rights or wrongs of any
other given standpoint or pro-ject than one's own. For example, in
the course of cultural negotiations I (and the various interpretative
communities that constitute the standpoint of that I) may come to
recognise – and the arguments of feminist epistemology may assist in
that recognition – aspects of my standpoint the implications and
operations of which I have not yet appreciated: the unacknowledged
power of my white, male and middle-class status, for example. Cultural
negotiations arise in and consist of the contestation of standpoints; this
is an aspect of their pragmatism. I may even be persuaded that to
refuse the implications of class, gender and ethnic origins in my
standpoint is incoherent with respect to the implications and operations
of other aspects of my standpoint: my living in a liberal democracy
committed (at least in theory) to the pursuit of tolerance with regard to
the beliefs of others, equality of opportunity, respect for other people's
property and justice for all. Or the implication might be considered
incoherent according to my Christian belief that in Christ there is
neither male nor female, Jew nor Greek. But if I remain unpersuaded
that the implications and operations of aspects of my standpoint
constitute social evils, and that standpoint-axes not shared, and
perhaps even condemned, by others nevertheless remain important
elements of my identity and sets of identifications – then there is no site

of judgement in cultural hermeneutics for proclaiming someone right or wrong.[84] Of course contestation does involve the recognition that others interpret things differently and each side of that difference is involved in a critique which may ultimately dismiss the other as wrong, or evil, or mistaken or objectionable. But such judgements can only be contingent upon the specific cultural negotiations. That does not mean that cultural hermeneutics is antinomian. Belonging to a liberal demo-cratic state means that one's standpoint is policed internally – by the value-laden language of civil rights, public accountability, community, welfare, for example – and externally – by the laws of the country and the institutions making, amending, ratifying, teaching and enforcing them. But those laws too are culturally specific. There is no morally superior standpoint from which Britain can condemn Holland in establishing the age of sexual consent between a male and a female at twelve years old, for example. That does not stop, in fact it provokes, contestation between various standpoints, but, and this is the point I wish to make, in the same way that goals and purposes are not intrinsic to cultural hermeneutics, neither is ethics. Ethics is intrinsic to pro-jects, it adheres to specific sets of values implicit and explicit in the cultural axes of standpoints; it is assumed. Generally speaking, people take this action rather than that action because they believe this action to be better. Others may ask, better for whom? Others may question the judgement of which action is better or the morality of either action. Either way, the language of better and best is indissociable from the language of the good. An assumed ethics is implicated in all cultural negotiations, but it is situationally determined. There is no intrinsic position in cultural hermeneutics for transcendental ethical judgements. Such judgements have to be suspended.

---

[84] This is evidently a worrying conclusion with respect to the perpetration of injustice and the aspirations of the judiciary towards the righting of wrongs. But let me offer a specific case – a standpoint orientated towards supporting the policies of the National Front Party. In a cultural hermeneutics other standpoints not sharing such convictions will contest the policies and their implications. They may point out their denial of basic tenets of liberal democratic thinking, for example. But there is no position from which to say such notions of government are wrong. When such policies (and their ramifications) are acted upon within a space governed by principles antithetical to their own then such behaviour will be condemned as antisocial, but a judgement, say, by a liberal democracy does not render liberal democracy the absolute form for governmentality. The judgement is contingent, announcing that such behaviour cannot be accepted within a society governed by the principles of liberal thinking.

SELF-REFLECTION

A question imposes itself here. 'I' have made several general claims about the nature of cultural hermeneutics. Two of these suggest that both the direction and purpose, and the ethics of engagement belong not to universal truths outside of the engagement. The truths are internal to the projects themselves. They constitute the grammar that dictates the kind and the nature of the cultural negotiations. The question is whether I am not, in fact, constructing a general hermeneutics, albeit of a radically different kind from Schleiermacher's. We can recall that what makes possible Schleiermacher's general hermeneutics – or Dilthey's – is an appeal to a fundamental ontology: the particular finds its meaning and significance in being part of the absolute being, the One. Put briefly, all beings have a place with respect to and are therefore utterly dependent upon absolute being. Am I simply inverting this ontology and appealing to what is now frequently called a metanarrative in which hermeneutical activity is necessary but secondary or epiphenomenal with respect to some anonymous and infinite alterity? To be specific, is the Christian pro-ject only one of a thousand different ways of telling the story of the endless exchange and production of signs which in and of themselves have no meaning, purpose or direction for they are simply indeterminate flows of libidinal energy, contingent constructions provoked by the void? If I were making such a case cultural hermeneutics would find allies among radical postmodern pro-jects such as Gilles Deleuze's and Jacques Derrida's – which, in their different ways, John D. Caputo, Mark C. Taylor and Don Cupitt have been providing with religious interpretations.[85] In this scenario, worlds are spun from the anonymous flux of signs and the desires which give rise to and perpetuate those signs *ad infinitum*, propelling them in manifold and unpredictable directions, rhizomatically. Cultures would constitute and be constituted by these shifting networks of semiotic forces, and each interpretative pro-ject would represent a specific act of the Nietzschean will to power and each interpretative community would simply be imaginary. Emmanuel Levinas gives this primordial background the existential term *il y a*, from which subjects tear themselves away in a violent self-assertion. Religiously, and this is where the projects of Caputo, Taylor and Cupitt coincide, to surrender oneself to living without truth, direction or determinate meaning is the mystical ideal. One approaches the sublime, the

---

[85] See my essay 'Postmodern Theology' in David Ford (ed.), *Modern Theologians*, 3rd edn (Oxford: Blackwell, 1997), pp. 585–602.

unpresentable, an infinite kenosis or deferral of meaning, an ultimate *Gelassenheit* or 'letting go'. For each of them, and here postmodern thinkers like Lacoue-Labarthe, Lyotard and Nancy[86] concur, works of art, especially abstract, minimalist works of art, articulate the near edge of this complete surrender to what Michel de Certeau called 'white ecstasy'.[87]

I have argued elsewhere that this anti-realism and antifoundationalism constitutes a postmodern form of nihilism that is not only atheistic but socially and politically aphasic. Nevertheless it is one more reading of the 'signs of the times', one more pro-ject in cultural hermeneutics. But my own story would challenge the coherence of this terminal ambivalence out of which we necessarily construct our local knowledges. And it is the manner in which I construct my case and contest such a reading that demonstrates that cultural hermeneutics is not making a universal claim founded upon a negative ontology. It also demonstrates, albeit in another way, how cultural hermeneutics avoids being classed as a form of judgemental relativism. For there can be more or less successful forms of contestation between standpoints where certain axes or truth-claims are shared. This account of cultural hermeneutics, like the radical constructivism of certain postmodern pro-jects, bases itself in semiotics and a sociology of knowledge, and is both anti-realist and antifoundationalist. But I would suggest such constructivism fails to do justice to either the nature of cultural transmission, transposition and transmutation or the nature of 'pro-jects' with respect to standpoints. What I mean by this is that where certain axes are shared by standpoints (and the radical interdependence of standpoints admits of incommensurability but not incompatibility),[88] then failure to account for some aspects of that shared axis would constitute a less adequate reading or cultural negotiation. This is similar to my earlier argument concerning strong and weak interpretations. A more successful reading would be one that accounted for many more of

---

[86] For Jean-François Lyotard see *The Inhuman*, trs. Geoffrey Bennington and Rachel Bowlby (Cambridge: Polity Press, 1991) and *Lessons on the Analytic of the Sublime*, tr. Elizabeth Rottenberg (Stanford: University of Stanford Press, 1994). For Jean-Luc Nancy see 'Finite History' in David Carroll (ed.), *The States of 'Theory': History, Art and Critical Discourse* (New York: Columbia University Press, 1990), pp. 149–172 and his book with Philippe Lacoue-Labarthe, *The Literary Absolute*, tr. P. Barnard and C. Lester (Albany: SUNY Press, 1988). For Philippe Lacoue-Labarthe see *Musica Ficta (Figures of Wagner)*, tr. Felicia McCarren (Stanford: Stanford University Press, 1994).

[87] See 'White Ecstasy', trs. Frederick Bauerschmidt and Catriona Hanley in Graham Ward (ed.), *The Postmodern God* (Oxford: Blackwell, 1997), pp. 155–8.

[88] See Richard Bernstein, *Beyond Objectivism and Relativism*, pp. 82–6.

the aspects of that shared axis and answered more of the questions raised by pro-jects emphasising that axis. 'Success' here can be measured by an increase in credibility such that other standpoints sharing that same cultural axis – in this case, the semiotic and sociological approach to knowledge – would be more persuaded of the correctness of one reading over another. For those sharing the same cultural presuppositions would understand through their own cultural negotiations the problematics of such presuppositions and recognise they were being less adequately treated in one case and more adequately treated in another. 'Success' then is an outcome of the economy of recognition. The incoherence of transcendentalising the nothing beyond the chains and tissues of signs, their iteration and exchanges, the nothing beyond the surfaces of such signs, is that this is a return to foundationalism and a universal judgement about the way things are. In fact, it rehearses the Kantian distinction between what is and the construction of what is (the realms of the noumenal and the phenomenal), adding to it a temporal dimension which, for Deleuze, say, or Lacan, issues from an analysis of libidinal desire. Desire perpetuates the chains of signs, locking them into an endless cycle of substitution for what is primordially lacking and absent. Where absence or the 'night of truth' (to use an expression employed by Michel Foucault) deconstructs our reasoned knowing, lack becomes a constitutive principle, what in transcendental philosophy is termed 'the condition for the possibility of'. Kant's *Ding an sich* is now refigured in terms of a foundational absence or a transcendental aporia, which, since it cannot be encountered as such (since it is *as a condition* unpresentable), renders all our semiotic negotiations rhetorical surfaces constructing virtual realities or reality-effects or meaning-effects. According to this *hermeneutica negativa* the various cultural hermeneutical pro-jects – feminist, Marxist, Christian, whatever – would all constitute arbitrary productions. Each standpoint and its pro-ject would be involved in judgemental relativism.

Now while I share with these radical hermeneutics the inescapability of interpretation, my account of cultural hermeneutics contests such a meta-narrative of the way things are. For this story fails, as I said, to pay sufficient attention to the nature of cultural transformations and the nature of standpoint-projects. In particular, this story of the local and radically contingent inscriptions of anonymous energies and flows is inadequately self-reflexive and has no account of agency.

Now let me further unpack these two catgeories of reflexivity and agency. First reflexivity: for all the attention to the diachronic axis of semiotic exchange – the accounts of deferral of meaning, supplementation, the endless substitutionary acts in an infinite kenotic economy – metaphysical claims about what is are being made, albeit negatively. These claims are the reverse side of modernity's preoccupation with presence and the sovereign autonomy of the reasoning subject. More particularly, what these projects on absence share with Kantian transcendentalism is what John D. Caputo calls a 'felicitous nominalism':[89] the division between what is (even if that ontology is understood negatively) and the constructed illusion we work with nevertheless.[90] Lack of presence and priority to the *tout autre* are only inversions of preoccupations with identity and the same. The metanarrative being forged here is a form of *ressentiment* – it is a reactive story about a negative idealism that turns semiotics into a means of aestheticising the real. There are three aspects of this metanarrative that need to be exposed in order to be reflected upon: first, this is a metaphysically driven nonfoundationalism (which raises the question of the metanarrative's coherence); secondly, the paradigm behind this metaphysics originates from particular standpoints in the negative theologies of Christian, Jewish and Islamic thinking; and, thirdly, those writing and accepting this story are not simply agreeing to a set of observations about the way things are but are, simultaneously, producing a world in which that is the way things are.

Let me give an example. The nihilistic metaphysics of Jean Baudrillard's work are explicit. He tells us in *Symbolic Exchange and Death* that 'violence is fundamental', everything participates in a play of 'functional variable[s]', '[n]obody produces any more' and the only 'law is indifference'.[91] He views this state of things as a development within the nature of signs and production itself – a history that he describes as the three orders of simulacra. He believes the only way forward in this evolving symbolic exchange that no one can evade is to push towards a catastrophe where all things collapse and become inverted.[92] Now what is absent from this narrative is the recognition that he, Baudrillard, is part of the production of simulacra. He is not just making observations about hyperreality, he is involved in the very production of the hyperreal. His standpoint is under-

---

[89] See *More Radical Hermeneutics* (Bloomington: Indiana University Press, 2001), pp. 6–7, 30.

[90] The felicity of nominalism is contestable. Certainly from a theological standpoint that accepts a fundamental relation between the uncreated creator and creation, and thinks through a theological anthropology in which the human and the divine co-operate (in some sense), the founding dualism of nominalism is far from felicitous. Nominalism stands diametrically opposed to incarnationalism.

[91] *Symbolic Exchange and Death*, tr. Iain Hamilton Grant (London: Sage, 1993), p. 4.

[92] Ibid.

reflected, and the Hegelian metaphysics (the universal dialectic) of symbolic exchange is unacknowledged. Baudrillard, and the same would go for a number of postmodern critical theorists, hypostasises his standpoint, and in doing so helps to construct the ideology for/of postmodernity. The more that ideology prevails the less reflexive it becomes. And this is the sublime object of ideology – to be rendered invisible or naturalised.

What I am arguing for is the need for a reflexive cultural hermeneutics. Standpoint epistemology, because it requires an analysis of shared axes or communities of knowledge, assists in this reflexivity. One becomes aware that in the attempt to understand and interpret, two other activities are also taking place simultaneously: first, there is a production of that understanding, a modification, a transformation occurring within and through that cultural negotiation; and, secondly, other pro-jects are being produced which will contest that understanding and interpretation, and enforce a recognition of standpoint. This is consonant with cultural pragmatics. The recognition of standpoint is a recognition of limitation or finitude. The story can and is being told in another way, elsewhere. Other production sites are in operation, and it is the interaction between all the various production sites that determines the nature of and changes within the field of what it is possible to believe in any culture. What Bourdieu calls the 'space of possibles', I will call the cultural imaginary. I will say more about transforming the cultural imaginary in the third part of this essay, when I examine Ricoeur's claim that '[w]ithout imagination, there is no action'.[93] For the moment what is significant is that the account I am constructing of cultural hermeneutics is more radical because more antifoundational than those reinscribing a negative ontology. For it rejects the negative metaphysics predicated, on my reading, on the Kantian divide between what is (the infinite indifference of what is always and only *tout autre*) and the symbolic orders (a linguistic adaptation of the Kantian categories) that create surfaces and façades. For these postmodern thinkers the surfaces and façades are necessary but ultimately veils woven to mask the determining and universal *indifferentia*.[94] The account of cultural hermeneutics outlined

---

[93] Paul Ricoeur, 'Imagination in Discourse and Action', tr. Kathleen Blamey, in Kathleen Blamey and John Thompson (eds.), *From Text to Action* (Evanston: Northwestern University Press, 1991), pp. 168–87.

[94] I am aware that although a number of postmodern thinkers appeal to concepts such as khora, the unpresentable, arche-difference, unreason, they are consciously aware that there is no access to these states in any pure sense. Derrida emphasises, for example, that there is no experience of difference as such, pure difference. Nevertheless, what I would argue is that they establish their own pro-jects with respect to a negative ontology even though they are aware that there is no immediate access to this ontology.

here also allows us to glimpse not only the necessary contestations between standpoints but also the possibilities of alliances. Some of these alliances may actually be at odds with certain assumptions about the pro-ject of the standpoint with respect to the wider cultural reception of that pro-ject. For example, the transcendentalising of aporia that issues from a commitment to infinite alterity is a cultural production governed by, aligned with and pitted against other forms of cultural production that contextualise it – economic, political, ethnic, and sexual. If, then, such theoretical productions recognised their own involvement in and promotion of (a) what Adorno called 'the liquidation of the individual'[95] and (b) what Guy Debord called 'the society of the spectacle',[96] then such theoretical productions would recognise how they are structurally related to various economic, political, and ethnic agendas quite at odds with the new liberating *jouissances* they pursue. There has yet to be a productive engagement between Fredric Jameson and Jean Baudrillard, or Jacques Derrida and Terry Eagleton, but the contradiction Eagleton so clearly articulates is significant:

It is a striking feature of advanced capitalist societies that they are both libertarian and authoritarian, hedonistic and repressive, multiple and monolithic. And the reason for this is not hard to find. The logic of the marketplace is one of pleasure and plurality, of the ephemeral and the discontinuous, of some great decentred network of desire of which individuals seem the mere fleeting effects, ... The political ambivalences of postmodernism match this contradiction exactly.[97]

If, then, postmodern radical hermeneutics tend towards viewing the culture they produce as universal (the way things are), as open to endless aporia (which is inevitable) but closed to fundamental self-reflexion, then my second reason for not endorsing their story follows from the first. To be reflexive would, in fact, require them to develop a more adequate concept of agency based upon the human characteristic of self-reflection and the capacity to work upon the world by continually reading and responding to it. Unlike my account of the economies of response and recognition in which human beings lose and find themselves, many postmodern critical projects are governed by a quietism of being more passive than passive or by an appeal to an endless diremption. Some recognise a tragic hermeneutics in which the individual is caught up in anonymous power-strategies that are productive and repressive in ways too complex to map or grasp. Where

---

[95] 'On the Fetish Character in Music and the Regression of Listening' in J.M. Bernstein (ed.), *The Culture Industry* (London: Routledge, 1991), p. 35.
[96] *The Society of the Spectacle* (Detroit: Red and Black, 1977).
[97] *The Illusions of Postmodernism* (Oxford: Blackwell, 1996), p. 132.

ethics does become an issue, it is a meta-ethical account that is offered in
which attention is drawn to the agony of endless responsibility in the face of
arbitrary choice (Derrida feeds this cat while bearing the weight of knowing
a thousand other cats are not being fed).[98] The action itself is rendered
meaningless and purposeless, for it isolates itself, being consumed entirely
by its contingency. The act does not relate *to*, situate itself *with respect to*,
other desires, other commitments, other givings, other refusals that contest
its isolation. But in the cultural hermeneutics I am outlining, action is never
arbitrary. For action is intrinsic to having a pro-ject, just as having a pro-ject
is already to be participating in cultural interpretation and a tradition of
critical enquiry. The pro-ject governs the direction of the engagement,
operating both at the level of the actant's aspiration (even though that
aspiration is culturally informed) and the standpoint's goals of social transformation. In fact, transformation is intrinsic to cultural negotiation, and
while the transformative operation puts the sets of identification of both
actant and standpoint into productive risk, that operation is not random,
but directed. Situations, relations and the persons making up those situations and relations cannot remain the same, and therefore agency and
intentionality, the pursuit of desired ends, are embedded in any
engagement.

  Though embedded the question still emerges about where the agency is
located, especially if we have rejected the Cartesian notion of the subject. If
we can speak of a standpoint as an epistemological community (as Lynn
Hankinson Nelson does in her own contributions to feminist epistemology), then where lies the agency, in the one who acts or in the standpoint?
While emphasising again the rejection of the sovereign individualism of the
modern subject, the account of cultural hermeneutics I offer would suggest
that within the standpoint there is a construction of agency. By that I mean
that just as the pro-ject is the practising of a truth-claim within a standpoint
so, in producing a pro-ject, that truth-claim constructs an agent. This is the
point where the different roles played by cultural axes and sets of identifications are clearly recognised. A Christian may engage with a govern-
ment-backed housing project because being a Christian commits that
person to the truth-claim that, in Christ's words, 'anything you did for
one of my brothers here, however humble, you did for me' (Matthew 25.40).

---

[98] 'How would you ever justify the fact that you sacrifice all the cats in the world to the cat you feed
at home every morning for years, whereas other cats die of hunger at every instant? Not to mention
other people?' *The Gift of Death*, tr. David Wills (Chicago: University of Chicago Press,
1995), p. 71.

This truth-claim then determines an engagement by a Christian with the poor, the homeless, the refugee, the dispossessed. Both agent and pro-ject are constructions of the standpoint or, more exactly, the way a person conceives the kind of action demanded by the pro-ject they are embarked upon and the cultural axes constituting the standpoint determines the kind of agent they are. There is no agent outside the commitment to act, the history of the formation of specific practices and the economies of response and recognition. It is in the engagement that the sets of identifications associated with a standpoint are made (and risked). One's view of oneself as agent is part of that set of identifications composing a standpoint and the practice of enquiry enjoined by that standpoint. So, in answer to the question where lies the agency – it lies in the very activity of standpoint interpretation by the actant.

What emerges from this dynamic account of culture, in which inflexions, reproductions, translations and transformations are affected from myriad standpoints, is the profound interrelational character of cultural hermeneutics. What occurs occurs in and through engagements and encounters between people or groups of people. Cultures are not autonomous spheres of activity over against the social, nor is the social an autonomous realm subtending the cultural. Cultures are the productions of social relations which, in turn, interpret the nature and value of those relations. As the one who acts and the type of action undertaken are mutually determined with respect to a standpoint, so the cultural and the social are inextricably bound. This is where my account differs from Foucault's understanding of governmentality and comes closer (without being identical) to Adorno's understanding of the culture industry.

For Foucault, governmentality (or the internalisation of a public surveillance constituted through various power-informed knowledges) is as pervasive and inescapable as it is anonymous. De Certeau was correct, in my view, to criticise governmentality for its top-down account of domination that forgets the personal practices which evaded its enforcements at local and grassroots levels.[99] While Adorno assumed the passivity of the subject

---

[99] See 'Foucault and Bourdieu' in *The Practice of Everyday Life*, tr. Steven Randell (Berkeley: University of California Press, 1984), pp. 45–60. I am aware that de Certeau's essay on Foucault is an early one, written before the movement made by Foucault towards understanding power as productive of pleasure (in his *History of Sexuality* work). Foucault himself recognised how his early work reaffirmed the 'repressive thesis'. Governmentality and biopower both came to be understood as disciplinary tools of domination and the production of life-affirming discourses. Nevertheless, de Certeau's appeal to personal agency – with his notion of *perruque* – underlines the anonymity of power in Foucault. In fact, the move towards decentralising power in the later work, and examination of the disseminated effects of power-knowledges, only reinforced that anonymity.

with respect to the anonymous and often seemingly abstract cultural powers (such as 'capitalism' or 'industry' or 'administration'), Foucault assumed a greater passivity by liquidating the subject itself. Because of the dynamic activity of standpoint-projects, the cultural hermeneutics I am presenting would emphasise that power is never anonymous. Power is fundamentally relational, as knowledge is relational (viewed in terms of epistemological communities). Power, and all its operations, is produced by persons and among persons as both de Certeau and Bourdieu insist. In turn, the power produced affects the understanding of what persons are or should be or could be. The operations of cultural power create the knowledge of identities and identifications. Foucault is good on the second half of this productive dialectic – 'the self is nothing else than the historical correlation of the technology built in our history'[100] – but forgets the first part: the recognition of being an agent.

Foucault's approach to critique implies dissolving the social into the cultural, and that severely limits the scope for transformation. Adorno, on the other hand, maintains the distinction between the social and the cultural, even whilst recognising the power of the cultural industry to get people to 'assimilate themselves to what is dead. And that is how they become disposable.'[101] Nevertheless, Adorno's (and Horkheimer's) critique of a totalitarian culture industry suffers from the same etiolated concept of agency. This is partly because of his critique of the bourgeois Cartesian 'subject'. Though treating music, film, radio, sport, television, newspapers and advertisements, Adorno says nothing about who runs this industry, how it is organised, of what it is composed and who does the composing. Though he insists throughout his analysis on the totalitarian character of a domination in which there is a 'consummated conflictlessness' that manifests 'the acceptance of the manipulation of needs by the might of production',[102] the strong association between domination and communication renders power too diffuse.[103] While rejecting the idea that the masses (with their lack of aesthetic taste) dictate to the media and proclaiming, therefore, that talk of a 'mass media' is a misnomer, he does not

---

[100] 'About the Begining of the Hermeneutics of the Self' in Jeremy Carrette (ed.), *Religion and Culture by Michel Foucault* (Manchester: University of Manchester Press, 1999), p. 181.
[101] 'The Schema of Mass Culture' in Bernstein (ed.), *The Culture Industry*, p. 95.
[102] Ibid., pp. 77–80.
[103] On the ambiguity of domination in Adorno (and Horkheimer), see Axel Honneth, *Kritik der Macht: Reflexionsstufen einer Kritischen Honneth, Gesellschaftstheorie* (Frankfurt am Main: Suhrkamp, 1985); Gillian Rose, *The Melancholy Science: An Introduction to the Thought of Theodor Adorno* (London: Macmillan, 1978); and Simon Jarvis, *Adorno: A Critical Introduction* (Cambridge: Polity Press, 1998), pp. 33–7.

examine the constitution of this media industry, its actions and the means it employs to disseminate its effects.[104] Attention is too quickly drawn to the fetishism of the products and masochistic logic of customers who see through them and yet are still compelled to buy and use them.[105] Adorno's concern is with interpreting the phenomenon itself, abstracting it from the very *verwaltete Welt* or matrix of administration that he inveighs against. The result is that the opacity of social relations and the abstract nature of labour – which Adorno claims are the common and depoliticising experiences of most people – are actually reinforced. The culture industry becomes faceless; power in late capitalism becomes faceless.   But capitalism is not faceless; and neither is the culture industry. Laying aside whether there is something monolithic called 'capitalism', economic and cultural operations are not abstract forms of power. You and I with our index-linked pensions, credit levels, bank accounts, property and mortgages are some of the faces of capitalism. The culture industry also is composed of women and men doing work and being paid for it – however grandly or badly. Both the economic and the cultural, then, issue from what the new historicist, Stephen Greenblatt, calls 'circulation of social energy'.[106] There is agency and that agency is effective. The work of Foucault and Adorno has been effective in bringing about cultural transformation. They have each fostered critical industries and discursive practices, and what has been disseminated in and through their production has been a force for change. The changes that have occurred may not be in accord with the changes they wished for, but then, in both their standpoint-projects the goals they wished their productions to achieve, the exact transformations they were calling for were highly under-defined.[107] Their critique was effective, even while it offered negative images of what might be alternative social and cultural possibilities. As to whether the changes their work brought about were good or bad, significant or insignificant, that would depend upon the standpoint-project engaging them. The extent to which a culture is transformed, from the perspective of cultural hermeneutics, is

---

[104] This is so even when he is being most empirical, as in *The Stars Down to Earth* when his examination of the ideology of dependence and semi-rationality begins with an astrology column in the *Los Angeles Times* by Carroll Righter.

[105] Theodor Adorno with Max Horkheimer, *Dialectic of Enlightenment*, tr. John Cumming (London: Verso, 1997), p. 167.

[106] *Shakespearean Negotiations* (Oxford: Oxford University Press, 1988), p. 5.

[107] In fact, Foucault's project seems to become increasingly descriptive as his *History of Sexuality* unfolds.

impossible to measure. Any measurement of it would be itself in terms of a specific standpoint-project. Nevertheless, the transformations themselves bear witness to effective agency. The effect may not be simply in terms of the author as biographical subject – the author Foucault, along with Roland Barthes,[108] saw as dead, though who, for cultural hermeneutics, remains to some extent as the focused agent within a standpoint. Cultures change through the various works operating within and upon them, the various engagements that I term cultural hermeneutics. Neither cultures, then, nor the powers at work constituting and deconstituting them, are anonymous.

A question arises here concerning the orientation of a standpoint-project and the cultural transformation effected by the project. That a transformation takes place is a fundamental corollary of cultural hermeneutics, but determining precisely the kind of transformation is not possible. For control and the power to determine ends are too widely disseminated across the cultural networks constituting any standpoint. This is where the risk of production takes place. This is not to suggest that in any given culture some standpoints and the pro-jects pursued within them do not dominate and colour the *Zeitgeist*. But I would suggest that there is probably less control than we think. For what is axiomatic to cultural transformation is interrelationality,[109] and the complexities of interrelationality are such that there is a continual struggle on behalf of the dominant trends to stay ahead and spin-doctor possible changes of cultural direction beyond their own conceived ends. Standpoint-projects cannot avoid the risk of production. This risk is twofold: (a) with respect to the identities and identifications of the standpoint (in cultural negotiation these will be modified and possibly abandoned); and (b) with respect to the pro-ject (that it may bring about that which is contrary to the standpoint orientation of the pro-ject). An offer of charity may have tragic consequences, for example.

---

[108] For Michel Foucault see 'What is an Author?' in *Language, Counter-Memory, Practice: Selected Essays and Interviews*, trs. Donald F. Bouchard and Sherry Simon (Ithaca: Cornell University Press, 1977), pp. 113–38. For Roland Barthes see 'The Death of the Author' in *The Rustle of Language*, tr. Richard Howard (Oxford: Blackwell, 1986), pp. 49–55.

[109] I say 'interrelationality' rather than, with Hegel, Habermas or Honneth for example, 'intersubjectivity' to avoid the idea that there are subjects prior to and outside of relations.

CONCLUSION WITH RESPECT TO CHRISTIAN PRAXIS

At the end of this examination we can see something of the structures of engagement, the processes by which cultures and, thereby, the public perception of what is true, change. This was the governing question of this second part of the essay. I opened this section by noting that a further question, fundamental to the development of a new Christian apologetics, sheltered beneath that initial question: how does the theological pro-ject (Christian, in this instance) become a transformative public practice with respect to the cultures that contextualise it? We are not quite in a position to answer that second question. We need to examine the way in which what is publicly believed is made believable. Having looked at standpoints and pro-jects we need to provide an account of how these come to an 'image' of themselves and recognise, through their self-representation, their cultural distinctivenesses and continuities. We have to investigate how any culture, and the standpoints that produce, reproduce and contest that culture, comes to an understanding of itself: how a *Zeitgeist* is not only produced but recognises itself. For this we need to analyse the way standpoint-projects (such as that performed by Christians living out their faith) relate to what a culture conceives itself both to be and to be possible. The economies of collective response need to be situated within the larger dreams of the cultural imaginary. Only then will it be possible to recognise the contribution made by these pro-jects to the transformation of culture. The key, as I quoted earlier, is found in Ricoeur's statement (which I now enlarge): '[B]eyond its mimetic function, imagination, even applied to action, has a projective function that is part of the very dynamism of acting . . . Without imagination, there is no action.'[110]

But, for the moment, let us return to the question of Christian praxis and some of the implications of our examination so far concerning stand-point-projects. For, having critiqued radical hermeneutics for embracing a nominalism and a negative ontology, and having refigured, for cultural hermeneutics, the concepts of intentionality and agency, we need to return to that important question of the relativity of standpoints. With respect to the Christian interpretation of culture, to Christian cultural hermeneutics, am I arguing that the Christian standpoint is a relative one? Is Christianity only one way to tell the story? If so, what happens to its universal claims? Another way of putting this would be to ask what kind of Christian

---

[110] 'Imagination in Discourse and Action', p. 177.

apologetics emerges from this account of cultural hermeneutics. Does theological hermeneutics, in this case Christian cultural hermeneutics, become a subset of a more general hermeneutics as it did with liberal hermeneutics from Schleiermacher (on Gadamer's reading) to Ricoeur? In which case what is so different about cultural hermeneutics at all?

I wish to make two important points. The first concerns there being no culture outside of cultural hermeneutics, outside interpretative stories and standpoint-projects. The second concern returns us, once again, to the spectre of relativism. First: there is no neutral, factual objective level called the pre-cultural or the raw experience of what is, upon which standpoints operate – Christian or otherwise. Interpretation, therefore, is not epiphenomenal: it constructs and constitutes lived experience and all lived experience contributes to and fosters cultures and the ongoing production of their transformations. It follows then that cultural hermeneutics is a participatory practice. And what standpoints participate in is the making of worlds through the telling and contestation of stories. This leads to the second concern with relativism. If asked the question, is Christianity only one way to tell the story of what is, then the only answer according to cultural hermeneutics is yes. There are many ways to tell the story of what is, some go in and out of fashion, gain or lose credibility, depending upon what other stories contextualise and so empower or disempower them. We have to recognise that some stories issue from events that are more powerful in terms of having longer-lasting discursive effects than other events. The events of Christ or Buddha, Moses or Mohammed are of a different order than the death of Queen Victoria or the Stonewall Riots. The stories narrating the events have had a profound impact over centuries. They have gathered a momentum where more recent events have not. And some events simply slip away altogether because, as Alain Badiou observes, an event 'compels us to decide a *new* way of being'.[111] There is if not a hierarchy, then, a calibration of events according to the extent to which they compel decisions that open a new way. All events are not the same; they are not relative. Furthermore, although there are other ways to tell the story of what is it does not follow that the judgements about the world made by this story are relative. Judgemental relativism is not a consequence of this account of cultural hermeneutics. As I said earlier in the essay standpoints are constituted through complex weaves of identifications. While, then, recognising there are other forms of identity and identification,

---

[111] *Ethics: An Essay on the Understanding of Evil*, tr. Peter Hallward (London: Verso, 2001), p. 41.

while recognising there are differences between, say, the Christian, the Hindu, and the atheist, that recognition does not necessarily weaken or erode those forms of identity and identifications. And we must again recall that these identities and identification are communal, not simply subjective. They are born within disciplines and practices, habits of thinking and living. From within a given standpoint, the judgement of other possibly antithetical standpoints might be either negative (they are wrong) or agnostic (we cannot say whether they are right in their interpretation of the world or wrong; we suspend judgement). Either way the judgement is not one concerning the relativity of world-views but *the relation of* one set of judgements about the world to another. This relation is not simply antagonistic. Relativism, in appealing to all judgements being equally valid, isolates and atomises positions, detemporalising them. Relational judgements are constantly being revised in the light of the new events they encounter and negotiate. Relational judgements are time-bound and made always in the context of other relational judgements that contest, affirm or are even indifferent to them. The Christian standpoint, the sets of identifications emerging from that standpoint and performed in any cultural activity engaged in on the basis of that standpoint, is produced and modified today in and through the recognition that there are other faiths being practised, other religious stories of the world and its salvation being told. Since the beginning of Christian practice, in its many different forms, this has always been so. It is because of this that Christianity never has a pure form. It is never identical with the image of its distinctiveness that it continually produces. For, like all stand-point-projects, it is syncretistic. Its own identity is constituted always and only *in relation to*. So a theological hermeneutics is not, on this account, a subset of a general hermeneutics. For there is no general hermeneutics, only specific acts of interpretation from complex standpoints. Nor are such theological hermeneutics doomed only to be relative, for they produce, rehearse and transform identities and identifications. They compose the sense of belonging, the sense that this is the best understanding of the world. They compose stories that compete with other stories for credence, but from within the set of stories that have shaped and continue to shape any given standpoint. The power of the stories of that standpoint lies in their capacity to outnarrate competing stories. There is no question of relativism, only relationality. There may be a question of dogmatic certainty (the belief that all other stories are wrong or inferior), but such a standpoint would effectively be counter-cultural.

I realise that I have not answered the question I raised above concerning what happens to the universalism of Christianity's claims. Let me be brief here because the answer proceeds from what we have said above. In brief then, any standpoint maintains claims to be valid while being aware of the different ways to tell the story of what is. The tension here between identification with and recognition of alterity would be productive for further cultural engagement in order to understand both the nature of the universalism involved in the claims and the degrees of difference in the other stories. For the Christian standpoint, this may be another way of putting Anselm's famous 'faith seeking understanding'. The tension nevertheless would remain, rendering all its judgements, like all other judgements, provisional. But it is the recognition of their provisionality that provides space for and demands ongoing change. Provisionality makes transformation necessary and possible – and that is where we take up our third question: what is the relationship between Christian discursive practices and the production and transformation of public truth or shared knowledge? In answering this question then the way is open to understanding, in a new way, the nature of Christian apologetics.

CHAPTER 3

The governing question III: what is the relationship between religious practices and cultural transformation?

We are now in a position to approach that third question: on the basis of the two previous examinations, how can we describe the relationship between Christian discursive practices and the production and transformation of public narratives of what is true or what Adorno calls 'monopolies of public opinion'?[1] As I have suggested, answering this question will also furnish us with an account of the apologetic nature of Christian discourse. That shared knowledges are in a continual state of transformation, I take as proven, but while the previous section dealt with the poetics or governing structures of that transformation and demonstrated its inevitability, the scope of the negotiations and exchanges fundamental to the nature of society and what exactly is being transformed still require analysis. Althusser, in his widely influential essay 'Ideology and Ideological State Apparatuses', informs us that the means of cultural production (education, but also other State apparatuses such as the Church and the army) 'ensure subjection to the ruling ideology or the mastery of its "practice"'.[2] But this observation begs a question which must also be answered in relation to shared knowledges of what is true (which I take as being very close to Althusser's 'ruling ideology'). That is, to what extent if at all can we talk of a coherent and unified object such as 'public opinion' or 'ruling ideology'? In the plethora of possible and affirmed opinions, in the dense overlapping (Althusser would say 'overdetermination') of values and perspectives that make up any complex production and reproduction of an ideology, to what extent can we abstract a certain homogeneity such that we can suggest

---

[1] *Introduction to Sociology*, tr. Edmund Jephcott (Cambridge: Polity Press, 2000), p. 15.
[2] *Lenin and Philosophy and Other Essays*, tr. Ben Brewster (New York: Monthly Review Press, 2001), p. 89.

this opinion is dominant or this ideology is ruling? And if we cannot, what then happens to the effect of Christian discourse (or any discourse) if what is being transformed by it is public (and executed with wide national or international media coverage) but highly local, dispersed and heterogeneous? What is the relationship between a local cultural negotiation and transformation, and more broadly accepted cultural mind-sets or ideologies?

From a Christian theological perspective we can raise these questions in an eschatological mode. If we are called upon to 'read the signs of the times', then we have to assume that these signs (when we can correctly discern them from the plethora of signs available and in constant production[3]) constitute a coherent 'message' and that these signs are publicly available for common reading and recognition. We have to assume that there is something we can call a *Zeitgeist*, a 'times', the characteristics of which can be sketched and specific articulations of which can be pointed to, and that a consensus of public opinion concerning these characteristics and articulations is available. This *Zeitgeist* constitutes an ethos of shared cultural knowledges, even ruling cultural assumptions. The sharing has to be pervasive and dominant. One cannot have two or three or four concurrent *Zeitgeister*, without compromising the very concept of there being 'a times'. But in a cultural scene characterised by its pluralism, syncretism and eclecticism it is not immediately evident that we can talk of 'a ruling ideology', public truth or *Zeitgeist*. It has then to be established to what extent and by what means there are shared cultural knowledges and ruling cultural assumptions. To what extent can we talk of 'public truth' or 'ruling ideology'?

Of course, for Althusser the one ideology that reproduced not only certain skills but also certain knowledges that worked for the subjection of the working classes was the ideology of the bourgeoisie or the capitalist. But to an extent this is the homogenising of myriad social, economic and cultural projects and labourings akin to Christian discourse claiming that the ruling ideology is 'secularism'. For where are the pure enclaves of secularism (or capitalism) to be found? Surely this is an idealist abstraction

---

[3] In his *Introduction to Sociology*, Adorno has a relevant discussion on determining whether the object of a cultural enquiry is 'essential' or not. He defines being essential not in epistemological or ontological terms, but rather 'the essential concerns the laws of motion of society, especially the laws which express how the present situation has come into being and where it is tending to go' (p. 25). These 'laws' manifest themselves in phenomena and interpretation discloses them. We can recall here the attention paid by de Certeau to 'silent laws' governing a discourse, referred to in section 1.

that denies something of the very 'overdeterminism' or complexity of any cultural activity.[4] It sets up and reifies a defining difference far too neatly. To understand something of the overdeterminism of 'secularism' (or 'capitalism') requires analysis of specific phenomena or activities taken to illustrate or be paradigmatic instances of such cases. But for every *Zeitgeist* established there will be found cultural and social practices that deny or question the rule of such a *Zeitgeist*. This is an axiom of the cultural politics examined in section 2. Analysis must take as its object then not just the phenomena, practices, beliefs and 'subjectivities' themselves, but what makes a sufficiently large number of people consider that these phenomena, practices, beliefs and 'subjectivities' identify the operation of a dominating *Zeitgeist*. What makes a belief in such a *Zeitgeist* possible? What are the discourses which nurture that credibility?

It would seem to me that the focus of an analysis of public truth (and its transformation) should not be the truths themselves so much as the pool of credible possibilities that make possible the belief that this truth is shared by significant numbers of people such that it warrants being understood as public rather than private, general rather than local. By the 'pool of credible possibilities' I intend something close to what several social scientists (among them, in their different ways, Benedict Anderson, Charles Taylor, Paul Ricoeur, Jürgen Habermas and Cornelius Castoriadis) have termed the 'social imaginary'.

IMAGINARY RELATIONS

Among men, the building and designing of cities have always included spaces that are shared, common spaces like the *agora*, a burial ground, a public way or the precincts of a sacred site in which exchanges took place that crossed the two dominant forms of social difference: generational difference and kinship difference. Sometimes these spaces were more 'democratic' – the market-place or the public park, for example – in admitting and allowing for a certain amount of crossing of gender, religious, ethnic and class difference. The polis, in requiring for its

---

[4] For Althusser the basis of overdetermination, which constitutes the complex process of the development of things, is displacement and condensation. These are Freudian categories manifesting a dialectical tension, a contradiction insofar as one works centrifugally and the other centripetally. This tension renders all social formations complex or (in Althusser's term) 'uneven'. It sets up a destabilisation out of which process emerges; but this destabilisation must affect the objects and events which act as moments within this process. See 'On the Materialist Dialectic' in *For Marx*, tr. Ben Brewster (London: Penguin Books, 1969), particularly pp. 206–18.

maintenance and continuance operations that negotiated various differences, needed to construct spaces for this negotiation, as if architects of the 'higher unity' constituting the city[5] recognised that it only functioned as a complex structure if spaces were designed for its self-reflection and for the exhibition of its ability to come together.[6] And it is in these negotiations, exchanges and reflections on its shared existence that a public is constituted. '[T]he criterion of publicness . . . means communication, whether in words or actions,' Habermas informs us.[7] But what is fundamental here is that though there might be certain anthropological, religious, economic, psychological and biological conditions that determine human beings coming into relation with each other, a 'public' is a construct, it is not a given. It is constructed through those 'words or actions'. It is constructed discursively. A 'public' is not simply a collection of people. It is already a statement about what being a person is. There has already taken place a certain socialisation prior to the arrival of the public as either concept or phenomenon.

We can ask a number of things about any particular construction, such as 'Who constructs this public, on whose behalf and who is excluded?' Such questions concern the cultural politics involved in the formation of the public and the necessary (even if implicit) boundaries that must be appealed to if *this* public is to be identifiable. For the moment, though, let us not examine the cultural and historical practices and conditions that produce a notion of the public realm, but rather what it is that is being constituted. Because I wish to argue that cultural transformation operates on the basis of something more primary than the pragmatics of cultural and historical practices and conditions. It operates, that is, from a belief in the relational nature of being human itself – which, of course, only discloses itself within particular sets of cultural and historical practices and conditions. The more fundamental question than 'how' the public is constructed is what discloses itself in the construction of the public. I suggest the answer to that question is the belief of being-in-relation; the belief in a certain social ontology that makes the public appear to be a natural phenomenon, a given. As I said, the public is already a statement about a belief in what people are. I emphasise the word 'belief', for what is key here is that there is a difference between the being-in-relation as an

[5] See Lewis Mumford, *The City in History* (Harmondsworth: Penguin Books, 1966), p. 40.
[6] It seems to me these spaces are severely compromised when, as is often the case today, they are constantly under CCTV surveillance.
[7] *Knowledge and Human Interests*, tr. Jeremy J. Shapiro (Cambridge: Polity Press, 1987), p. 238.

anthropological and biological *a priori* and the being-in-relation that is produced in, and conditions the possibility for, the construction of the public.

We must tread carefully here, for I do not wish to suggest any bipolarity between nature and culture. There are various accounts of what it is to be human, and we have learnt too much from historians, gender critics, and sociologists of science to accept naïvely accounts of the physiology of being human as providing transparent descriptions of what is natural. But there is a difference between a relation with a lover, a friend, a sibling, and one's child and a relation between two members of the public. There is a difference in the quality of the relationship that issues from greater intimacy with the former than the latter. Both relations are mediated. That is: the accounts given of different relations and how we understand and even value them are culturally and historically coloured. But both relations are mediated in different ways such that, following Benedict Anderson, I would call the first relation familiar and the second imaginary. My practices of everyday living with the former involve high degrees of physical contact, of co-presence. My practices of everyday living with the latter involve, to use Anderson's understanding of the 'imaginary community', believing a relation exists between us when we might never meet or know each other's names.[8] Each of these relations enables us to use the language of 'we': 'we are going on holiday to Scotland', on the one hand, 'we, the citizens of . . .' on the other. But the 'we', and the knowledge about what constitutes that 'we', issues from a different set of spatial relations and exchanges. With the familiar relation there is contact, an appeal to tactile and sensate life-forms. In the imaginary relation there may be little or no contact. In fact the very distances involved only serve to deepen the imaginary nature of the relation, giving it more scope, rendering it more amorphous.

I realise these two categories – the familiar and the imaginary – are abstractions; that any number of relationships fall between the two; that the categories are, at best, heuristic.[9] But the point I wish to make is fourfold:

---

[8] *Imagined Communities* (London: Verso, 1991), p. 6.
[9] As both Lacan and more recently Slavoj Žižek have made us aware, the very closest of sexual relations is 'plagued by fantasies' – to use Žižek's phrase. In both the familiar relation and the imaginary one there is the Other, and the construction and negotiation of this Other. Since then all relations are organised around this dialectical tension and fantasy is one way of negotiating this tension, 'fantasy tells me what I am to my others' (Žižek, *The Plague of Fantasies* (London: Verso, 1997), p. 9). All relations are then caught up with the operations of the imaginary. Hence Žižek moves quickly from the most intimate relationship to the function of ideology in various forms of institutionalism (national, military, ecclesial, etc.).

first, that what the public constitutes is a set of imaginary relations, what Charles Taylor recently has called 'the crucial fiction';[10] secondly, that any particular historical and cultural understanding of the public is inseparable from an implicit account of being human and being in relation; thirdly, that relations are *believed* to hold and so the imaginary relation must be a credible relation, a relation that can be believed in; fourthly, that the credibility of such an imaginary relation depends upon a degree of analogy that can be made between the imaginary and the familiar or model relation. More needs to be said here to clarify that final claim.

What I am suggesting is that we measure the credibility of a relationship by our models of the perfect, working relationship. These models are culturally specific. So, if Lacan is right that in the West at present this perfect relationship is governed by an ideal of sexual congress, then the credibility of relationships for us is in proportion to the degree of social intimacy they seem to afford.[11] We develop our sense of the model relationships, the ones we trust in, partly by experience of successful and unsuccessful familiar relationships, partly by observing and interpreting other relationships around us, and partly by current ideologies of relation and our response to them. The ideology of the family and parental relations would be an example of this. The ideology of the heterosexual relation at the heart of contemporary mediatised views of 'romance' or 'love' would be another example. The credibility of imaginary relations, then, is measured by criteria learnt and internalised by familiar ones and extended or transferred analogically. Hence, those who wish to manipulate public truth employ, as a marker of the credibility of their claims, references to and images of familiar relations. They seek to generate a belief in the imaginary relation by associating it closely with the familiar one. Two examples will suffice, both from different stages in the development of the body politic. The first is the emphasis placed upon the sovereign as being the head of the national body, the one who thinks and rules over the various other organs or offices. The second is an association

---

[10] *Modern Social Imaginaries* (Durham, N.C.: Duke University Press, 2003), p. 96. I would like to thank Charles Taylor for allowing me to read the manuscript for this book and raise questions about the social imaginary with him.

[11] Of course, this state of affairs in which a high degree of intimacy is the marker of a relationship that can be believed in also recognises that most relationships rarely can meet this criterion or meet it only on occasions. A 'credibility gap' opens between that which is the perfect model (the fulfilment of which can be most trustworthy) and the facts of the case. The gap fosters a social cynicism about relationships. For, on the one hand, there is a longed-for ideal, while, on the other, all too much evidence of the failure to find many examples of the ideal. Our views of relationships, I suggest, move between these poles of idealism and cynicism.

made between the micro unit of the heterosexual family and the macro unit of the nation in the ideology of the nation state, in which one safeguards and legitimates the other. These kinds of associations may begin by seeming metaphorical, but the extent to which they are believed in and internalised as true or cultural givens corresponds to the degree to which the association can be understood literally.[12]

Having understood that what the construction of the public is attempting to do is get people to believe they belong to a certain kind of community, persuade them that they stand in solidarity with the values and norms of that community, we can now return to that other set of questions concerning 'how' a public is constituted. The fourth point I made with respect to imaginary relations and their dependence for credibility on familiar ones already moves us from the 'what' to the 'how'. But it becomes much clearer now that 'imaginary relations' and 'believing' are inextricably associated with the rhetorics of persuasion and how these rhetorics are received. What is at stake in the employment of these rhetorics is authority. It would seem that two further enquiries now become necessary – an enquiry into the rhetorics and their employment and an enquiry into the principles generating both the rhetorics and their reception. The first is an enquiry into the constitution of a public with shared beliefs and the second into the dynamics of desire and imagination with respect to generating and believing such beliefs. To return to our earlier set of questions in a slightly modified form: 'Who constructs this public, on whose behalf, who is excluded and how does this construction come to be believed?'

THE CREATION OF THE PUBLIC SPHERE

If we accept the thesis of Habermas's important early work, *The Structural Transformation of the Public Sphere*,[13] then, in the West, the construal of the public is a construction dating from the end of the seventeenth century. From the subtitle of the book (*An Inquiry into the Category of Bourgeois Society*) we can infer that this public is informed by notions of being human and being-in-relation that are inseparable from categories such as 'liberal humanism', 'bourgeois property-owners', 'human rights' and 'democracy'.

---

[12] One can note here how, in contemporary advertising and marketing, 'belief' in a product is frequently solicited through an appeal to explicit forms of sexual intimacy. Again, the imaginary relation (with a product) is being forged through associating it with the most familiar.

[13] All references to this work are taken from *The Structural Transformation of the Public Sphere: An Inquiry into the Category of Bourgeois Society*, tr. Thomas Burger (Cambridge: Polity Press, 1989).

The notion of there being a 'public' is developed alongside the security, through religion, of a sphere of private autonomy and the creation of public and depersonalised forms of state authority ('a *permanent* administration and a *standing* army'[14]). To the trend towards the internalisation of 'religion'[15] can be added the insistence (by thinkers like John Locke, for example) on the right to property and the proliferation of private housing. The first condition for the emergence, then, of a public is the ability to police people who have become privatised. The second condition, which Habermas sees developed in England more than anywhere else in Europe in the early eighteenth century, is the existence of organs for publishing opinions. With the daily press and the circulation of various journals, concomitant with the emergence of a public sphere was a sphere for public reflection. A number of early journalists like Daniel Defoe, Joseph Addison, Richard Steele and Samuel Johnson took upon themselves the role of public educator – defining a moral ethos, styles of social behaviour (manners) and the conception of a common humanity.[16] Journalists and pamphleteers were the new secular priests of a new civic order. The effectiveness of this emerging 'public opinion' can be gauged by the debates between Defoe, say, and the British parliaments – debates which continually threatened to shut down Defoe's printing presses. Essential to the developing notion of the public was the possibility of participation. With the establishment of the daily newspaper there arose public reflection on all the political issues of the day.

We must stop to reflect here upon the character of this public sphere. It was founded paradoxically, as I have said, on the atomisation and privatisation of civil society – in fact Habermas views the emergence of this sphere as the 'completion' of that privatisation.[17] Secondly, with respect to its composition, it was an organ for certain class interests: commodity owners with 'rights'. We might say the first human right to be established was the right to own property (and demand the protection of that right from public authority). As Habermas points out this class bias entrenched the concept

[14] Ibid., p. 18.
[15] See my *True Religion* (Oxford: Blackwell, 2002). Habermas has been criticised for paying too little attention to the role of religion in the construction of the public sphere. See David Zaret, 'Religion, Science, and Printing in the Public Spheres in Seventeenth Century England' in Craig Calhoun (ed.), *Habermas and the Public Sphere* (Cambridge, Mass.: MIT Press, 1992), pp. 212–35.
[16] The belief in a common humanity can be traced back through the Renaissance to figures like Pico della Mirandola and the advocates of a universal 'religion' on an anthropological basis (Ficino, Grotius, and Herbert of Cherbury, for example).
[17] *The Structural Transformation*, p. 75.

of a public sphere in an ineradicable tension: 'The public sphere of civil society stood or fell with the principle of universal access. A public sphere from which specific groups would be *eo ipso* excluded was less than merely incomplete; it was not a public sphere at all.'[18] The tension here lies in the fact that the rationale of 'public sphere' demanded the continual need to extend access, on the one hand, while the right to private property that made a person, to use a contemporary idiom, a 'stakeholder' in civic society was a protective means for the limitation of personal damage, on the other. Thirdly, as the case of Defoe illustrates, public opinion wrestled with State authority, and State forms of censorship: there emerged legislative limits within which the bourgeoisie had the freedom to speak. Fourthly, the public sphere was founded upon what Habermas terms a culture of debating (*Kulturräsonierend*).

It is with respect to this culture of debating that Habermas argues for a major transformation in the public sphere. 'The public sphere in the world of letters was replaced by the pseudo-public or sham-private world of culture consumption.'[19] To some extent one might expect such a view from a thinker following in the footsteps of Adorno, but other literary and social analysts would concur.[20] Habermas views this change as an effect of the laws of the market governing commodity exchange and social labour. The vehicle for the change is the press.[21] This is significant, for while there are economic transformations that affect production and consumption, in the move from the citizen as 'rational and critical debater' to the citizen as 'consumer', what is also changed is structures of feeling and sensibility. There is a new understanding of what it is to be human and to be in relation to other human beings. We might see this transformation as an unfolding of the logic of tensions that composed the public sphere: the atomisation of individuals is reinforced by the narcissism of citizen as consumer who now designs his or her own lifestyle, manners and morals; a consumer culture radically extends the right to private ownership. Privatisation leads to depoliticisation. But the vehicle for the transformation is persuasive rhetorics which, I would argue, effect changes in that 'space of possibles' Bourdieu examined; changes in the cultural imaginary. In a consumer culture there are technologies for what Habermas calls 'manipulative publicity'[22] and competition is extended

---

[18] Ibid., p. 85.
[19] Ibid., p. 160.
[20] See particularly Richard Sennett, *The Fall of Public Man* (New York: Knopf, 1977).
[21] *The Structural Transformation*, pp. 180–95.
[22] Ibid., p. 178.

now into the very domain of public opinion. Habermas observes, some-what lugubriously:

Publicity once meant the exposure of political domination before the public use of reason: publicity now adds up the reactions of an uncommitted friendly disposition . . . One may speak of a refeudalization of the public sphere . . . public relations already assumes a 'political' character, subjects even the State itself to its code. Because private enterprises evoke in their customers the idea that in their consumption decisions they act out their capacity as citizens, the State has to 'address' its citizens like consumers. As a result, public authority competes for publicity.[23]

We speak then in the plural today of public spheres, of a variety of organised public opinions in competition. These are what I would call public narratives of what is true, or what is the case. These public spheres are locked into the competitiveness and self-inflation of public relations, the setting of a public agenda, and their concern is to win public trust or public confidence. What is at stake here is not so much the truth of the matter or even the debate – it is credibility. The anxiety over credibility is actually a testimony to the doubts that any 'public' can now be constituted – even as a fiction. Nevertheless, while we must continually be aware that the major tendency of a consumer culture is hyper-individualism that exacerbates depoliticisation and enervates participation in critical debate, I would suggest there is a significant affinity between the organisation of public truths and standpoint-projects. They are not identical because there is much more self-reflection and agency involved in a standpoint, whereas one's public opinions of what is the case can be founded upon unquestioned assumptions about how to act and what to think. Habermas points out that the effect of public relations orchestrating and organising public opinion is integration or what Antonio Negri would call the reduction of 'dialectical possibilities to zero'.[24] Habermas ends his thesis with something of a call to action: '[T]he communicative interconnectedness of a public can be brought about only in this way: through a critical publicity brought

---

[23] Ibid., p. 195. A number of people have responded critically to Habermas's lugubrious conclusion and the project he then sets himself, which is how to render the public sphere more critical and re-establish the culture of debate. Some have questioned whether the public sphere has degenerated as much as Habermas believes. Others have pointed to aspects of power and institutional networks that Habermas neglected and attention to which would deepen the analysis he offers. (See Calhoun (ed.), *Habermas and the Public Sphere*.) I am evidently accepting Habermas's analysis of the decline of participation and 'critical publicity'.

[24] *Time for Revolution*, tr. Matteo Mandarini (New York: Continuum, 2003), p. 41.

to life within the intraorganisational public sphere.'[25] I will go on to suggest, in the last part of this essay, that a cultural ethics is only possible on the basis of resistance to the hyper-individualism and depoliticisation that prevents the further erosion of that 'critical publicity'. Cultural ethics is only possible where critique is possible. As Habermas's work indicates, the public sphere was always an agonistic sphere. It is now also a competitive set of spheres. The question raises itself: what is the competition for? Bourdieu would no doubt say symbolic power, in its various guises. But I wonder if we can be more precise than this. The competition between persuasive rhetorics concerns the power to shape belief, the power to *make* credible. This, it seems to me, rests upon the energising and transformation of the imagination and the reorientation of desire. We come then to the second of our enquiries.

RHETORIC AND AUTHORITY

A number of modern social scientists and philosophers have written about social imaginaries. I have mentioned the influential account by Benedict Anderson, but before and after him there are accounts by Cornelius Castoriades, Paul Ricoeur and Charles Taylor, among others. As we will see, these thinkers differ in their approach to social imaginaries, but to varying degrees each of them emphasises the role that sign-exchange or representation plays in establishing a particular social imaginary. When Habermas commented upon the importance of the press it was in relation to the nineteenth century. There are now, of course, considerably more developed media. Nevertheless, any notion of there being a shared cultural space in which beliefs are generated is dependent upon the productions of the various media. These productions can have an effect, because they represent value-laden accounts of the encounters and exchanges between people who cannot be co-present to each other. This means that the nature of the public sphere – who composes it, what images of the social circulate within it, what debates or questions govern it, etc. – will be determined by the forms of mediation available, and how widely these are available. Anderson draws attention to the role played in the constitution of an image of a homogenous state by the press, the census, maps, and the founding of museums. Again, he is thinking about the nineteenth century. We might add the composition of histories and genealogies, and the

---

[25] *The Structural Transformation*, p. 249.

development of transport and postal systems, and telecommunications. Technology then is crucial to the construction and transformation of the public sphere because it generates and transforms our understanding of the social.

We can begin with a definition of the social imaginary taken from Charles Taylor's recent volume *Modern Social Imaginaries*. He describes it as 'the ways in which [people] imagine their social existence . . . the way ordinary people "imagine" their social surroundings . . . that common understanding which makes possible common practices'.[26] Taylor makes clear the involvement of the social imaginary with rhetoric and representation; how it is 'expressed in theoretical terms . . . carried in images, stories, legends, etc.'.[27] A social imaginary then is both a cultural product – of theories, images, stories, legends, etc. – and a producer (of a people's understanding of the social life they participate in). It functions as a constitutive fiction on two levels. First, it presents the fiction of there being a society at all. If Habermas insists that now we cannot tell the extent to which what is called 'public opinion' has been manufactured, Taylor points to the constitutive fiction of there being a collective agency known as the public. Secondly, this fiction itself perpetuates further images, stories, discourses and practices that constitute and disseminate the imaginary. Taylor suggests this fiction becomes culturally pervasive through two means. First, it operates through the cognitive faculty of the imagination, affecting people's thoughts, dreams, conceptions of what is possible, structures of feeling, etc. As such 'imaginary' is a synonym for 'imagination'. This will be important later, for the term 'imaginary' is understood differently, and with important consequences, in the work of Castoriades, Althusser and Lacan. Secondly, 'people take up, improvise, or are inducted into new practices. These are made sense of by the new outlook, the one first articulated in the theory; this outlook is the context that gives sense to the practices.'[28] On the basis of this constitutive function Taylor claims such imaginaries 'are never just ideology'.[29] I take this claim to mean not that they operate outside of ideology, but that they operate in ways far more subtle than the implementation of sets of dogmatic ideas. The world-orders they imply have been internalised by a common imagining ('a mutually

---

[26] *Modern Social Imaginaries*, p. 16.
[27] Ibid.
[28] Ibid., p. 20.
[29] Ibid., p. 113.

recognized common mind'³⁰) such that they are naturalised and appear to most as unquestioned fact.

By 'fiction' here neither Charles Taylor nor I would wish to imply that social imaginaries are insubstantial; only that they have no ontological foundation, they are ways of *making* sense, they are forms of *poiesis*. To employ a Freudian term that is related to the productive use of fantasy, social imaginaries are forms of 'illusion' (*Illusion*).³¹ These constitutive fictions are ways in which those negotiations with difference so primary to civic life are conducted in and across large political units. But there are questions about this fictitiousness that neither Taylor nor Anderson appears to address. They concern the relationship between fiction, persuasion and the formation of belief, and they arise when Taylor employs a phrase like 'the effective social imaginary'. What makes one 'fiction' effective and another ineffective or less effective? What governs the persuasive power of a social imaginary? Of course we can detail the institutions that forge and induct people into these new practices; we can provide accounts of what Foucault called the 'technologies of the self'.³² We can point to the sites of pastoral power and production (the judiciary, parliament, the academy, parenting, the Church, etc.). But such accounts could only tell us something about what made a certain social imaginary over time an effective (as in, pervasive and powerful) one. Effectiveness here concerns the pervasiveness of the institutional power-structures such that larger and larger numbers of people come to make sense of their social existence in the same way. But what is it that persuades people? How do people come to 'a mutually recognized common mind'? With Hegel in mind and Taylor's own work on the politics of recognition, what are the operations in the achievement of 'recognition'? What is recognised and how is it recognised?

What I am suggesting here is that there is an important need to understand the discursive operations involved in the creation and transformation of these imaginaries such that they become effective, ineffective or less effective. There are persuasions, conversions, changes of mind, acts of will, displacements of desire involved in these recognitions of commonality that constitute the public belief in what is true; there are relations and exchanges

---

³⁰ Ibid., p. 67.
³¹ See Freud's essay 'The Future of an Illusion' as an illustration.
³² See his essay, 'Technologies of the Self', trs. Robert Hurley et al., in *Michel Foucault: Ethics. The Essential Works of Foucault* 1954–84, ed. Paul Rabinow (Harmondsworth: Penguin Books, 2000), pp. 223–51.

at local levels that determine effectiveness and that are responses to the effectiveness of a certain social imaginary. This is what we need to investigate if we are to understand how a rhetoric gains, fails to gain or loses its authority. We need to examine more closely than either Taylor or Anderson that crucial faculty of the imagination and the way it operates not just on cognitive but on somatic levels.[33]

IMAGINATION AND ACTION

We begin with the work of Paul Ricoeur. For Ricoeur has also been explicitly concerned with social imaginaries (*l'imaginaire social*) and most particularly with the relations between rhetoric and action; what he terms a 'poetics of the will'.[34] The previous section of this essay examined one relation between rhetoric and action, that of desire, and we will return to this through Ricoeur's own early interest in Freud. But for the moment it is specifically Ricoeur's examination of the imagination and its relation to the transformation of a social imaginary that concerns us.

Like Taylor, Ricoeur understands 'imaginary' in terms of the work of imagining, but unlike Taylor Ricoeur has a more dynamic, creative and synthetic understanding of the imagination. If the imagination is not simply a mental faculty for Taylor it is not fully articulated as a transformative operation. Ricoeur explicitly relates the imagination to *poiesis*. The social imaginary is the practical functioning of the imagination in and between people. But Ricoeur makes a further connection that Taylor either assumes or neglects: that rather than the imagination being understood as involved in reproducing weak or shadowy forms of perception (the

---

[33] There are times when Taylor almost suggests the mental and the practical are two distinct operations; when he seems to accept that theories and ideas give birth to practices. It is exactly at this point that we need to gain some clarity on the relationship between thought, imagination and the practices of everyday life. See the work of the neurobiologist, Antonio Damasio, for an account of the profound interrelationality between thought, feeling, imagination, representation and practices. *Looking for Spinoza* (London: Heinemann, 2003).

[34] *Poetics of the Will* was the projected title of Ricoeur's third and concluding volume in his trilogy *Philosophy of the Will*. The first volume, *Le Voluntaire et l'involuntaire*, was published in Paris in 1950. This was followed ten years later by the second volume, *Finitude et culpabilité*. This second volume was to comprise three parts. The first part, *L'Homme faillible*, and the second, *Le Symbolique du mal*, both appeared, but neither the third part of this volume nor the third volume of the trilogy appeared. Ricoeur's thinking took another direction after his investigations into symbol and myth, turning instead to a consideration of metaphor and narrative.

Humean view of imagination[35]), 'our images are spoken before they are seen'.[36] Language makes possible what we see. In this way, Ricoeur relates the imagination to his productive theory of metaphor – that is, that metaphor (and therefore imagination) is associated with semantic innovation: 'Imagining is above all restructuring semantic fields.'[37]

Ricoeur's theory of metaphor is most thoroughly developed in *Interpretation Theory: Discourse and the Surplus of Meaning*[38] and *The Rule of Metaphor.*[39] Ricoeur develops this theory existentially, insofar as the new level of awareness brought about by the suspension of the reference of ordinary language returns us, Ricoeur believes, to a more primordial recognition of 'our profound belonging to the life-world'.[40] Insofar as this theory suggests the erasure of the literal level of meaning by the challenge of a semantic shock that the metaphorical produces with respect to predicates, it has not been without its critics.[41] The rich surplus of meaning as a result of the metaphorical process seems to privilege a poetic use of language over an ordinary use or, to use Ricoeur's terms, second-order reference over primordial reference. This privileging has a strong Romantic background as, similarly, does the ontological value given to the experience of this surplus of meaning. The theory requires the identification of a literal level of meaning, in fact requires the dualism of literal–metaphorical that suggests a prior acceptance of a certain correspondence theory of language. Is there such a thing as the literal? Can it be so clearly distinguished from the metaphorical? Part of the problem here concerns the relationship between reference (predication) and mimesis – a problem Ricoeur courageously tackles in his first volume of *Time and Narrative.*[42] This later work noticeably

---

[35] This is distinguished from the Kantian understanding of the imagination that is productive with respect to meaning since it synthesises and schematises sensations, enabling us to make sense and come to an understanding of them.

[36] 'Imagination in Discourse and Action' in *From Text to Action*, tr. Kathleen Blamey, eds. Kathleen Blamey and John Thompson (Evanston: Northwestern University Press, 1991), p. 171.

[37] Ibid., p. 173.

[38] Fort Worth: Texas Christian University Press, 1976.

[39] Tr. Robert Czerny (Toronto: University of Toronto Press, 1977).

[40] *Imagination in Discourse and Action*, p. 175.

[41] See Hans Frei, 'The "Literal Reading" of Biblical Narrative in Christian Tradition: Does It Stretch or Will It Break?' in Frank McConnell (ed.), *The Bible and The Narrative Tradition* (Oxford: OUP, 1986), pp. 36–77; and Graham Ward, 'Biblical Narrative and the Theology of Metonymy', *Modern Theology*, Vol. 7 no.4 (July 1991), pp. 335–50.

[42] Trs. Kathleen McLaughlin and David Pellauer (Chicago: University of Chicago Press, 1984), pp. 52–87.

drops the language of reference and predication in favour of three levels of the mimetic process – the prefigured (the perceived *as*), the configured (the written) and the refigured (the read) – which suggests all representation is metaphorical; and there are degrees of that metaphoricity. It is also interesting to note how, in his later work, particularly *Oneself as Another*,[43] the positive ontologising of the experience of surplus is also rendered more aporetic and open to various interpretations. The essay 'Imagination in Discourse and Action', which constitutes the starting point for this present investigation, predates both *Time and Narrative* and *Oneself as Another;* the explorations of those later works can be used productively, I think, with respect to how the generative power of the imagination enables us to *make* sense of the world and our experiences of it, and transform or restructure the social imaginary.

What imagination does is glimpse the new possibilities for meaning that metaphor provokes. If, as I argued earlier (on the basis of Heidegger and Wittgenstein) we do not see, we only see *as*, then imagination enables us to see differently, to glimpse alternative and perhaps better possibilities. Since seeing *as* infers that such seeing is implicated in figuration – that is, seeing *as* infers seeing *by way of,* seeing *analogically,* seeing *metonymically,* seeing *metaphorically,* seeing *synecdochically,* etc.[44] – then the dynamic power of imaginative conception is inextricably linked to the power of language to provoke new ways of seeing and sense-making. Imagination facilitates not only the continual rethinking of any one social imaginary. It is the imagination that enables the adaptation from religious concepts of 'society' (the Jesuits) to the secret societies of the eighteenth century (Freemasons) to civic society, say. It is imagination that wrestles to conceive future possibilities for liberal democracy in late capitalism. Imagination, then, enables us to fashion different social imaginaries. These imaginaries might develop critically, constructively and sometimes incommensurately alongside each other – rather like the standpoint-projects we discussed in the last section. More schematically, Ricoeur argues (and in a way which owes

---

[43] Tr. Kathleen Blamey (Chicago: University of Chicago Press, 1992).

[44] There is much that could be developed here. For insofar as there are different rhetorical figures – catachresis, metonymy, metaphor, irony, etc. – so there are different modes of seeing *as*. Epistemology here is governed by language-use – the worlds we describe (as writers) and the worlds we enter into (as readers) issue from the various figurations of that imaginative seeing *as*. Since most acts of writing are a complex blend of many different forms of figuration, then the worlds that are seen and entered into are correspondingly rich in meaning and connotation and invoke continually reflective and imaginative interpretation.

much to the abiding influence on his thinking of Aristotle and Hegel) that there are two opposing dynamics within any social imaginary – the one ideological, that seeks social integration and the *status quo*; the other utopian, that seeks to disrupt or open up the limitations of the ideology.[45] But if we relate social imaginaries back to standpoint-projects then something far more complex and generative emerges. For standpoint-projects, as socially engaged activity, will inevitably presuppose forms of valued, less-valued and even downright negative sociality. So if, as I suggested in the last section with respect to standpoint identification, any individual can belong to several different standpoint-projects, then it follows that we are each working with (both in the sense of participating in and resisting) not two but several social imaginaries.

Allow me to develop this with respect to Christian praxis. To some extent Ricoeur himself has done this in a number of less well-known essays published in *Esprit* and *Le Christianisme social*.[46] But I wish specifically to relate his thinking back to the nexus of several standpoints within which the self is situated and out of which the identity and agency of that self emerges, as outlined in section 2. I live in the West within some form of liberal democracy that accepts the sovereignty of the nation state and, at least on paper, the rights of human beings to free association, the ownership of property and self-determination (subject, in the exercising of those rights, to infringing neither the rights of my neighbours nor the laws of the country). I am also aware that several social scientists have identified dramatic changes currently taking place to democratic processes. Some have announced the triumph of liberal democracy;[47] some have perceived the demise of liberalism;[48] some have spoken of a post-democratic condition.[49] I am, then, aware of a past social condition and aware also of different conceptions of how sociality in the West is changing. Nevertheless, as things stand and as a parent I find my life easier than some because sociality in liberal democracy privileges the family unit defined as the heterosexual unit and privileges, most would tell me, my white male status. I am aware this society may be experienced very

[45] *Imagination in Discourse and Action*, p. 182.
[46] See the five essays grouped under the subtitle 'The Christian and Society' in *Paul Ricoeur: Political and Social Essays*, eds. David Stewart and Joseph Bien (Athens, Ohio: Ohio University Press, 1974), pp. 103–97.
[47] Francis Fukuyama, *The End of History and the Last Man* (Harmondsworth: Penguin Books, 1992).
[48] John Gray, *Post-Liberalism: Studies in Political Thought* (London: Routledge, 1993).
[49] See Ronald Jeremiah Schindler, *The Frankfurt School Critique of Capitalist Culture: A Critical Theory for Post-Democratic Society and its Re-education* (Aldershot: Ashgate, 1998).

differently from other positions within it. As such, I am then already caught up in several conceptions of the social. Furthermore, I am also a socialist and a Christian. The socialist works to expose forms of social injustice and oppression; structural inequalities that support and foster systemic exploitation of the work force to the advantage of plutocrats and market-profiteers. As such, the socialist would draw attention to, and seek the readdressing of, the privileging of one form of sexuality and one understanding of family. The socialist would also critique continuing aspects of racial and gender discrimination, aspects of economic policy that generated rather than alleviated various forms of poverty, and political and cultural processes eroding democratic participation, exacerbated by the unequal distribution of the world's goods. The socialist too, then, works with an alternative social imaginary; works towards a utopic horizon and, I would say, is permanently a revolutionary with respect to the *status quo.* The Christian might share many of the socialist's convictions – a future hope, a perfected sociality, notions of justice and freedom from oppression, possibly a teleology. The Christian might also share much of the socialist's social imaginary, but not necessarily – as the Christian thinkers convinced of the justice, even righteousness, of market-economics demonstrate.[50] For the Christian's social imaginary is eschatologically coloured by language of the Kingdom, by liturgical practices such as the eucharist within ecclesial bodies, by teachings with respect to discipleship, the treatment and identification of one's neighbour and the relation of this world to the heavenly one, and by relations (or non-relations) between Church and State. While the socialist's imaginary involves immanent examinations and critique of the present social order, the Christian's imaginary is governed by transcendent conceptions of the Good and the Just that can only be worked out immanently through and in co-operation with the workings of grace. The Kingdom to come, for Christians, is God's. It cannot therefore simply be built with human hands.

There are, of course, many different imaginings of the social, its current condition, its ideal perfection and the manner in which it may move from one to the other in both socialism and Christianity. My point is only to demonstrate how our lives inhabit, simultaneously, several different social imaginaries, and our living crosses back and forth through them all. In fact, some of them are probably not even articulated, because the social terrain

---

[50] Most recently the work of Michael Novak and Max Stackhouse. See D. Stephen Long, *Divine Economy* (London: Routledge, 2000), pp. 35–87 for an interesting discussion of their work (and others) with respect to questions of ecclesiology.

they propose is so internalised it has become invisible: like my being white, like my moving mainly among people of a professional class. What this means is that social imaginaries are never stable. They are as constantly shifting as time and context. They are continually being negotiated, questioned, recognised, forgotten, dreamed of, and aspired to. Each encounter with what is other to our social imaginaries calls for a reshaping of them all. When I watch Afghans being bombed, when I read of people starving in Ethiopia, when I hear of farmers and metalworkers in Senegal and Zambia losing their livelihood because of Western modes of global trading, when I leave a good meal after preaching at an Oxbridge college and meet a homeless person curled into a tight ball, sleeping on the street – my collocation of social imaginaries is engaged and demands to be refigured. I am confronted with forms of living that, to return to Ricoeur, 'engender[s] the imaginary'.[51]

Now one can distinguish, at the cultural level, between social imaginaries that are dominant and those that are marginal, even marginalised. The market-led democracy is more pervasive than any socialist hopes for social justice and the redistribution of wealth; more pervasive too than the Christian convictions of peaceable communion and the Kingdom. Nevertheless, at the more local level, the dominance of a 'ruling ideology' may well find successful forms of resistance. My point is not that there are no cultural hierarchies among various social imaginaries, but rather that those hierarchies, simply because of the existence of other imagined social possibilities and other forms of imaginary relations, are destabilised. To return to the language of Charles Taylor, the borders between the effective (the dominant social imaginary) and less-effective or ineffective (other marginal forms of conceiving and living the social life) can never be sealed. This rendering porous of the borders separating the dominant from the utopian is the work of the imagination, the labour one might say, the *poiesis*.[52] I would, following Ricoeur, see that it is the imagination that makes possible such destabilisations, fostering ongoing transitions, readjustments, painful juxtapositions and transformations. Imagination enables us to forge new connections, new relations between social imaginaries and standpoint-projects, new bonds between those who are

---

[51] 'Imagination in Discourse and Action', p. 172.
[52] Where the existence of a real or true state of affairs is most insisted upon there indeed ideology can be said to rule. The social imaginary becomes the given and it is blind to its own metaphoric processes. And to the extent that any authority needs to legitimate itself publicly then any ideology aspires to such a blindness, aspires to an internalisation so profound that no rethinking outside its own logic becomes possible. And the possibilities for critique die out.

themselves implicated in those imaginaries and pro-jects. The work of the imagination with respect to a social imaginary is transformative, utopian and critical of ruling interests and values.

Ricoeur returns us then to standpoint-projects by demonstrating how imagination is associated with cultural transformations and critical engagement. In fact, he explicitly claims that 'imagination ... has a projective function that is part of the very dynamics of acting'.[53] This 'projective function', as we have seen in section 2, works with an anticipation for the future, and 'is involved in the very process of motivation'.[54] It is in this sense that Ricoeur views action as rooted in imaginative possibility. To slightly rephrase an aphorism written in the Book of Proverbs: without a vision the people are frozen, like Dante's conception of the extremities of Hell. The imagination empowers us to act. It enables us to glimpse the surplus that is excessive to the *status quo*. Hauntingly, and agonisingly, Ricoeur makes a staggering remark which, I suggest, he fails to examine fully and which is central to the argument I am making in this essay: 'There remains to be discerned, in the freedom of the imagination, what could be termed the imagination of freedom.'[55] What possibilities for freedom there are are intimately linked with the space for the play of the imagination.

There is another place in the text where Ricoeur makes an observation that he does not follow through and it leads us to the next stage of my argument. He writes that, prior to the 'imaginative variations of "I can"', a project passes 'through the figurability of my desires' (*la figurabilité de mes désirs*).[56] This is the only point in the essay when any observation about desire is made, and it is difficult to understand whether this phrase refers to 'the capacity of my desires to receive representation' or 'the figurative powers of my desires'. Although Ricoeur provides a rich, Kantian-based analysis of the role of the imagination, its motivating power and its social consequences, he does not investigate how the imagination is provoked to engender, other than pointing to the product of such engendering: poetic language. The imagination is profoundly associated, for Ricoeur, with language, with discourse. The imagination mediates between *poiesis* and praxis. In fact, in an earlier essay in the same volume, The Model of the Text: Meaningful Action Considered as a Text', he examines the extent to which 'the object of [the social sciences] shares the same characteristics

---

[53] 'Imagination in Discourse and Action', p. 177.
[54] Ibid.
[55] Ibid., p. 178.
[56] Ibid., p. 225 in French.

[*offre quelques-uns des traits constitutifs*] as a text'.[57] But imagination is not simply a 'dimension of language'[58] that informs the will to act. Imagination, motivation and action are more profoundly rooted in desire. Ricoeur does not unravel the relations between desire, motivation, language and imagination. To go further, he does not show how imagination operates in an economy that relates *poiesis*, eros and praxis. This is what we must now examine.

Not that Ricoeur is a stranger to the discourse of eros. Indeed, what is interesting is the way in which Ricoeur wrote an in-depth study of the relationship between language, eros and social praxis in the early 1960s. In his detailed textual study, *Freud and Philosophy: An Essay on Interpretation*,[59] he acknowledges the primordiality of desire and how, prior to his own thinking, Freud had discovered the association between desire, intersubjectivity that is constitutive of desire (one always desires what is other that oneself), and communication that bridges desire and the other. '[S]exuality gives rise to imagination and to speech,' he wrote.[60] And, in a later essay, the 'analytical experience is desire coming into discourse'.[61] Because of these observations, Ricoeur is able to hold the view that Freud had already understood that the behaviour of human beings (not only psychic but social) had a strong affinity with the disciplines of textual interpretation.[62] In the early 1960s he would even define the imaginary as 'cover[ing] all kinds of mediations implied in the unfolding of desire'.[63] He seems here on the very brink of understanding how operations of the imaginary were encompassed by the Freudian sense of the verb *phantasieren*. In a section of his book on Freud, Ricoeur examines Freud's investigations into 'primal fantasies' – like the murder of the father that sets up the primal longing for a father figure. He argues that these primal fantasies cannot be reduced to historical events for they are forms of mytho-poetic thinking. The 'father figure is not simply a return to the repressed . . . [It] constitutes the true overdetermination of authentic

---

[57] *Du texte à l'action: Essais d'herméneutique, II* (Paris: Editions du Seuil, 1986), p. 183.
[58] 'Metaphor and the Central Problem of Hermeneutics', tr. and ed. John B. Thompson in *Hermeneutics and the Human Sciences* (Cambridge: Cambridge University Press, 1981), p. 181.
[59] It was published in France as *De l'interprétation: Essai sur Freud* (1965), which signals the true focus of the book, not Freud, but Freud's hermeneutics. It was translated into English by Denis Savage (New Haven: Yale University Press, 1970).
[60] Ibid., p. 271.
[61] 'The Question of Proof in Freud's Writing' in *The Philosophy of Paul Ricoeur: An Anthology of his Work*, eds. Charles E. Reagan and David Stewart (Boston: Beacon Press, 1978), p. 202.
[62] Ibid., p. 192.
[63] Ibid., p. 188.

symbols.'[64] The imagination works creatively here to figure an archaic, anthropological longing for God, for transcendence.

Nevertheless, his later essay on the imagination withdraws not only from the language of desire but from a language that blurs the distinction between imagination and fantasy. Ricoeur's concept of the imagination, like his anthropology, remains profoundly Kantian.[65] The Kantian imagination is *Einbildung*, its operation an *Einbildungskraft*. Ricoeur works from this notion of imagination. The imagination here is dynamic and synthetic compared to the Humean idea of images as weak representations of perceptions, but its actions are circumscribed (by the real as the *Ding an sich*). The question is, why does Ricoeur retreat from a relationship between eros and the imagination? It is an interesting question to pursue because it bears upon why, in this argument, we must turn from the notion of social imaginary to cultural imaginary.

Put briefly, for Freud, neither *Illusion* nor *phantasieren* are moral categories; and Ricoeur, like Kant before him, wishes to see a teleological connection between moral judgment and the synthetic powers of the imagination. As Ricoeur observes, '*L'imaginaire ne connaît pas de censure*'; of itself it is unable to make judgments. It can, as we have seen, create connections (between conflicting world-views and between people) and what Ricoeur wants is for imagination's 'letting new worlds shape our understanding of ourselves'.[66] But there is no guarantee that the operations of the imagination will always be creative and have positive, liberating effects. And that guarantee is even further removed when the imagination is associated not simply with the rational reflections of the subject (as in Kant) but with the radical deconstitution of that very reflective subject by the unconscious. Ricoeur noted, 'The reading of Freud is also the crisis of the philosophy of the subject. It imposes the dispossession of the subject such as it appears primarily to itself in the form of consciousness. It makes consciousness not a given but a problem and a task.'[67]

We come here to a core question for this essay as it emerges in the work of Ricoeur. It is a question worth pursuing with Ricoeur, not

---

[64] *Freud and Philosophy*, p. 542.

[65] For a more detailed study of the category of imagination in Ricoeur's thinking see Richard Kearney, *Poetics of Imagining* (London: Routledge, 1981), 'The Hermeneutical Imagination (Ricoeur)', pp. 134–70; *The Wake of the Imagination* (London: Hutchinson, 1988), pp. 392–439; and 'Narrative Imagination: Between Ethics and Poetics' in Richard Kearney (ed.), *Paul Ricoeur: The Hermeneutics of Action* (London: Sage, 1996), pp. 173–90.

[66] 'Metaphor and the Central Problem of Hermeneutics', p. 181.

[67] 'A Philosophical Interpretation of Freud' in *The Philosophy of Paul Ricoeur: An Anthology of his Work*, p. 170.

because I think he is able to present us with an answer but rather because I think he wishes to maintain, in order for *poiesis* not to dissolve the moral question, in order for aesthetics not to subsume ethics, a notion of agency. As I suggested in section 2 over against either Foucault or Adorno, in project-orientated, standpoint praxis there remains a notion of intention, though intention is not simply annexed to a strong construal of the subject as agent. The subject is located within a field of identifications, a web of interrelations, a 'space of possibles' and the stories that it tells of itself. This is not the self-authenticating, self-legitimating subject of Cartesianism – the subject at the centre of 'the philosophy of the subject'. Ricoeur, and others have said this, remains committed to this Cartesian subject, even though he treats that subject in the wake of Hegel's dialectical understanding of the subject in history and Husserl's enquiries into apperception and intersubjectivity in *Cartesian Meditations*; even though his later work is governed by a narrative understanding of selfhood in which we are continually the writers and readers of the stories of our lives. He is wary then of those who wish to dissolve the subject into a field of forces, be those forces Freudian drives, Foucauldian powers or Althusserian apparatuses. This is the key to his brilliant reading of Althusser's work in *Lectures on Ideology and Utopia*, delivered at the University of Chicago in 1975. Here he criticises Althusser for his 'emphasis on anonymous entities without subjects'[68] and likens Althusser's notion of the 'field' of ideology within which any thinking and writing takes place to the Freudian concept of the Id.[69] What Ricoeur finds disturbing about the unconscious – and this is what determines his rejection of a Freudian understanding of the imagination and desire – is both its atemporality and its antinomianism. The unconscious makes meaning pragmatic; it makes all recognition mis-recognition.[70] It opens an abyss of bottomless interpretation such that it laughs hysterically at Ricoeur's attempts to develop a science of

---

[68] Ed. George H. Taylor (New York: Columbia University Press, 1986), p. 119.

[69] Ibid., p. 121. Later in the *Lectures*, Ricoeur examines the utopian writing of Charles Fourier. Fourier, an advocate of open sexual relations, makes the forgotten passions the basis for new modes of living, and Ricoeur sees in his work also a close association with the Freudian Id (p. 305). The unconscious presents the possibility of a fundamental licentiousness.

[70] Recognition is an important Hegelian concept for Ricoeur. In recognition there is shared understanding; there is communication. This draws him towards Habermas, who, finally, he is critical of, but nevertheless they share the 'need [for] a utopia of total recognition, of total communication, communication without boundaries or obstacles', *Lectures on Ideology and Utopia*, p. 151.

interpretation. The unconscious raises the Nietzschean spectre of the Dionysian. 'Fancy borders on madness.'[71] So while Ricoeur wishes to accept that any thinker thinks within a cultural field such that so many ideas are already presupposed and therefore resist the radical transparency of that thinker's thinking to himself or herself – nevertheless to give too much emphasis to this determinative and anonymous field of powers has 'dreadful consequences for the theory of meaning, because what is meant in a field if it is meant by nobody?'[72] Who owes this meaning? Who is responsible for its shape, its legitimation, its justification and its destiny? Ricoeur wishes to insist upon a social *poiesis*, and a surplus of significance, but the imagination can only work constitutively if it remains governed by a will; a will that is set in motion by a motivation. It is a will that remains individual and individualising. To act within a motivational framework is to act rationally and accountably.[73]

While my understanding of 'intention' bears some resemblance to Ricoeur's notion of 'motivation' – in that they are central to rescuing a sense of agency from the anonymity of what Althusser and Foucault would call the *dispositifs* that give form and therefore meaning to any action or behaviour – a fundamental difference remains. Ricoeur locates 'motivation' at the heart of his poetics of individual willing – human beings choose to act in some ways/circumstances and refuse to act in others. I locate 'intention' at the level of the pro-ject orientation of a standpoint; in terms, that is, of the teleology of a standpoint action that is carried out by an individual identifying with that standpoint. The difference here is not simply that of individualism versus corporatism, for a standpoint constitutes the individual's sense of agency. What is fundamentally different is a recognition that 'motivation' (and the values that motivate) are not independent of cultural context, but arise only from within sets of cultural

---

[71] Ibid., p. 310.

[72] Ibid., p. 119.

[73] It is interesting to note how in Ricoeur's earlier philosophical approach to psychoanalysis he attempts, with reference to an article by Anthony Flew, to ally the Freudian unconsciousness to rationality. While stating that Freud's contribution was to extend the notions of motive, desire and intention into the spheres of the unknown and the involuntary, he adds: 'but this extension would not change the basically psychological or mental, i.e. intentional, character of the stream of motivation.' We can talk of 'unconscious motivations' and therefore the 'object of analytic therapy is to extend the patient's area of rationality, to replace impulsive conduct by controlled conduct', *Freud and Philosophy*, p. 361. But such an interpretation relies upon a fundamental homogeneity between the unconscious and consciousness such that one 'is its relative other, and not its absolute other', p. 430. This is a very optimistic reading of Freud.

possibilities and values. In motivation something is believed, and believed in strongly enough to affect behaviour, but Ricoeur refers to motivation as if it operated solely under the individual's willing. The conscious is always in control. Again this testifies to Ricoeur's lingering Cartesianism, while intentional standpoint is an attempt to think agency outside such a Cartesianism.

If then, in this pro-ject, I am wishing to explore and insist upon the association of *poiesis* to praxis, while placing imagination and desire at the heart of transformative possibilities for a culture – two of the forces that displace the subject conscious of his or her own motivations – then I must address the question Ricoeur puts to Althusser. This question is: '[W]hat kind of relation exists between a field and a thought?'[74] What kind of agency are we speaking of when what is pursued is a change to what I call the cultural imaginary? What kind of agency labours in transformative hope? In section 2 of the essay I proposed that the standpoint actually constructs and presupposes a notion of the agent and the kind of actions expected of that agent or which fulfil the nature of that agency. The question is whether this is sufficient an understanding of agency for an ethical pro-ject. Upon the answer to this question much depends. In fact the very notion of the social is at stake. Anderson, Taylor and Ricoeur speak of the social and the imaginary as if the social itself is not in question. And they can only do so because of a humanism (based upon some notion of existential co-presence) that is presupposed. They presuppose those individual volitional subjects who are subsequently in relation one to another by choice. If, then, any strong notion of such subjects begins to unravel when the action of any agent is located within larger economies, forces or a nexus of cultural possibilities that Althusser names 'overdetermination', then what happens to the notion of the 'social'? Can the social itself be rescued from the determinism of the cultural? Is cultural ethics simply an oxymoron?

We must arrive at an answer to this question, but for the moment I only wish to point out that Ricoeur's critical response to Althusser's emphasis on the field just does not do justice to the complexity of the question. He observes that Althusser appears to have a causal relationship in mind. That is, that the ideological field determines all possibilities for what the thinker is able to think. Ricoeur offers another model for the relation, his 'motivational framework, a conceptual framework' that can be understood to

---

[74] Ibid., p. 120.

offer any thinker 'a kind of reserve, a resource of possible thoughts'.[75] But to view the circumstantial, cultural field as a reserve or a resource requires more transparency on the part of the thinker, almost approaching a God's-eye view, than even Ricoeur's notion of the narrated-self can accommodate. What we are wrestling with here is the extent to which the individual will can be rescued from the crisis of the subject that necessarily ensues when consciousness is situated within movements of desire, power, knowledge and embodied response that subtend consciousness and rationalisation. So although Ricoeur is aware of the dreadful consequences to meaning and motivation that follow from the emphasis upon the field, he does not seem able to provide an adequate account of how those consequences can be avoided; why the relation of individual thought to ideological field is necessarily governed by choice with respect to a conceptual resource. What becomes clearer is why he cannot pursue an account of the imagination unfettered from the will and why he is coy with respect to the role of desire in *poiesis* and praxis.

Psyche, Logos and Koinonia[76]

The work of the French social scientist, Cornelius Castoriadis, shows no such coyness, probably because he was trained and eventually practised as a psychoanalyst. It is his long-term project of investigating and transforming the social imaginary with respect to imagination, desire and the institutions they give rise to that I enlist to take my own argument one step further. For Castoriadis also has a vision, a hope that finds expression in the urgency and directness of his prose. He moves freely between Freud, Marcuse and Lacan, producing an account of a profound relationship between the individual (*psyche*) and the social (*koinonia*) imaginary that makes comprehensible transformative social praxeis and the aspiration to freedom. For his account of the social imaginary is foundational for his construal of intersubjectivity. The imaginary, or the reserve of imaged possibilities with which the imagination works, is twofold, for Castoriadis. Somewhat like Coleridge, he distinguishes between the second imagination that is reproductive, synthetic and imitative and the primary or radical imagination

---

[75] Ibid., p. 121.

[76] Whilst these three notions are central to what I am developing in terms of a cultural hermeneutics and arise from the previous set of analyses, they also happen to be the name of the three sections that make up Cornelius Castoriadis's important collection of six essays *Les Carrefours du labyrinthe* (Paris: Editions du Seuil, 1978; trs. Kate Soper and Martin H. Ryle, *Crossroads in the Labyrinth*, Brighton: Harvester Press, 1984).

that is the condition for the possibility of all thinking.[77] His debt here is not to psychoanalysis but Aristotle. But in developing his account of the radical imagination the unconscious as the discourse of the Other that constitutes the ego becomes central. It is here that he is indebted to Lacan; although Castoriadis does not develop Lacan's understanding of the *réel* as the absolute Other.[78] But otherwise, his reading of Lacan is good. The unconscious is viewed as generating the primary imaginary, 'the content of this imaginary being related to the discourse of the Other'.[79] It seems itself to be the scene of an endless conflict between the drives and reality, but it 'invests' an imaginary reality that functions as 'this spring in the depth of ourselves from which flow both alienating phantasies and free creation truer than truth, unreal deliria and surreal poems, this eternally new beginning and ground of all things, without which nothing would have a ground'.[80] It is the imaginary that defines for the subject both 'reality and desire'[81] – its own and the world's. It is the imaginary that makes possible the realm of the symbolic (both in terms of language and, more generally, all the organised social institutions predicated upon what Habermas would call communicative action). The symbolic constitutes a realm of the Logos, both in terms of language, or more properly discourse, and reasoning that remains shot through with, because reliant upon for its existence and continuation, the radical imaginary. As Castoriadis puts it (and this is close to Lacan): '[I]t is because radical imagination exists that "reality" exists *for us.*'[82] In this he is pushing far beyond Ricoeur's Kantian framework, for sense impressions themselves are illusory, the product of the radical imagination that *gives form* 'to something which, "in itself", has no relation to that form'.[83] The radical imaginary determines significations at both the individual and the social level. We exist, then, individually and collectively within streams of presentations that are somatic as well as psychic and so also inseparable from affects, intentions, drives and desires.

---

[77] 'Radical Imagination and the Social Instituting Imaginary' in *The Castoriadis Reader*, ed. David Ames Curtis (Oxford: Blackwell, 1997), pp. 319–20.
[78] He comes closest to it when he writes about an 'indeterminacy' and 'an undifferentiated chaos' that give rise to primordial questions which it is 'the role of imaginary significations' to provide an answer for. *The Imaginary Institution of Society*, tr. Kathleen Blamey (Cambridge: Polity Press, 1987), pp. 146–7.
[79] Ibid., p. 103.
[80] Ibid., p. 104.
[81] Ibid., p. 103.
[82] 'Radical Imagination', p. 321.
[83] Ibid., p. 323.

Individually and collectively we create and transform our worlds out of the operations of this imaginary.

There are two moments in the operations Castoriadis outlines that demand further consideration for this project. The first is the move from the *psyche* to *koinonia*, and the second is the passage from imaginary to symbolic.

The relationship between self-image and world-image lies first in the capacity of the unconscious to cathect representations such that human beings enjoy representational pleasure more than organ pleasure.[84] This might 'explain' pornography as a social phenomenon, but for Castoriadis it leads to the important conclusion that 'projective schemata and processes have precedence over introjective ones'.[85] The individual imaginary that exists in and as various schemata is, then, orientated to externalising what gives form and meaning to itself. But these schemata are already socially mediated such that in the process of socialisation, when 'the psyche is forced to abandon (never fully) its pristine solipsistic meaning for the shared meanings provided by society',[86] a negotiation and readjustment takes place. 'Socialized individuals are walking and talking fragments of a given society; and they are *total* fragments: that is, they embody, in part actually, in part potentially, the essential core of the institutions and significations of their society.'[87]

There is some slippage in Castoriadis's language here: references to 'pristine solipsistic meaning' and even 'total' seem to overstate the case. His earlier statements in *The Imaginary Institution of Society* are clearer: the intersubjective relation is played out in each individual because his or her unconscious constitutes the discourse of the Other. So that any subject's understanding of himself or herself always participates in significations that surpass him or her, rooting them in 'society and history, even as the subject realizes his autonomy'.[88] The individual *psyche* is then always situated within, while not being simply reduced to and absorbed by, social imaginary significations. Thus the imaginary and its operations define, for Castoriadis, what it is to be a human being at all. Imagination is no longer, as for Ricoeur, a Kantian faculty

[84] Ibid., p. 329.
[85] Ibid., p. 330.
[86] Ibid.
[87] Ibid., p. 332.
[88] *The Imaginary Institution*, p. 107.

of consciousness (however productive); rather is it 'the fundamental determination of the soul'.[89]

We might relate this account of the subject to my account in section 2 about the processes of identification that constitute a standpoint within which the subject comes to self-understanding. We can allow Castoriadis's psychoanalytical account (which he himself always terms a pathology of the soul) to deepen that earlier account, allowing us to proceed with demonstrating how, then, this *psyche* (both individual and collective) determines the symbolic. Unlike Lacan, Castoriadis does not narrate the moves between the imaginary and the symbolic through an account of the mirror-stage, although he cites Lacan's seminal text on the mirror-stage in *Ecrits*. The symbolic is somehow – and he is not clear about this – inchoate in the social imaginary in the way the unconscious is already a discourse of the Other. The unconscious, that is, appears to be both formed and informed by 'significations to which the individual has been exposed from the moment of conception and even before'.[90] The symbolic is a supplement of the imaginary (which is always social because it is projective). As such,

[t]his element – which gives a specific orientation to every institutional system, which overdetermines the choice and connections of symbolic networks, which is the creation of each historical period, its singular manner of living, of seeing, of conducting its own existence in the world, and its relations with this world, this original structuring component, this central signifying–signified, the source of that which presents itself in every instance as an indisputable and undisputed meaning, the basis for articulating what does matter and what does not, the origin of the surplus of being of objects of practical, affective and intellectual investment, whether individual or collective – is nothing other than the *imaginary* of the society or of the period considered.[91]

Castoriadis comes close here to rewriting Hegel's *Volksgeist* in terms of semiotics and psychoanalysis.

Two important points are raised by this passage. First, symbolic structures are always overdetermined because they continue to participate in a radical imaginary that can never be grasped as such. This imaginary connotes much more than the symbolic denotes and can only be recognised

---

[89] 'Psychoanalysis and Philosophy' in *The Castoriadis Reader*, p. 356. Castoriadis, in developing his account of the imaginary in both philosophical and psychoanalytic terms, is fond of rehearsing how, for Kant, the imagination is always and only *productive*. Kant never describes a *schepferische Einbindungskraft*.

[90] *The Imaginary Institution*, p. 102.

[91] Ibid., p. 145.

obliquely and indirectly. Symbolic structures cannot be reduced to their functional determinations, despite the intrinsic inertia and self-protection of institutionalism.[92] Secondly and partly on this basis, the actual symbolic structure of a society is always only one of any possible number of potential symbolic structures, and what precipitates this actualisation is contingent not necessary. The historically embedded practices of everyday life will transform one epoch into another, invest certain objects with value (giving less value to others) only to have this evaluation revised, and view certain opinions and behaviours as *de rigueur* at one moment and, subsequently, question the assumptions of such opinions and behaviours. We can recognise this to be a faithful account of what occurs as social norms change. We can understand through this account a concept such as 'fashion' or 'being in vogue'; a concept that we came across in section 1 when treating the reception over time of Barth's theology. Theologies too are subject to fashion. But Castoriadis also presents us with a way of understanding the pathology (individual and collective) informing such transformations of fashion. Everything is already being revised and revisable. This means that, on the one hand, new imaginary significations can change the institutional structures of a society, and, on the other, new institutional structures mark the emergence of new imaginary significations. There is then a twofold work for those projects involved in developing transformative practices of hope: the work of generating new imaginary significations and the work of forming institutions that mark such significations.

The important corollary of the two moments I have been elucidating – the individual and the collective *psyche* and the relationship between the social imaginary and the genesis of symbolic structures – is that, for Castoriadis, society as organised institutions that embody social imaginary significations is a self-creation continually undergoing transformation. It is not that there is potential for transformation through imaginative, that is metaphorical, *poiesis* – as it is for Ricoeur. The *poiesis* is always in process because the symbolic is always a singular expression whose meaning cannot be totalised. For, '[t]o recall, as a mere image, what we said about the sense of autonomy for the individual: we can no more eliminate or absorb the unconscious than we can eliminate or absorb the unlimited and unfathomable ground upon which every society reposes'.[93] The questioning of the social imaginary is always already under way for the imaginary already actively contains the possibilities for its own transformation.

[92] Ibid., p. 110.
[93] Ibid., p. 113.

A question remains: what determines the direction of the transformation of the social imaginary and the symbolic structures it modifies, razes and erects? This is a particularly pertinent question when the radical imagination of the unconscious is viewed in itself as indeterminate and unfathomable. We might ask this question in a modified and less ambitious way (to begin with): what constrains the transformations of the social imaginary? Castoriadis helps us to answer this question, for he outlines four forms of constraint upon changes that direct social transformation.[94] There are 'external' constraints such as natural habitat, the grammars of any language that already prescribe how things are to be represented and the functionality of institutions. There are 'internal' constraints such as the nature of the *psyche*, for example, and the way it cathects socially created and valued objects. There are 'historical' constraints such as the past of practices and their remembrance, the traditions and heritages as they are continually being rewritten. Finally, there are 'intrinsic' constraints. Here Castoriadis is again abstract to the point of being elusive, but his main point seems to be that because social imaginary significations and the institutions they engender give meaning and shape to the individual and collective *psyche* they must be 'coherent'. They answer to specific human needs and questions. This coherence does not exclude the possibility of internal divisions and contestations as long as these do not fatally endanger the 'enigmatic unity and substantive kinship between artifacts, beliefs, political regimes, artistic works, and, of course, human types belonging to the same society and same historical period'.[95] Hence institutions like slavery, the extended family, missionary societies, the belief in angels, or the divine right of kings etc. each make sense within certain cultures at certain times in their history. We might rephrase this final constraint in terms of Michel de Certeau's question, 'What makes a belief believable?' A certain archaeology of cultural assumptions and discursive connections makes possible the explicit espousal, employment and dissemination of certain truths, goods, values and significances.

In section 2 we noted similar analyses of constraints in Foucault's archaeology of discourses and Bourdieu's account of acquiring capital in a field of symbolic production. But given these constraints what determines the specific direction of the production of new social imaginaries and new institutions? There are I suggest certain pointers towards answering this question. I will sketch three of them.

---

[94] 'Radical Imagination', pp. 333–6.
[95] Ibid., p. 335.

First, the institutional emergence of the new, its entry into the symbolic, does not necessarily coincide with its genesis but there must exist a logical relation between that genesis and that emergence. We can put this into Christian theological terms drawn from the New Testament. There is temporality as *chronos* and there is temporality as a specific opportunity for acting or *kairos*. What I take this to mean culturally is that the new often emerges at a time of cultural crisis, when the break-up of accustomed ways of handling, explaining or giving meaning to certain phenomena triggers a search for new paradigms of interpretation. So, for example, the 1970s have been viewed in the West as being a time of considerable cultural change such that in the wake of various events, from the tearing up of the GATT agreement, to the development of new electronic technologies, to the acceleration of a pluralism that criticised liberalism for its ethnocentricity, to the promulgation of new anti-humanist philosophies, a new *Zeitgeist* announced itself to which labels such as 'postmodernism', 'late-capitalism' and 'post-industrialism' have been applied. But the production of this new cultural scene did not come *ex nihilo*. Diverse and seemingly unrelated elements of this scene were already in place – the impact of Nietzsche's thought, the waves of immigration into the West after the Second World War following new demands upon the labour markets, the advances in telecommunications developed by the military, etc. But certain cultural triggers cathect these elements. In other words, the emergence of the new accorded with a certain cultural logic that we can piece together after the event. The *kairos* is not dialectically opposed to the *chronos*, but a new concretisation of elements that already coexist gives rise to an intensity that refigures how a culture recognises and identifies itself. In time this *kairos* is reabsorbed into the *chronos*, and the combination we could call history. '[S]ociety is intrinsically history,' Castoriadis writes.[96] Therefore the possible directions for social transformation are already available in some inchoate way; they already part of the social imaginary. What cannot be predicted are the triggering events that turn these elements into symbolic institutions. This, of course, gives legitimation to the political work of 'spin-doctors' whose jobs are to identify or create what the trends are

---

[96] *The Imaginary Institution*, p. 371. I think this notion can be compared to the materialist understanding of time developed by the Italian political thinker, Antonio Negri. Time for Negri is not a medium, and not a spatial envelope for acts and events, it is 'real composition' and 'productive force'. *Time for Revolution*, pp. 36–7.

or should be, then predict the future trajectories of such trends and develop policy with respect to these predictions. To return to Ricoeur's emphasis upon poetic language, not every user of language coins new words, develops new vocabularies, but from what is already available new sentences can be generated, new moods defined, new aesthetic experiences composed.

This returns us to the role of the discursive and raises a second pointer concerning the direction of transformation, with respect to a clarification concerning mimesis. In stating that the new arises from an original concatenation, and consequent intensification, of elements already there within a culture we need to ask what facilitates or brings about this concatenation. This is where we need to distinguish between reproduction and creation, repetition and *poiesis*. When the dominant thematics of a culture are simply rephrased we get more of the same. So, for example, the realistic novel as a literary genre has continued, little changed, from Defoe to Donna Tartt. Different aesthetic endeavours are involved in its production but the portrayal of social drama as such has changed little. The genre is reproduced, and that a culture still entertains such reproduction (and novelistic realism remains marketable) is an indication that something in Western culture, despite the major historical events of the nineteenth and twentieth centuries, remains the same. Perhaps there is a continuing belief in the truth of positivist and empiricist philosophies which equate what is with what is out there. But I would reserve for the label *poiesis* what happens when the novel form is taken over by a James Joyce or a Gabriel Garcia Marquez or an Elias Canetti. Something new emerges; another kind of genre of literature appears that is difficult to catalogue in terms of familiar cultural expectations. One might say the same about the Gospels – they are neither histories, nor biographies, nor chronicles, nor fables in the manner in which such genres were available for imitation. They institute something new in literary terms; they issue from new imaginative connections that have demanded new symbolic forms. The logical heart of such *poiesis*, and Castoriadis recognises this, is an 'essential indetermination' that 'obviously does not mean that the indetermination is total'.[97] Until it is done no one could have predicted its possibility. The move from A to B involves an encounter with what is other, with the discourse of the other. Of course, there are

---

[97] Ibid., p. 199.

degrees of reproduction and of *poiesis* – a Gustav Flaubert, a Thomas Mann, a Toni Morrison inflect the genre of the realistic novel in original ways without necessarily breaking out of the form itself. Nevertheless, I would suggest the direction of transformation that occurs from changes in the social imaginary is dictated in part by *poiesis* – new creative associations made, new relational actions that generate modifications (and some of them major) in social institutions or new institutions altogether. The imaginary is changed both by and through these creative works which do not operate upon the symbolic or rupture the symbolic, but occur in and through the way the symbolic is always overdetermined and opening up the imaginary that subtends it.

If we take this further, keeping the uniqueness of the Gospel-genre in mind, we could say that what galvanises this *poiesis*, giving it a specific orientation, is a new desire, inseparable from a new word, intuition, intimation or communication that offers itself. The new wine will not fit into the old wineskins. The new connection, I suggest, is not made at the level of rational thought; it is not a mental determination like the solving of a puzzle. It is made in the imaginary itself – in the dreaming and day-dreaming, in the surrender of the ego to the stream of presentations issuing from the discourse of the unconscious as this is fed by the myriad embodied experiences of worlds both lived and continually composed. The effect of the making of something new is surprise, even awe. *Poiesis* is an affective form of saying; a saying that is profoundly invested in what Austin and Searle have elaborated as illocutory and perlocutory speech-acts. *Poiesis* is an event (*Ereignis*); production is only an occurrence (*Geschehen*). To adapt Ricoeur, *poiesis* affects change in the social imaginary in the way that a new metaphorical expression (Milton's 'blind mouths', for example) alters the way the world is conceived. *Poiesis* does not present an argument as much as offer a vision – a way of seeing the world differently. After Shakespeare, after Turner, after Pert we began to dream differently, and the structures of what we desire and think possible are modified. After Moses, after Jesus, after the Prophet we also began to dream differently, and the structures of what we desire and think possible are modified.

For the moment let us develop this account of *poiesis* in another direction by stating that *poiesis*, like representation more generally, is inseparable from desire. Desire, along with its corollary, affectivity (pleasure/pain), would then constitute the third of our factors determining the specific direction of the production of new social imaginaries and new institutions. Castoriades writes, 'Representation, affect, and desire are mixed together in a *sui generis* fashion, and in general it is impossible, except in trivial cases, to separate them one from another.'[98] But if the subject (both individual and collective) is situated within a malleable flux of such representations, affects and desires, then *poiesis* – which is a specific creative symbolic practice – involves the sublimation and orientation of desires towards new hoped-for affects in, through and by particular representations. Desires are only ever in operation in a work. To return to an argument I raised towards the end of section 2 – desire does not work in, through and because of lack. If desire is always already represented and names itself only in that representation then it has already found that towards which it is orientated. In the Freudian vocabulary of Jean Laplanche and J.-B. Pontalis, 'The phantasy . . . is not the object of desire, it is a scene . . . It does not represent the desired object to itself, but instead it is represented as participating in the scene.'[99] The representation itself resolves the desire *for something*, because the desire already *is something*: its intention is realised in and as a particular scene. Desire is continually being sublimated and staging itself; it is not available *as such*. It only has appearance in and through its sublimations. But insofar as desire is already instantiated in the figures and schemas of the imaginary it too must continually undergo alteration. The forms of sublimation are continually over-determined and therefore in a process of being transformed. The scenes of desire or intention continually shift. We saw something of this in the last section with respect to intention and pro-jects. As the standpoint-project involves itself with various forms of con-testation and affirmation, other views and similar views, the object of the pro-ject is restaged, re-imagined. But we need to deepen the account of desire here. For desire can never be reduced to the goal of a pro-ject; just as representation can never be reduced to what the words denote. If desire is always and only in and as a scene, then what in that scene is taken as the focus or interpretative centre for understanding desire? Take a dream or a piece of poetry: which figures in the dream or poem

---

[98] 'Psychoanalysis and Philosophy', p. 355.
[99] 'Fantasme originaire, fantasmes des origines, origine du fantasme', *Les Temps Modernes*, no.215 (April 1964), p. 1968.

warrant more attention than others?[100] This cannot be answered cate-gorically. In any given work, then, desire is disseminated across a represented scene and as such it is plural and pluralising, though neces-sarily sublimated to make these representational connections rather than those, fix upon these signs rather than those. Desire relates to intention and pro-ject as the imaginary relates to the symbolic; it operates at the border between the *psyche* and the *soma*.

What does this mean with respect to particular practices as they issue from established standpoints? Let me be specific again with respect to Christian social practices. Formally, Christian desire can be said to be fourfold. Three forms of this desire can be summed up in Jesus's rehearsal of the heart of the Jewish law: '[Y]ou shall love the Lord your God with all your heart, and with all your soul, and with all your mind . . . [Y]ou shall love your neighbour as yourself' (Matthew 23.37–8). Desire is orientated towards God, self and neighbour (the Sermon on the Mount adds 'enemy'). These are not three forms of desire, nor three objects of desire, but, and in terms of the account of the social imaginary we have been detailing, these are three representa-tions of desire. They exist as three representations at the level of the symbolic and the grammatical, but in the imaginary where God, self and neighbour begin and end is impossible to say – they are irreducible and polysemous. Each of these points of reference is also a place where other unconscious desires are cathected; each composes a dense point of imaginary significances. Castoriadis, speaking specifically of Christ, calls

---

[100] I am aware that Freud tackled this question with respect to dreams, and through years of practice of interpreting them and observation came to formulate certain proposals not only in the famous *Interpretation of Dreams* but in essays like 'Remembering, Repeating and Working-Through', 'The Dynamics of Transference', 'Constructions in Analysis', and 'Analysis Terminable and Interminable'. But I am not treating here questions such as the influence of repression, the suggestions of the analyst, the production of compensatory illusions, fetishism or the impact of everyday events on the shaping of dreams. Freud understood that what he was searching for in dreams was the staging of the forgotten experience of childhood locked away in the unconscious. This became the hermeneutical net through which a particular patient's dream-material was sifted, determining what figures or actions or backgrounds could be put to one side as insignificant or less significant. When we are dealing with a collective *psyche*, a social imaginary, some of the same mechanisms may apply. Freud himself developed the view, in Habermas's words, of the 'cultural tradition as the collective unconscious' (*Knowledge and Human Interests*, p. 282). In fact, more generally, the Frankfurt School critiques of capitalist culture frequently used psychoanalytic terms to explore the 'scene' before them. Freud's work enabled them to investigate institutional and systemic distortions and the operation of illusion as false consciousness, in an examination of power and ideology. But, certainly with Adorno, the analytical tools Freud fashioned were uncoupled from Freud's concern with childhood experience. Furthermore, in treating the collective unconscious we are not handling one individual's pathology, which makes the processes of discernment and judgement infinitely more complex.

them 'imaginary pole[s]'.[101] Furthermore, as representations, they are bound to larger fields of Christian reference – the Scriptures: their stories, injunctions, poetry, visions, polemics; the Church: its history, traditions, liturgies, institutionalism, preaching, failings; a particular *Weltanschauung*: salvation, sin, the Kingdom, genesis, apocalypse, creation. As desires and affects, they are bound to the experiences of being faithful, the experiences of believing in 'the substance of things hoped for' but which are not yet seen; believing in that which is promised. This 'standing in grace', in hope believing 'against hope', engenders a distinctive set of experiences and practices. Paul gives us an insight into the turbulence in which Christian desire is situated and the subjects such experiences form, when he speaks of how Christians 'are justified by faith' so that 'we rejoice in our sufferings, knowing that suffering produces endurance, and endurance produces character, and character produces hope, and hope does not disappoint us, because God's love has been poured into our hearts by the Holy Spirit which has been given to us' (Romans 5.3–5). The Holy Spirit is the present pledge of the fulfilment that is yet to come. But we note the range of passions into which Christian desire is pitched and the struggle that must be endured such that pain and joy, hope, fear of disappointment and doxology are all experienced. We also note the fourth form of desire that we have not yet spoken of, when Paul writes above 'God's love'. With this fourth form of desire, the impenetrable desire of the Other, then we traverse the imaginary; we traverse all the scenes of desire. Slavoj Žižek speaks of such a traversal as 'synonymous with confronting the opening, the abyss of the Other's impenetrable desire'.[102] For Žižek, after Lacan, this desire of the Other is profoundly wounding and traumatic. It is an encounter with the *réel* that is unbearable. Its effect is to reorganise radically the scenes of fantasy. It does not terminate the operations of the imaginary, but rather propels them to new reworkings. For the desire of the Other is unsustainable; the abyss cannot be lived with as such.

Christian desire, then, is not one. Its orientation is long-term (and eschatological), short-term (dealing with issues that are present to hand), interim (investing in personal and corporate future states) and radically other. Desire is complex, multi-focused and held to be maintained by a power that is greater than that of any individual or even collective. It is

---

[101] *The Imaginary Institution*, p. 266.
[102] *The Plague of Fantasies*, p. 31.

continually reading, rereading and composing the world in which it operates; fashioning from the flux of the social imaginary representations for the intimation of a future state it yearns for but does not yet possess. Christian desire rehearses in the public and cultural domain the ordeals of the lover who is not yet sure of his or her relationship to the beloved; it is open also and continually to all the fears of madness, delusion and paranoia.

In *A Midsummer Night's Dream* Duke Theseus sums up this collocation between the imaginary, desires, affects and *poiesis*:

> Lovers and madmen have such seething brains,
> Such shaping fantasies, that apprehend
> More than cool reason ever comprehends.
> The lunatic, the lover, and the poet
> Are of imagination all compact:
> One sees more devils than vast hell can hold;
> That is the madman. The lover, all as frantic,
> See's Helen's beauty in a brow of Egypt.
> The poet's eye, in a fine frenzy rolling,
> Doth glance from heaven to earth, from earth to heaven;
> And as imagination bodies forth
> The forms of things unknown, the poet's pen
> Turns them to shapes, and gives to airy nothing
> A local habitation and a name.
> Such tricks hath strong imagination
> That if it would but apprehend some joy,
> It comprehends some bringer of that joy;
> Or in the night, imagining some fear,
> How easy is a bush supposed a bear?
>
> (Act V sc. 1, 4–22)

Poiesis names desire, names the experience of desiring in 'local' and particular ways; it names the practice of 'strong imagination'. In *poiesis* the imaginary is 'bodie[d] forth' such that 'forms of things unknown' and 'airy nothing' are given shape. What Aristotle called the practical imagination (*phantasia bouleutike*),[103] while drawing upon what is available and already rendered significant in the world (bushes and bears, Helen and Egypt), translates them into something new. It is in this way that *poiesis* as an imaginative praxis transforms the social. More specifically, what this praxis does is to open up new possibilities, new relationships between objects, new significances for objects (because of these new relationships),

---

[103] *De Anima*, tr. Hugh Lawson-Tancred (Harmondsworth: Penguin Books, 1987), III, 9–12.

new ways to perceive, desire, interpret and rethink the world. The forging of new possibilities I view as inseparable from the structuring of hope. But before examining these practices of transformative hope more closely we need to pay heed to Shakespeare's observation, even warning, about the 'tricks' of 'strong imagination'. For, like Puck the fairy in Shakespeare's play, there is a wildness, even a mischievousness, about 'strong imagination'. All imagining may be creative, but not all imagining fosters the flourishing of sociality. The rabid imaginings of the psychopath or the reasoned imaginings of those designing landmines and H-bombs or the unrestrained greed of the capitalist hardly encourage social practices of transformative hope. Such imaginings promote violence, fear, aggression, jealousy, paranoia. In his letter to the Galatians St Paul outlines a different set of virtues that should characterise human sociality: 'love, joy, peace, patience, kindness, goodness, faithfulness, gentleness, self-control' (5.22–3). These are the fruit of 'walking' by the Spirit – that is, disciplined practices that involve self-reflection, recognition, discernment, correction, prudence and a tradition of practical knowledge. These are available not only in Christianity, which is obviously the context of Paul's admonition. They are available in the practices of other faiths. They are also available in certain secular standpoints. But without training in these practices, and the understanding of their significance that comes from such training, then the tricks, mischievousness and wildness of 'strong imagination' can disrupt and challenge the social imaginary in ways that, rather than nurturing relations, tear and rend them.[104]

We will return to this training later when we develop the ethics of cultural hermeneutics and Christian *poiesis*. For the moment we can observe that the work on the social imaginary by Cornelius Castoriadis takes us one step closer to answering the central question of this section: how can we describe the relationship between Christian discursive practices and the production and transformation of public truth or shared knowledge? He does this by deepening our understanding of the association between *psyche*, *koinonia* and *logos*. If, as he asserts, the 'imaginary . . . is the logical and ontological condition of the "real" . . . a condition for all thought',[105] then the work of the radical imagination (not as

---

[104] We can note here that Freud did insist we are responsible for what we imagine, and that such responsibility was an aspect of self-knowledge. See 'Some Additional Notes on Dream-Interpretation as a Whole', Vol. XIX of the *Collected Works of Sigmund Freud*, tr. James Strachey (Harmondsworth: Penguin Books, p. 133.

[105] *The Imaginary Institution*, p. 336.

Einbildungskraft but *Bildungskraft*) is the basis upon which all discursive practices, public truth and common knowledge are made possible. Furthermore, Castoriadis's work puts into place what can sometimes be effaced in the work of Foucault and Adorno on cultural production and its politics: the particularity of institutions. The social exists in and through the institutions that construct its world of significations, which is concomitantly its world of values. For Castoriadis there are two fundamental and correlated institutions – language and what he terms *teukhein* (from which we get 'technique'). These two forms of institution institutionalise. Working together they socialise the individual who already 'is a social institution',[106] disciplining the subject in attitudes, gestures, practices, comportments and know-how. The subject is never reducible to this particular language code and these particular techniques because the imaginary as a primary representative flux overdetermines the signs and symbols that schematise and gives it form.[107] 'Representation is radical imagination. The representative flux is, makes itself, as self-alteration, the incessant emergence of the other in and through the positing [*Vor-stellung*] of images or figures, an imaging which unfolds, brings into being and constantly actualizes what appears retrospectively, to reflective analysis, as the pre-existing conditions of its possibility: temporalization, spatialization, differentiation, alteration.'[108]

This constantly changing 'magma of imaginary significations'[109] creates and fabricates the social, 'otherwise a social revolution is impossible'.[110] As I said earlier, Castoriadis's concern is founding, for him, the preontological and prelogical basis for social transformation. Socialism is a viable possibility because capitalists are individuals who have been socially fabricated[111] and the social is never simply where it thinks it is. It is always to some degree alienated and other; and this alienation and otherness can challenge all hegemony. The social imaginary gives purpose to and makes sense of labours such as Castoriadis's own striving for better social conditions more

---

[106] Ibid., p. 247.
[107] There is no getting behind 'representation' for Castoriadis, which is probably why he has little to say about Lacan's concepts of the '*réel*' and the '*objet petit à*', though he sometimes speaks of a primordial madness from out of which logic and reasoning arise.
[108] *The Imaginary Institution*, p. 329.
[109] *The Imaginary Institution*, p. 210; see also his essay 'The Logic of Magmas and the Question of Authority' in *The Castoriadis Reader*, pp. 290–318.
[110] *The Imaginary Institution*, p. 311.
[111] Ibid., pp. 319–20. This is why he rejects any Marxist notion that the economy or class divisions dictate the institutional structure of society. All institutional structures are subject to change, class and economics are both social fabrications.

equitably shared. He concludes his magisterial *The Imaginary Institution of Society* with: 'The self-transformation of society concerns social doing – and so also politics, in the profound sense of the term.'[112] But with respect to the wild workings of 'strong imagination', there is nothing in Castoriadis's project that evaluates the products of the social imaginary; there is nothing that could offer a resistance to the imaginings of a Hilter, a Stalin, a Caligula, a Julius II or an Idi Amin. For the dangers of the practices of 'strong imagination' lie not simply in what they produce but in the relationship between what they produce and the particular social needs.

Castoriadis does offer an albeit slim psychoanalytical account of good and evil: at the level of the unconscious and the social imaginary good is pleasurable and evil is painful. Leaving aside the collapse of ethics into aesthetics, and how we classify a growing number in late capitalist society who enjoy pain,[113] since, for Castoriadis, the ultimate pleasure psycho-analytically is an impossible return to a primary autism, before the splitting of the self and its subsequent entry into the social – the good so conceived politically and socially is some totalitarian state cleansed of all alterity. Recognising that this return is an impossible (and dangerous) fantasy, and that the imaginary keeps open plural possibilities for future social change, is an important corrective. But there still needs to be a greater examination of the range of transformations possible and how they cohere with, adapt to and shape social needs. As I have pointed out, some transformations (and concomitantly some needs) are socially more beneficial than others. To facilitate that examination we have to return to a question that has haunted this essay: what makes a belief believable?

As I have argued, *after* the event we can examine why this set of ideas or practices had wide appeal while others did not. We can delineate an archaeology of discourses (*à la* Foucault); we can map out the field of symbolic production (*à la* Bourdieu). But it is not always possible to predict what beliefs will become believable. For the believability of beliefs lies in what those beliefs facilitate more widely – what satisfactions, appeasements, consolations, coherences (all of them different pleasure affects) they offer to the needs of the society in which they appear. Not

---

[112] Ibid., p. 373.
[113] See Adorno and Horkheimer's chapter 'Juliette or the Enlightenment and Morality' in *Dialectic of Enlightenment*, Adorno's essay 'On the Fetish Character of Music and the Regression of Listening' in *The Culture Industry* and my own 'Theology and Cultural Sadomasochism', *Svensk Teologisk Kvartalskrift*, Arg. 78 (2002), 1–10.

that these needs are not themselves produced. New needs arise as new possibilities are opened; *poiesis* not only creates new connections, it creates new orientations for desire and new possibilities for the satisfaction of that desire. Beyond the satisfactions demanded biologically, needs too are defined by the social imaginary. New institutions may gain popular backing because they satisfy social needs, but they also provoke and define such needs. I suggest that this is the place where the contestation of standpoints, which I said was inevitable, becomes culturally creative. When a set of new perceptions and relations issues into a series of representations and finally takes on more extensive institutionalisation, there have to be evaluations. These evaluations are not from one point of judgement only, in terms of some crass and reductive censorship, but from a number of standpoints – defining their own pro-jects with respect to this new practice of the imagination. There has to be what I would call a cultural pathology that attempts to examine critically not only what is being offered, but the dialectic between the social need that is being appealed to and the social need being brought into being. Only in this way can mass deception and the injustices of false consciousness be made evident and open to account. This is the very task that the discursive practices of standpoints must undertake. The Christian standpoint, for example, is not simply involved in an act of self-definition; it is involved in a critical and cultural act of discrimination and judgement with respect to how it understands itself and the worlds in which its practices are embedded. It too must undertake the work of cultural pathology (rather than define itself over against the cultural orders that face and challenge it) – this is fundamental to its apologetic task. And the examination here of what fails to gain public attention and credibility is as important and insightful as any examination of what succeeds. Standpoints make possible public discussion and evaluation, and enable there to be a series of critical gazes maintained on the products expressing and transforming the social imaginary. Standpoint critiques enable there to be judgements made on 'strong imagination' – even if such judgements are contested. With respect to the 'seething brains' that apprehend more than they comprehend, these other standpoints can offer the lover or the madman critical perspectives on their predicament. This discursive action undertaken by various standpoints maintains the possibility that cultural transformations are governed by hope.

What then of the distinctive contibution made to these transformations (and their directions) by religious practices? Despite referring on several occasions to religion – and the Christian religion in particular – and despite his own recognition that religion is a social institution like any other and irreducible (to trafficking in illusions, false consolations and wish-fulfilments), the concern of Castoriadis is not with the ways in which the institutions and disciplinary practices of a religion can transform the social. But he enables us to situate a particular cultural imaginary that is religiously informed with respect to the socially fabricated world-view, the common knowledge by which the society or *koinonia* identifies itself. Societies exist only in and through a sense of coherence that can be shared. They have to hold together an 'open multitude of individuals, acts, objects, functions'.[114] And so to some extent the particular religious imaginary (and its institutions) will cohere with (in order to continue existing within) the wider set of social significations. Even, say, a counter-cultural religious movement finds its place, can only find its place, within the sets of schemas, or common frames of reference, figures, images and institutions that constitute and organise a society's *kosmos idios.*

It might be argued that to think through the distinctive contribution of religious practices – in my case Christian practices – of piety on the basis of Castoriadis's work is to capitulate to psychoanalysis as a foundational, explanatory discourse. But there remains a remarkable correlation between the anthropology Castoriadis sketches of *homo poeticus* as a creature of imagination and Judaeo-Christian theological anthropologies that emphasise that human beings were made 'in the image of' and are then essentially image-makers and makers through imitation. Furthermore, as Castoriadis's account of the soul makes clear, Freud rethinks Aristotle and Plato: he stands within a line of thinking that would include all the Judaeo-Christian tradition has thought about concerning the soul.[115] What is needed in order to understand how societies arrive at the values they hold in common and how these values are changed over time is an account of cultural production. It is the nature of that production that has been the concern of this essay. What psychoanalysis (conceived in terms of both an account of the subject and an account of the social) provides is a place from which such production can be thought. Castoriadis might challenge the statement made by Deleuze and Guattari that '[The unconscious] represents nothing, it produces everything. It means nothing, but it works,'[116] on the ground that, for him, 'the unconscious exists only as an indissociably

[114] *The Imaginary Institution*, p. 369.
[115] See 'Epilegomena to a Theory of the Soul which has been presented as a Science' in *Crossroads in the Labyrinth*, pp. 3–45.
[116] *Anti-Oedipus: Capitalism and Schizophrenia*, trs. Robert Hurley et al. (London: Athlone Press, 1984), p. 109.

representative/affective/intentional flux'.[117] But what each of these socialist thinkers would accept is that the source and origins of production lie within that deep and remote realm of the *psyche* or the soul Freud terms the 'unconscious'. Christian theology would only concur – history issues out of the heart of human making and being. Psychoanalysis, then, offers a schema for understanding another aspect of the human condition – it offers ways of enriching first an anthropology and, secondly, an ethnology: what it is to be human and what it is to be human in this cultural setting or social imaginary.

THE CULTURAL IMAGINARY

Until this point I have in the main adopted the term 'social imaginary' as it is used by the social scientists I have been concerned with, but I have wished to speak about the cultural imaginary. Why do I see the shift from social to cultural imaginary as important and what is the character of this shift? Why the move from social to cultural? There are two principal reasons. First, because in the writings of these social scientists who employ the term 'social' there is, it seems to me, a continual slippage between the social and the cultural. The slippage occurs because of the imbrication of the social within the cultural. That is, our conceptions of social order are culturally governed – there is not one without the other. But not to reflect upon the slippage is to aid the conflation of the social and the cultural. Along with Adorno, I view this conflation as dangerous. The cultural is a symbolic domain governed by processes of exchange and syncretistic transformation. It is the domain of the aesthetic. An increasingly aesthetic world-view has been emerging in the West with the radical critiques of modernity and what has been termed the re-enchantment of the real.[118] The new visibility of religion in public life is one aspect of this re-enchantment, but as Adorno (after Marx) pointed out, capitalism has always been caught up in a certain spiritualising of the world. Throughout my analysis I have been at pains to emphasise it is people who act, people who fashion and employ symbols. The most pressing concern about the conflation of the cultural with the social is that people as standpoint agents disappear, politics disappear, and the advocacy and pursuit of alternative modes of living also disappear. Perhaps the emphasis by the social scientists I have been considering on 'social imaginary' testifies to the fact it is people

---

[117] *The Imaginary Institution*, p. 274.
[118] See Zygmunt Bauman, *Intimations of Postmodernity* (London: Routledge, 1992), pp. vii–xxviii.

who dream, imagine, desire, create, imitate, etc. It is people who have conceptions of belonging or being marginalised, who relate to their kin, their friends, their neighbours and their colleagues. But there is no concept of a person that is not culturally mediated, and therefore no concept of belonging, kinship or friendship that it is not culturally mediated. So while we cannot dissolve agency into cultural determinism, we have to recognise that the imaginary realm is culturally conditioned. So, secondly, I use 'cultural imaginary' to draw a distinction between the social and the cultural.

In the past, the distinction between the social and the cultural issued from a more fundamental distinction between being and doing or making; ontology, on the one hand, praxis on the other. The social concerned people in their immediate relations with each other, while the cultural was viewed as that which members of the social order made. The cultural was understood to be the expression of that society's moral and intellectual values, its ideology. Human beings congregated and through the institution of their various relationships formed the social and then these social gatherings produced civilisations or forms of civil living. Thus the cultural is epiphenomenal and the social as the concourse of individual men, women and children (not always if ever equally valued) is foundational. This understanding of culture remains embedded in German discourse on *Kultur* – for example in Freud's famous essay 'Civilization [*Kultur*] and its Discontents'. It is the same with the French *culture* which also relies upon a distinction between the primitive or given state of things and the cultivated, the raw and the cooked. In both German and French, the discourse on culture is intimately associated with education, the arts, and the media.[119] It would not, therefore, make sense in either German or French to speak of the cultural imaginary in the way I am understanding that imaginary, as a creative resource for the formation of images of sociality. Hence both Ricoeur and Castoriadis refer to *l'imaginaire social*. Ricoeur can justify his use of the term because for him there is an ontological condition that all symbolic action refers to. There is the *Ding an sich* that the act of appropriation or refiguration re-engages; it is this re-engagement that opens up the reader/interpreter to the other. But for Castoriadis the ontological is itself a product of the social imaginary. There is no action that is not symbolic action; no given that is not already so profoundly

---

[119] This view of culture – pictured so clearly in Walter Benjamin's 'Theses on the Philosophy of History' as spoils that are held aloft in a triumphal parade – gives rise to functional or instrumental conceptions of culture.

mediatised[120] that 'as such it is almost non-existent'.[121] There is society only where there is institution; the individual is himself or herself one such institution. '[T]he idea of a given, assignable organization of nature (and one that is essentially, that is, ontologically, simple) which society could take up part by part or progressively, is simply an incoherent fantasy of a certain stage of Western science,' Castoriadis writes.[122] There is, then, no immediate 'face-to-face relation' or 'positioning of agents in circumstances of co-presence' – conditions that offer 'ontological security' for the social and distinguish it from the cultural.[123] Given then the development of the 'cultural' in terms of symbolic world-views, by anthropologists in the wake of structuralism and the linguistic turn in modern philosophy, the social and the cultural are inseparable where, as Castoriadis observes, 'every society must produce its life and socially organize this production'.[124] He may employ at different times both 'social' and 'cultural', 'society' and 'culture', but where there is no distinction between being and doing then the terms slide one into the other. The imaginary – the extensive fund of imaged possibilities – offers several potential forms for sociality.

I wish then to use the term cultural imaginary in this way and for this reason, understanding its operation to be more foundational than the various forms of society it institutionalises. But the danger here is the effacement of any particular phenomenon that can be called 'society'. Where society is identified as an imaginary community, a shared world of symbolic exchanges that continually informs the socialising processes of those nurtured and disciplined within its purviews and practices, what is the difference between saying 'this society' and 'this culture'? The question does not arise when talk of 'society' presupposes some territorial or linguistic boundaries: all those who belong to this polis or that nation state, for example, or all those who speak this one language. But with increasing globalisation, migration of labour-forces, shifting populations of refugees and the dissemination of certain first world languages (American English and Spanish most insistently) we are seeing the erosion of such boundaries.

---

[120] This is a term used by Habermas to speak of the organisation of social life.

[121] *The Imaginary Institution*, p. 236.

[122] Ibid., p. 231. It is no accident, therefore, that culture as *Kultur* and *culture* arises at the same time as Nature is being defined in increasingly empirical and positivistic terms. On the changing sense of culture, see Raymond Williams, *Culture and Society: 1780–1950* (London: Chatto and Windus, 1959).

[123] See Anthony Giddens, *The Constitution of Society* (Cambridge: Polity Press, 1984), pp. 83–9.

[124] *The Imaginary Institution*, p. 26.

This is what I meant by saying we have to recognise something about the historical circumstances in which we stand. Famously, we have statements by those in the tradition of Hayek, Friedman and Margaret Thatcher to the effect that there is no such thing as society. The danger of this parallel rise of culture and demise of society is that politics – or the dealings among and between human beings about the ways they are being governed and should be governed – becomes aestheticised. By aestheticised here I mean the production of false consciousness through dominant cultural rhetorics whose aim is to dazzle with the spectacular, divert or entertain; the production of anodyne cultural objects that mask or appear to resolve conflict rather than express and give it form.[125] We move from a public sphere in which debate and calling to account is important for the ongoing processes of democracy, to a public sphere in which various factions fight to gain public trust and accreditation. We have seen earlier in this section that Habermas has observed such a shift: citizens become customers who need to be satisfied and forms of governance become providers of services. The satisfied customer is then free to design his or her own lifestyle under the illusion of his or her own sovereign autonomy. Politics is rendered invisible; masked beneath relations of authority and jurisdiction based upon 'consumer satisfaction', a tranquillising rhetoric of transparency and caring. The pacified customer is the depoliticised one; in exchange for certain gratifications (and satisfaction is one such gratification) customers retreat into their private worlds where, they are assured, the genuine meaning and value of their lives reside. The truculent customer, on the other hand, is viewed as aggressive, violent or psychotic; his or her resistance is characterised as nihilistic, anarchistic or terrorist.[126]

There need to be, then, new understandings of what constitutes the social and society as distinct from the cultural and culture, but it cannot be on the grounds of some myth of the given; human beings in some immediate and 'raw' mode of cohabitation. The cultural imaginary as that magma of social significations makes many forms of sociality possible, makes possible then new construals of 'society'. And I would see religious traditions, which long have retained theological accounts of *societas*, as having a major contribution to make here

---

[125] I would understand the exaltation of kitsch as emblematic in such a culture: where surface is celebrated as surface. A culture of reflective surfaces eludes penetrating analyses that would foreground difference, alterity, and contestation – all the marks of an active imaginary.

[126] This situation marks the triumph of liberalism's utopian dream (and the end of history): the 'public' role of the state is to secure the sacred values of the private, the household gods.

to public discourse and to the transformation of the cultural imaginary. They have resources for the repoliticisation of cultural agents; resources for new humanisms. Without that repoliticising, then, systemic dissatisfaction cannot be registered in a way that demands and forces change. For 'satisfaction' means that you, I, they, we, he or she have nothing left to complain about. And yet it is the visibility of complaint, of contestation between standpoints, that is vital for cultural transformation to come about. It makes manifest the irreducibility of the imaginary and the symbolic institutions it engenders. It makes manifest what Fredric Jameson (after Ernst Bloch) terms the 'overlapping modes of production' that give rise to 'nonsynchronous [*Ungleichzeitigkeit*] development'.[127] In this making visible of complaint, antagonism or contestation lies not only a future for politics and democracy, but cultural transformation *tout court*. A culture of 'satisfaction' is a culture where aesthetics have become anaesthetics, because what it aims at is the erasure of desire: that is, stasis (or death). Viewed as antagonistic to standpoint-projects, it denies those things that in the last section we noted involvement in such pro-jects fashions: construals of identity, agency, intentionality and temporality (as historicity). Fundamentally, it denies materiality. What attention to the contestation and partial alliances between standpoints allows, then, is a focus upon association, intersubjective practices, exchange and interactive relations between identities – all the hallmarks of material *Gemeinschaft* and what I think Antonio Negri would describe as 'a new proletarian practice of time'.[128] The focus would not be upon some reified abstraction called 'society', but the very operation of sociality as it is produced in, through and across cultures. This is a sociality issuing from the 'radical imagination, the representative flux' that constitutes what I am now calling the cultural imaginary.

---

[127] *The Political Unconscious* (London: Routledge, 1983), pp. 83–5. See also Ernst Bloch, 'Nonsynchronism and Dialectics', *New German Critique*, no.11 (Spring 1977), 22–38.

[128] See Negri's *Time for Revolution*, p. 21. There are some overlaps here between Negri's development of Marx's idea of the 'real subsumption' of the social by capitalism in which difference is erased and my construal of the 'culture of satisfaction'. There would also be some overlap between his understanding of internal resistance and my development of the cultural imaginary as continually destabilising institutional forms of hegemony. In fact, Negri too locates the possibilities for revolution in the practical imagination, what I term *poiesis*. See also my essay 'The Commodification of Religion', *The Hedgehog Review: Critical Reflections on Contemporary Culture*, Vol. 5 no.2 (Summer 2003), 50–65.

THE CHRISTIAN TRANSFORMATION OF THE CULTURAL
IMAGINARY

We come now, finally, to answer to our question about Christian discursive practice or *poiesis* and the production and transformation of public accounts of what is true. What is the relationship between religious activity and cultural transformation? But first let me emphasise that *poiesis* is not solely a Christian or a religious activity. For standpoint-projects are manifold and each is a social institution issuing from the flux of the cultural imaginary. It is through the pro-jects and interaction of standpoints that public narratives are formed and win credibility. But, as the return to the specificities of Christian *poiesis* illustrates, because some standpoints have more profound histories than others they have, first, a greater persistence within the cultural imaginary and they are, secondly, more embedded within institutional structures. Certain forms of *poiesis* then can have (not *a priori* because other restrictions apply) more transformative impact than others, depending upon the historical conditions of a particular cultural ethos. I would argue that Christian *poiesis* has today the potential for considerable impact on public accounts of what is true because of two prevailing conditions. The first condition is the cultural shift registered in such words as 'postmodernity', 'late-capitalism', 'post-industralism' and 'post-secularism'. The new visibility of religion has created new receptivities to religious pieties. The sociologist Peter L. Berger has noted (in a way that calls for the rewriting of theories of secularism) that 'the assumption that we live in a secularised world is false. The world today . . . is as furiously religious as it ever was, and in some places more so than ever.'[129] The second prevailing condition is the long-term indebtedness of cultural traditions in the West to Christianity's ideas, myths, motifs, symbols and practices. Terry Eagleton has recently pointed out how 'religious mythology survives modernity . . . that the gods stage a come back in the form of Reason, providence in the shape of scientific determinism, and nemesis in the guise of heredity. Infinity lingers on in sublimity.'[130] But the 'religion' and the 'gods' here are specifically associated with Christianity. Christianity in both demythologised (secularised) and remythologised forms profoundly inhabits the Western cultural imaginary – which through successive waves of

---

[129] 'The Desecularization of the World: A Global Overview' in *The Desecularization of the World*, p. 2.
[130] *Sweet Violence: The Idea of Tragedy* (Oxford: Blackwell, 2003), p. 225.

immigration and colonial expansion is no longer simply Western at all. Both the word 'secular' and the modern construal of 'religion' are the products of Christian reflection. The contemporary cultural imaginary is therefore already fertile with Christianity in a manner not available in the climates of positivism and atheism that followed the Second World War.

So far in this essay we have been enquiring into the mechanics of cultural transformation, but we must also enquire into both the contents of these practices and what they produce. For it is with respect to the specific contents of standpoint-projects that the cultural imaginary is modified in one way rather than another. Althusser remarks in his essay 'On Materialist Dialectic' that Marxist political practice, 'like any other practice, also produces transformations (which are not *knowledges*, but a revolution in *social relations*)'.[131] I would not wish to be too rigid in distinguishing *knowledges* from *social relations*, for it seems to draw too firm a line between the cultural and the social in a way that my own concept of *poiesis* resists. But it does seem to me to be a useful distinction about the modes of production in transformative practices. We might then analyse Christian praxis in terms of the knowledges it produces and the way those know-ledges continually affect existing and constitute new social relations, and new desires within those relations, while recognising that the praxis itself involves social relations that will affect and determine the subsequent shapes of those knowledges. In doing this I suggest a critique of certain forms of social transformation will be articulated that can reorientate the magma of the cultural imaginary towards alternative social possibilities. For example, Castoriadis speaks of a transformative pro-ject 'orientated towards fostering the autonomy of all, this transformation being accom-plished by the autonomous action of all human beings, such as they are produced by current society'.[132] As my examination of Castoriadis demon-strated 'autonomy' is an awkward category in his work. For he argues cogently for an intersubjectivity that constitutes the basis of praxis and renders such praxis (and the freedoms it aspires to) comprehensible. But as a category with close associations with the philosophy of the liberal subject, I suggest an analysis of Christian praxis would reveal that the goal of the transformation is not simply the realisation of personal sovereignty. Neither would it be simply the opposite: some form of communitarianism. An analysis of Christian praxis would articulate a critique of both positions

---

by giving expression to economies of response, relation and desire that
continually exceed the autonomous agent in terms of both their meaning
and their consequences in the constitution of reciprocal and communal
identities, while never losing sight of the scandal of the particular, in this
case the singular calling of this person and that. I say 'scandal' here because
any testimony to the singularity of one's calling with respect to the great
theological schema of salvation history must wrestle continually with both
humiliation and hubris. The Christian critique that is articulated would
call into question the extent to which teleologies of transformation with
respect to either individual autonomy or communism can be (a) achiev-
able; (b) desirable; and (c) transformative in terms of hope for better
human flourishing. It would, though, recognise that these criticisms – of
achievability, desirability, transformability – are historically contextual-
ised. Castoriadis, for example, in defending the orientation of the transformation he seeks, believes he is examining demands and aspirations
'decipher[able] . . . in actual history. . .'

> If we assert the tendency of contemporary society towards autonomy, if we want to
> work for its realization, this is because we are asserting autonomy as a mode of
> being of humans, that we are ascribing value to it, that we recognize it as our
> essential aspiration and as an aspiration that surpasses the peculiarities of our
> personal constitution, the only one that can be defended publicly with lucidity and
> coherence.[133]

Castoriadis defends the orientation of his transformation with respect to an
intersubjectivity that belies the category of the subject's autonomy on the
basis of (a) an essentialised anthropology (an assurance that he knows what
the human condition *is*) and (b) a public rationality (that there is consensus
about what this human condition *is*). This may have been possible in the
mid 1970s. I doubt it is possible in the climate of today's post-liberalism
and sceptical humanism. I suggest that where we stand culturally today
essentialist anthropologies, much like appeals to a universal nature, are no
longer tenable and that appeals to a public rationality come up against
MacIntyre's question: 'Whose rationality?' The Christian critique, then,
that issues from the examination of contemporary Christian *poiesis* will also
have to defend itself against the charge of being arbitrary, and defend itself
along lines Castoriadis drew. That is, it is not arbitrary because its relevance
lies in the relationship it bears to questions our contemporary culture is
already asking about itself. But, in that defence, it appeals to other

---

[133] Ibid., p. 100.

categories that it offers for public accreditation and provides an account of interrelationality that is not based in an essentialised and universalised humanism.

As a standpoint-project Christianity, then, approaches the world critically. The critique issues from both its ethical and its eschatological vision. By ethical here I refer to Christianity's conceptions of the God's goodness, beauty and justice, conceptions incarnated in Christ whom Christians are called to imitate. The ethical vision provokes judgement with respect to distorted and distorting forms of social relation: that is, social relations that do not reflect God's goodness, beauty and justice, but rather manifest violent inequalities,[134] exploitations and subjugations. The ethical vision also provokes the advocacy of new possibilities in Christ. Redemption realises a new creation in which social relations are conceived in terms of a love that fosters human flourishing and community. The horizons of this ethical vision are eschatological. That is, the ethical vision looks toward an end-times in which a realm is established where all creation finds its true goodness, beauty and justice by being enfolded into, rather than alienated from, the Godhead. In fact, the ethical vision maintains, proleptically, the eschatological resurrection of all creation that is the measure by which the various world-orders are compared.

Christianity's critique of the world is not simply negative. The critique itself participates in the redemptive operation such that true critique issues in the establishment of hope, not scepticism nor cynicism. Of course, there is no immediate recognition of the truth of any critique. There is only the labour of discernment and the operation of faith; the striving to recognise what is true. Nevertheless what characterises Christian critical practices in the world, Christian *poiesis*, is a governing soteriology that pursues social transformation by means of opening up new utopian possibilities in the prevailing cultural *Zeitgeist*. These critical and transformative practices

---

[134] I speak of 'violent inequalities' not 'inequalities'. All may be equal in the sight of God, but all are not equal with respect to the world. Modern democracy was founded on a Judaeo-Christian principle of equality from the divine perspective – see John Locke and Thomas Paine. But when democracy set aside its theological axioms and pursued 'equality' on the grounds of all people being human, it created a radical tension between the all-too-evident inequalities among human beings and a universal condition of being human fashioned in the historical and ethnic particularities of the West and its Enlightenment. The mediator in this tension was the language of 'rights' – and the problems with 'rights' talk and pluralism continue. It is not inequality as such that I believe is wrong – certainly from a Christian perspective all are equal as made in the image of God, though not all have the same gifts or the same calling. It is the violences that issue from the maintenance by some of systemic inequalities that provoke judgement from the perspective of Christianity's ethical vision.

affect and reorientate the cultural imaginary. The credibility of what they suggest is always subject to other conditions. Where the dominant world-view is secular and positivist, then these practices struggle for a recognition of their significance. But, as I said above, in a cultural climate characterised as 'post-secular' and 're-enchanted', their effect may be much more profound.

At the heart of these transformative practices I have placed 'hope'. Charles Péguy, in his wonderful poem *La porche du mystère de la deuxième vertu*, imagines God speaking about love (the first virtue) and hope (the second):

Charity, says God, that doesn't surprise me.
It's not surprising.
These poor creatures are so miserable that unless they had a heart of stone, how
   could they not have love for each other . . .
But hope, says God, that is something that surprises me.
Even me.
That is surprising.
That these poor children see how things are going and believe that tomorrow
   things will go better.
That they see how things are going today and believe that they will go better
   tomorrow morning.
That is surprising and it's by far the greatest marvel of our grace.
And I'm surprised by it myself.[135]

Hope is orientated towards a future condition and it is inseparable from desire. So what is produced by these transformative practices of hope and desire in terms of both knowledge and social relations is a manifestation of the eschatological. Put another way, what is produced is the positioning of any desiring, knowing and relating (all knowledge being a knowledge-in-relation) in terms of its perfection in Christ. Not that this perfection is absent now and realised later, either in some Hegelian organic dialectical movement in which the contingent becomes the necessary or in the abrupt and violent arrival of a new and eternal order into the temporal. The perfection is already realised in Christ, and we are already in Christ – just as the Kingdom is already among us. But there is a working out of the salvation wrought in Christ; there is an incorporation (through a submission) whereby all things are returned to Christ. Christian praxis participates

---

[135] Translation *The Portal of the Mystery of Hope*, tr. David Louis Schindler, Jr (Edinburgh: T&T Clark, 1996), p. 6.

in this eschatological incorporation; in an economy of salvation that is inseparable from an economic working of the Trinitarian love in and through creation. The working of hope makes present a future doxology, while simultaneously realising a past promise; just as the present itself is only given to us through a relation both to the future expectation and to the remembered past. One might say here that the very operation of the eschatological is the formation of relation, true social relation; for relation can only be realised in the extent to which it participates in the love of Christ. The social is and can be social only insofar as it is constituted *in Christo*. From the Christian standpoint, there is no other body. In fact, one might suggest that what transformative practices of hope and desire produce is embodiment; they fashion the body of Christ.

The working of hope, then, is not an abstract principle but always an embodied one – where embodiment recognises what I called in *Cities of God* (after Julia Kristeva) 'transcorporality'. That is, because the boundaries between physical bodies, civic bodies, social bodies, sacramental bodies and the body of Christ are fluid (and therefore vulnerable one to another), then practices of hope move in and through one body affecting all the others. It is people who hope, and such hoping is always a labour (an expenditure of energy, a channelling of choice, a disciplining of desire) that involves a many-faceted resistance (a resistance against despair and doubt, a resistance against what is seen in favour of what is unseen, a living beyond what is apparent or evident or given). It is the labouring in hope that distinguishes that hope from wishful thinking and fantasy. There is a disciplining that issues from that labour. Hope is never passive; its desires are always political and politicising. While in a sense it abides, bearing the weight of a present imaginary, and securing moments of being-at-rest-with, hope is always discerning, searching out, sifting through, pressing its nose into the future. To hope is always to pro-ject, to be involved and implicated in specific pro-jects, to live pro-jectively, to practise the future like practising a foreign tongue. When I speak then of transformative practices of hope, that 'hope' is the medium, the content and the object of the praxis. Its desire awakens the imagination to new possibilities and fosters an ethos whose values transcend the merely evident. In their various ways, this is what the philosophers of desire from Freud to Lacan, Deleuze and Castoriadis have taught us: the imaginary is located in an economy of desire. The imaginary produces new objects of desire. Hope, while learning patience, is always hungry. It activates and energises, producing pro-jects and stand-points of resistance to the *status quo*. I would suggest that Christian hoping is the paradigm for Western hoping, secularised from the twilight of

Christendom onwards, in various utopian and socialist dreams. St Paul characterises creation as 'subjected in hope [*hupotazanta ep' elpidi*]' (Romans 8.20), where *hupotatto* has the sense of 'to arrange in order'. Hope, in the Christian world-view, is structured into the orders of creation. But, he continues, 'Hope that is seen is not hope' (Romans 8.24). Hope abides then in a not seeing that nevertheless reaches beyond itself, escapes the realm of the possible. Maurice Blanchot writes perceptively about the event of hope with respect to constituting relations: 'Hope bespeaks the possibility of what escapes the realm of the possible; at the limit, it is relation recaptured where relation is lost.'[136] Where there is no hope there is paralysis; for hope calls for abiding in a place of vision, a walking through the valley of shadows while clinging to the scandal of the impossible. In the Letter to the Hebrews we are told, 'By faith Abraham obeyed when he was called out to a place which he was afterwards to receive as an inheritance; and so he went out, not knowing where he was to go. By faith he sojourned in the land of promise, as in a foreign land . . . For he looked forward to the city which has foundations, whose builder and maker is God' (11.8–10). It is not that Christians abide in this world and dream of its full restoration in Christ. Exactly the opposite: Christians, like Abraham, 'sojourn in the land of promise', while suffering the contradiction between that promise and the surrounding foreignness.[137] It is a suffering that is not borne passively but lived actively in labouring for the subjection of all that is distorted and sinful to the ethical, spiritual and political orders of that promise. The cultural imaginary is challenged and changed by that labouring.

This leads to a theological reflection: that all theological discourse has to negotiate suffering, alienation and dispossession. In fact, theological discourse, which on my account is what all Christian practice is, is born from this negotiation. Theological terms like God, beauty, justice and the good might be tossed about, played with like so many x's and y's in a logician's game. But theological discourse is formed only in and as passion – and passion is complex and wounding and sometimes wonderful. Since Jesus Christ is the one in whose footsteps all Christians follow, then the crucifixion of Jesus Christ is not one moment on the way to redemption, such that Christ could still have remained Christ had he rejected the cup he knew was offered to him in Gethsemane. He had to drink it to the dregs.

---

[136] *The Infinite Conversation*, tr. S. Hanson (Minneapolis: University of Minnesota Press, 1993), p. 41.
[137] This suffering of the contradictory is given a Christian inflection here but it pertains to all standpoint-projects. Althusser observes that 'contradiction is the motor of all development' (*For Marx*, p. 217).

Only on the other side of wrestling with the scandal of the impossible is the announcement of resurrection possible. The Church born from the wrestling is an extension of that incarnation, that crucifixion and that resurrection. So theological discourse labours with impossibility and the tears and tearings of faith, driven on by hope to stay its course. Hope, like love, endures all things and baptises all action undertaken in its name, redemptive.

Theological discourse relates then to the productive transformation of culture by directing such transformation towards a transcendent hope. It works not only to participate in but to perform the presence of Christ. In and through its working the cultural imaginary is changed, and alternative forms of sociality, community and relation are fashioned, imagined, and to some extent embodied. I say 'to some extent' not only because Christian practices are not inoculated against distortion. Like all practices, they are enacted through the finitudes and vicissitudes of human beings. But I say 'to some extent' because, as Castoriadis shows, the magma of the imaginary exceeds its institutional performances. Furthermore, Christian practices are bound to other practices such that the question can arise: when is a practice Christian and when is it not? There are certain transformative practices that are not governed by hope; violent practices of all kinds from abusive anger, to rape and the waging of war. One can only judge a practice by the kind of transformations it produces – the kind of knowledges that build rather than destroy social relations.

Of course, Christian praxis is partial, both in terms of it being only one praxis (even one theologically orientated praxis) among many and in terms of it being closed to certain options on the grounds of its pre-given grammar of the faith. Nevertheless, this praxis operates with respect to society as a whole. The conception of this totality is important. The totality is not co-extensive with the nation state. Rather, it is co-extensive with a totality that is global and transhistorical – nothing less that the community of the redeemed past, present and future. This totality is not closed since the conception of the Kingdom that is operative in Christian praxis is one that is understood without being comprehended; it is a belief that knowledge has yet to gain. In the sense that belief already possesses its object of belief, though not in full, the totality Christian praxis works with is constitutive, not regulative: the totality is continually being realised. But insofar as the completion of this totality exceeds all that Christian praxis can do and all that it can grasp, there remains an ineluctable pragmatism about all Christian doing and making. But it is a pragmatism that works out of and towards a universal, or a normativity that issues from

participation in the operations of the Godhead. The nature of this normativity is as impossible as the operations of the Godhead itself to comprehend. It is lived as faith and entrustment – which are inseparable from
hope. In the groundlessness of the human condition it is God alone who is
normative. Christian pragmatism, which responds to the local and the
contingent in the name of the eternal, continually calls forth reflection
upon its responses to each new negotiation and, in such reflection, produces a transformed relation to the object in that negotiation (and therefore transforms the object itself). In fact, the local and contingent is
vouchsafed only in the name of the universal and eternal that 'made of it
this *"particularity"* '.[138] As such, the partiality of Christian praxis is not a
'lack', but a condition for an ongoing transformative labour that renders
the concrete concrete, saving the singularity of things. In fact it is this
pragmatism necessitated by its partiality and its inability to comprehend
the totality that stalls Christian triumphalism in all its senses. This pragmatism constitutes a cultural ethics whose goal is the social flourishing of
all and the voicing of a creature's own doxology in being created as this
particular being.

We have, I believe, answered those three questions that were the starting
point for this essay: from where does the theologian speak? What are the
processes by which cultures and, thereby, the public perceptions of reality
change? What is the relationship between Christian discursive practices
and the production and transformation of public truth or shared knowledge? What can emerge from *this* pro-ject is, first, a new engagement of the
theologically informed practices of the Christian with the larger social
world that contextualises him or her: a new apologetic task. Secondly,
from this engagement will emerge a new vernacular – a language that is
neither 'churchy' nor 'secular', for these are no longer the poles for its own
self-understanding. This will be a public discourse, inscribing a cultural
ethics, in which the theological finds its place as a voice already engaged in
contributing to the production of public truth. No doubt for some time to
come the recognition of its right to take such a place may be contested – by
those who maintain the autonomy of the secular – but eventually this
vernacular will constitute a new *ekklesia*. *Ekklesia* here designates not only
those who are called out (*ek-kaleo*), but also a set of political, ethical and

---

[138] The words again are Althusser's (*For Marx*, p. 218). Althusser is examining Marx's alleged
inversion of Hegel's dialectic, and pointing to how Marx's dialectic facilitates a reflection on the
crux of Hegel's dialectic. We cannot travel far into this matter other than to say that the
universalism of Hegel's dialectic is rooted in a Trinitarian theology.

theological relations working passionately (in the rich sense of that word) in the *agora*, in anticipation of a city yet to come.

People who speak thus make it clear that they are seeking a homeland. If they had been thinking of that land from which they had gone out, they would have had opportunity to return. But as it is, they desire a better country, that is, a heavenly one. Therefore God is not ashamed to be called their God, for he has prepared for them a city.

(Hebrews 11.14–16)

Bibliography

Adam, Karl (1926), 'Die Theologie der Krisis', *Hochland*, no.23 (June), 271–86.

Adorno, Theodor (1983), *Prisms*, tr. Samuel M. Weber. Cambridge, Mass.: MIT Press.

(1991), 'On the Fetish Character in Music and the Regression of Listening' in J.M. Bernstein (ed.), *The Culture Industry*. London: Routledge.

(1994), *The Stars Down to Earth*, ed. Stephen Crook. London: Routledge.

(2000), *Introduction to Sociology*, tr. Edmund Jephcott. Cambridge: Polity Press.

(2001) 'The Scheme of Mass Culture' in Richard J. Bernstein (ed.), *The Culture Industry*. London: Routledge. 61–97.

Adorno, Theodor with Horkheimer, Max (1997), *Dialectic of Enlightenment*, tr. John Cumming. London: Verso.

Agamben, Giorgio (1999), *The Man Without Content*, tr. Georgia Albert. Stanford: University of Stanford Press.

Althusser, Louis (1969), *For Marx*, tr. Ben Brewster. London: Penguin Books.

(2001), *Lenin and Philosophy and Other Essays*, tr. Ben Brewster. New York: Monthly Review Press.

Anderson, Benedict (1991), *Imagined Communities*. London: Verso.

Anderson, Pamela Sue (1998), *Towards a Feminist Philosophy of Religion*. Oxford: Blackwell.

Anscombe, Elizabeth (1957), *Intention*. Oxford: Blackwell.

Aristotle (1976), *Ethics*, tr. J.A.K. Thomson. Harmondsworth: Penguin Books.

(1987), *De Anima*, tr. Hugh Lawson-Tancred. Harmondsworth: Penguin Books.

(1991), *Poetics*, trs. W. Hamilton Fyfe and W. Rhys Roberts. Cambridge, Mass.: Harvard University Press.

Badiou, Alain (2001), *Ethics: An Essay on the Understanding of Evil*, tr. Peter Hallward. London: Verso.

Balthasar, Hans Urs von (1951), *Karl Barth. Darstellung und Deutung seiner Theologie*. Cologne: Verlag Jakob Hegner.

Barth, Karl (1946), *Natural Theology: Comprising 'Nature and Grace' by Emil Brunner and the Reply 'No!' by Karl Barth*, tr. Peter Fränkel. London: The Centenary Press.

(1956–75), *Church Dogmatics*, 14 volumes. Edinburgh: T&T Clark.

(1961), *The Humanity of God*. London: Collins.

(1962), *Theology and Church: Shorter Writings 1920–1928*, tr. Louise Pettibone Smith. London: SCM.

(1963), *Der Römerbrief*, 1st edn. Zurich: EVZ-Verlag.

(1964), *Revolutionary Theology in the Making: Barth–Thurneysen Correspondence, 1914–1925*, tr. James D. Smart. London: Epworth Press.

(1973), *Karl Barth–Eduard Thurneysen Briefwechsel*. Band I, 1913–1921. Zurich: TVZ.

(1974), *Karl Barth–Eduard Thurneysen Briefwechsel*. Band II, 1921–1930. Zurich: TVZ.

(1981), *Karl Barth – Martin Rade: Ein Briefwechsel*. Gütersloh: Verlagshaus Gerd Mohn.

(1982), *Karl Barth – Rudolph Bultmann: Letters 1922–1966*, ed. Bernd Jaspert, tr. Geoffrey W. Bromiley. Edinburgh: T&T Clark.

(1982a), *A Late Friendship: The Letters of Karl Barth and Carl Zuckmayer*, tr. Geoffrey Bromiley. Michigan: Eerdmans.

(1989), 'Concluding Unscientific Postscript on Schleiermacher' in *Karl Barth, the Theologian of Freedom: Selected Writings*, ed. Clifford Green. London: Collins.

(1990), *The Göttingen Dogmatics: Instruction in the Christian Religion*, I, tr. Geoffrey W. Bromiley. Grand Rapids: William B. Eerdmans.

(2001), *Protestant Theology in the Nineteenth Century*, trs. Brian Cozens and John Bowden. London: SCM.

Barthes, Roland (1986), 'The Death of the Author' in *The Rustle of Language*, tr. Richard Howard. Oxford: Blackwell.

(1990), *The Pleasure of the Text*, tr. Richard Miller. Oxford: Blackwell.

Baudrillard, Jean (1993), *Symbolic Exchange and Death*, tr. Iain Hamilton Grant. London: Sage.

Bauman, Zygmunt (1992), *Intimations of Postmodernity*. London: Routledge.

Beintker, Michael (1987), *Die Dialektik in der 'dialektischen Theologie' Karl Barths*. Munich: Ch. Kaiser Verlag.

Berger, Peter L. (1999) (ed.), *The Desecularization of the World: Resurgent Religion and World Politics*. Grand Rapids: William B. Eerdmans.

Bernstein, Richard J. (1972), *Praxis and Action*. London: Duckworth.

(1983), *Beyond Objectivism and Relativism*. Oxford: Blackwell.

(2001) (ed.), *The Culture Industry*. London: Routledge.

Blanchot, Maurice (1993), *The Infinite Conversation*, tr. S. Hanson. Minneapolis: University of Minnesota Press.

Bloch, Ernst (1977), 'Nonsynchronism and Dialectics', *New German Critique*, no.11 (Spring), 22–38.

Bonhoeffer, Dietrich (1963), *Sanctorum Communio*, tr. R. Gregor Smith. London: Collins.

Bourdieu, Pierre (1977), *Outline of a Theory of Practice*, tr. Richard Nice. Cambridge: Cambridge University Press.

(1983), 'The Philosophical Establishment' in Alan Montefiore (ed.), *Philosophy in France Today*. Cambridge: Cambridge University Press.

(1991), *The Political Ontology of Martin Heidegger*. Oxford: Polity Press.

(1993), *The Field of Cultural Production: Essays on Art and Literature*, ed. Randal Johnson. New York: Columbia University Press.

(1996), *The Rules of Art: Genesis and Structure of the Literary Field*, tr. Susan Emanuel. Cambridge: Polity Press.

Bowie, Andrew (1998), 'Introduction' to his translation of Schleiermacher, *Hermeneutics and Criticism*. Cambridge: Cambridge University Press. vii–xxxi.

Bullivant, Keith (ed.) (1977), *Culture and Society in the Weimar Republic*. Manchester: Manchester University Press.

Busch, Eberhard (1976), *Karl Barth: His Life from Letters and Autobiographical Texts*, tr. John Bowden. Philadelphia: Fortress Press.

(1978), *Karl Barth und die Pietisten: Die Pietismuskritik des jugen Karl Barths und ihre Erwiderung*. Munich: Chr. Kaiser Verlag.

(1982), 'Autobiographical Sketches of Karl Barth' in *Karl Barth–Rudolf Bultmann: Letters 1922–1966*, ed. Bernd Jaspert, tr. Geoffrey Bromiley. Edinburgh: T&T Clark.

(1986), 'Theologie und Biographie: das Problem des Verhältnisses der beiden Grössen in Karl Barths Theologie', *Evangelische Theologie*, no.6, 325–9.

(1986a), 'Deciding Moments in the Life and Work of Karl Barth', trs. Martin Rumscheidt and Barbara Rumscheidt, *Grail*, no.2, 51–67.

(1988), 'Memories of Karl Barth' (an interview made in November 1985) in Donold Kim (ed.), *How Karl Barth Changed My Mind*. Grand Rapids: Wm. B. Eerdmans. 9–14.

(1988a), 'Gelebte theologische Existenz bei Karl Barth' in Heidelore Köckert and Wolf Krötke (eds.), *Theologie als Christologie: Zum Werk und Leben Karl Barths: Ein Symposium*. Berlin: Evangelische Verlagsanstalt. 170–92

Caputo, John D. (2001), *More Radical Hermeneutics*. Bloomington: Indiana University Press.

Carrette, Jeremy (1999) (ed.), *Religion and Culture by Michel Foucault*. Manchester: University of Manchester Press.

Casanova, Jose (1994), *Public Religions and the Modern World*. Chicago: University of Chicago Press.

Castoriadis, Cornelius (1978), *Les Carrefours du labyrinthe*. Paris: Editions du Seuil.

(1984), *Crossroads in the Labyrinth*, trs. Kate Soper and Martin H. Ryle. Brighton: Harvester Press.

(1987), *The Imaginary Institution of Society*, tr. Kathleen Blamey. Cambridge: Polity Press.

(1997), *The Castoriadis Reader*, ed. David Ames Curtis. Oxford: Blackwell.

Certeau, Michel de (1984), *The Practice of Everyday Life*, tr. Steven Randell. Berkeley: University of California Press.

(1988), *The Writing of History*, tr. Tom Conley. New York: Columbia University Press.

(1997), 'White Ecstasy', trs. Frederick Bauerschmidt and Catrona Hanley in Graham Ward (ed.), *The Postmodern God*. Oxford: Blackwell. 115–18.

Chapman, Mark D. Chapman (2001), *Ernst Troeltsch and Liberal Theology: Religion and Cultural Synthesis in Wilhelmine Germany*. Oxford: Oxford University Press.

Code, Lorraine (1991), *What Can She Know? Feminist Theory and the Construction of Knowledge*. Ithaca: Cornell University Press.

(1995), *Rhetorical Spaces: Essays in Gendered Locations*. London: Routledge.

Collins, Patricia Hill (2000), *Black Feminist Thought: Knowledge, Consciousness, and the Politics of Empowerment*, 2nd edn. London: Routledge.

Corset, Paul (1987), 'Premières rencontres de la théologie catholique avec l'oeuvre de Barth (1922–32)' in Pierre Gisel (ed.), *Karl Barth: genèse et reception de sa théologie*. Geneva: Labore Fides. 151–90.

Crimmann, Ralph P. (1981), *Karl Barths frühe Publikationen und ihre Rezeption*. Bern: Peter Lang.

Debord, Guy (1977), *The Society of the Spectacle*. Detroit: Red and Black.

Deleuze, Gilles and Guattari, Felix (1984), *Anti-Oedipus: Capitalism and Schizophrenia*, trs Robert Hurley et al. London: Athlone Press.

Derrida, Jacques (1995), *The Gift of Death*, tr. David Wills. Chicago: University of Chicago Press.

Eagleton, Terry (1996), *The Illusions of Postmodernism*. Oxford: Blackwell.

(2003), *Sweet Violence: The Idea of Tragedy*. Oxford: Blackwell.

Edwards, Mark, Goodman, Martin and Price, Simon (eds.) (1999), *Apologetics in the Roman Empire: Pagans, Jews, and Christians*. Oxford: Oxford University Press.

Engert, Joseph (1923–4), 'Metaphysik und Historismus im Christentum', Hochland, no.21, 507–17.

Fish, Stanley (1980), *Is There a Text in This Class? The Authority of Interpretive Communities*. Cambridge, Mass.: Harvard University Press.

Fisher, Simon (1988), *Revelatory Positivism? Barth's Earliest Theology and the Marburg School*. Oxford: Oxford University Press.

Foucault, Michel (1975), *Birth of the Clinic: An Archaeology of Medical Perception*, tr. A.M. Sheridan Smith. New York: Vintage.

(1977), 'What is an Author?' in *Language, Counter-Memory, Practice: Selected Essays and Interviews*, trs. Donald F. Bouchard and Sherry Simon. Ithaca: Cornell University Press.

(1991), 'What is Enlightenment?' in *The Foucault Reader*, ed. Paul Rabinow, tr. Catherine Porter. Harmondsworth: Penguin Books. 32–50.

(1991a), *Discipline and Punish: The Birth of the Prison*, tr. Alan Sheridan. Harmondsworth: Penguin Books.

(1999), 'About the Beginning of the Hermeneutics of the Self' in Jeremy Carrette (ed.), *Religion and Culture by Michel Foucault*. Manchester: University of Manchester Press.

(2000), 'Technologies of the Self', trs. Robert Hurley et al., in *Michel Foucault: Ethics. The Essential Works of Foucault 1954–84*, ed. Paul Rabinow. Harmondsworth: Penguin Books. 223–51.

Frank, Manfred (1977), *Das individuelle Allgemeine. Textstrukturierung und Interpretation nach Schleiermacher*. Frankfurt am Main: Suhrkamp.

(1997), 'Introduction' to Schleiermacher's *Hermeneutik und Kritik*. Frankfurt am Main: Suhrkamp.

Fraser, Nancy (1997), *Justice Interruptus: Critical Reflections on the 'Postsocialist' Condition*. London: Routledge.

Frei, Hans (1986), 'The "Literal Reading" of Biblical Narrative in Christian Tradition: Does It Stretch or Will It Break?' in Frank McConnell (ed.), *The Bible and The Narrative Tradition*. Oxford: Oxford University Press. 36–77.

(1992), 'Eberhard Busch's Biography of Karl Barth' in George Hunsinger and William C. Placher (eds.), *Types of Christian Theology*. New Haven: Yale University Press. 147–63.

Freud, Sigmund (1953), *The Interpretation of Dreams*, tr. James Strachey, vols IV and V of *The Standard Work of Sigmund Freud*. London: Hogarth Press.

(1962), 'Some Additional Notes on Dream Interpretation as a Whole', tr. James Strachey, in vol. XI of *The Standard Work of Sigmund Freud*. London: Hogarth Press. 125–36.

(1964), *The Future of an Illusion*, tr. James Strachey, vol. XII of *The Standard Work of Sigmund Freud*. London: Hogarth Press. 3–56.

(2001), *Die Traumdeutung*. Stidenausgabe. Band II. Frankfurt am Main: Fischer Verlag.

Fukuyama, Francis (1992), *The End of History and the Last Man*. Harmondsworth: Penguin Books.

Gadamer, Hans-Georg (1975), *Truth and Method*, trs. Garret Barden and William G. Dörpel. London: Sheed and Ward.

Gay, Peter (1968), *Weimar Culture: The Outsider as Insider*. New York: Harper Torchbooks.

Geertz, Clifford (1973), 'Thick Description: Toward an Interpretive Theory of Culture' in *The Interpretation of Cultures*. New York: Basic Books, Inc. 3–30.

Giddens, Anthony (1984), *The Constitution of Society*. Cambridge: Polity Press.

Gisel, Pierre (1987), 'Receptions protestantes et questions ouvertes' in Pierre Gisel (ed.), *Karl Barth: genèse et reception de sa théologie*. Geneva: Labore Fides. 247–74.

Gorringe, Timothy (1999), *Karl Barth: Against Hegemony*. Oxford: Oxford University Press.

Gray, John (1993), *Post-Liberalism: Studies in Political Thought*. London: Routledge.

Greenblatt, Stephen (1988), *Shakespearean Negotiations*. Oxford: Oxford University Press.

Grimm, Jakob and Wilhelm (1854), *Wörterbuch*. Leipzig: Verlag von S. Hirzel.

Habermas, Jürgen (1987), *Knowledge and Human Interests*, tr. Jeremy J. Shapiro. Cambridge: Polity Press.

(1989), *The Structural Transformation of the Public Sphere: An Inquiry into the Category of Bourgeois Society*, tr. Thomas Burger. Cambridge: Polity Press.

Haraway, Donna (1991), *Simians, Cyborgs, and Women*. London: Free Association Books.

Harding, Sandra (1991), *Whose Science? Whose Knowledge?* New York: Cornell University Press.

(1993), 'Rethinking Standpoint Epistemology' in Linda Alcoff and Elizabeth Potter (eds.), *Feminist Epistemologies*. London: Routledge.

Hartstock, Nancy (1998), *The Feminist Standpoint Revisited and Other Essays*. Boulder: Westview Press.

Hegel, G.W.F. (1968), 'Church and State' in *Community, State and Church*, trs. A.M. Hall et al. Gloucester, Mass.: Peter Smith.

(1977), *The Phenomenology of Spirit*, tr. A.V. Miller. Oxford: Oxford University Press.

(1991), *Elements of the Philosophy of Right*, tr. H.B. Nisbet. Cambridge: Cambridge University Press.

Honneth, Axel (1985), *Kritik der Macht: Reflexionsstufen einer Kritischen Gesellschaftstheorie*. Frankfurt am Main: Suhrkamp.

(1995), *The Struggle for Recognition: The Moral Grammar of Social Conflicts*, tr. Joel Anderson. Cambridge: Polity Press.

Hood, Robert E. (1985), *Contemporary Political Order and Christ: Karl Barth's Christology and Political Praxis*. Allison Park: Pickwick Publications.

Horkheimer, Max (2002), *Critical Theory: Selected Essays*. New York: Continuum.

Hunsinger, George (ed.) (1976), *Karl Barth and Radical Politics*. Philadelphia: Westminster Press.

(2000), *Disruptive Grace: Studies in the Theology of Karl Barth*. Grand Rapids: William B. Eerdmans.

Husserl, Edmund (1960), *Cartesian Meditations: An Introduction to Phenomenology*, tr. Dorion Cairns. Dordrecht: Martinus Nijhoff.

Jaggar, Alison M. (1983), *Feminist Politics and Human Nature*. Brighton: Harvester Press.

Jameson, Fredric (1983), *The Political Unconscious*. London: Routledge.

Jantzen, Grace (1998), *Becoming Divine*. Manchester: Manchester University Press.

Jarvis, Simon (1998), *Adorno: A Critical Introduction*. Cambridge: Polity Press.

Kant, Immanuel (1960), *Religion Within the Limits of Reason Alone*, trs. Theodore M. Greene and Hoyt H. Hudson. La Salle, Ill.: Open Court Publishers.

(1999), '*Was ist Aufklärung?' ausgewählte Kleine Schriften*, ed. Horst D. Brandt. Hamburg: F. Meiner Verlag.

Kearney, Richard (1981), *Poetics of Imagining*. London: Routledge.

(1988), *The Wake of the Imagination*. London: Hutchinson.

Kearney, Richard (ed.) (1996), *Paul Ricoeur: The Hermeneutics of Action*. London: Sage.

Kniesche, T. and Brockmann S. (eds.) (1994), *Dancing on the Volcano: Essays on the Culture of the Weimar Republic*. Columbia: Camden.

Köbler, Renata (1987), *Schattenarbeit: Charlotte von Kirschbaum. Die Theologin an der Seite Karl Barths*. Cologne: Pahl-Rugenstein Verlag.

Lacan, Jacques (1989), *Ecrits*, tr. Alan Sheridan. London: Routledge.

Lacoue-Labarthe, Philippe (1994), *Musica Ficta (Figures of Wagner)*, tr. Felicia McCarren. Stanford: Stanford University Press.

Lakeland, Paul (1982), *The Politics of Salvation: The Hegelian Idea of the State*. Albany: SUNY Press.

Laplanche, Jean and Pontalis, J.-B. (1964), 'Fantasme originaire, fantasmes des origines, origine du fantasme', *Les Temps Modernes*, no.215 (April).

Levinas, Emmanuel (1974), *Autrement qu'être ou au-delà de l'essence*. The Hague: Martinus Nijhoff.

Long, D. Stephen (2000), *Divine Economy*. London: Routledge.

Lubac, Henri de (1967), *The Mystery of the Supernatural*, tr. Rosemary Sheed. New York: Herder and Herder.

Lyotard, Jean-François (1991), *The Inhuman*, trs. Geoffrey Bennington and Rachel Bowlby. Cambridge: Polity Press.

  (1994), *Lessons on the Analytic of the Sublime*, tr. Elizabeth Rottenberg. Stanford: University of Stanford Press.

Marion, Jean-Luc (1991), *God Without Being: Hors-Texte*, tr. Thomas Carlson. Chicago: University of Chicago Press.

Marquardt, Friedrich-Wilhelm (1985), *Theologie und Socialismus: Das Beispiel Karl Barths*. 3rd edn; Munich: Chr. Kaiser Verlag.

Martin, Marty E. (1988), 'Barth' in Donald Kim (ed.), *How Karl Barth Changed My Mind*. Grand Rapids: Wm. B. Eerdmans. 102–7.

Marx, Karl (1975), 'Towards a Critique of Hegel's *Philosophy of Right*' in *Karl Marx: Early Writings*, trs. Rodney Livingstone and Gregor Benton. London: Pelican Books.

McCormack, Bruce (1995), *Karl Barth's Critically Realistic Dialectical Theology: Its Genesis and Development*. Oxford: Oxford University Press.

Milbank, John (1995), *The Word Made Strange*. Oxford: Blackwell.

Milbank, John, and Pickstock, Catherine (2001), *Truth in Aquinas*. London: Routledge.

Minear, Paul S. (1988), 'Rich Memories, Huge Debts' in Donald Kim (ed.), *How Karl Barth Changed My Mind*. Grand Rapids: Wm. B. Eerdmans. 47–51.

Miner, Robert (2004), *Truth in the Making: Creative Knowledge in Theology and Philosophy*. London: Routledge.

Mumford, Lewis (1966), *The City in History*. Harmondsworth: Penguin Books.

Nancy, Jean-Luc (1990), 'Finite History' in David Carroll (ed.), *The States of 'Theory': History, Art and Critical Discourse*. New York: Columbia University Press. 149–172.

Nancy, Jean-Luc with Lacoue-Labarthe, Philippe (1988), *The Literary Absolute*, trs. P. Barnard and C. Lester. Albany: SUNY Press.

Negri, Antonio (2003), *Time for Revolution*, tr. Matteo Mandarini. New York: Continuum.

Nelson, Lyn Hankinson (1990), *Know Knows: from Quine to a Feminist Epistemology*. Philadelphia: Temple University Press.

Niebuhr, H. Richard (1951), *Christ and Culture*. New York: Harper & Row.

Nietzsche, Friedrich (1956), *Genealogy of Morals*, tr. Francis Golffing. Garden City, N.Y.: Doubleday.

Nowak, Kurt (1987), 'Die antihistorische Revolution: Symptome und Folgen der Krise historischen Weltorientierung nach dem ersten Weltkrieg in Deutschland' in H. Renz and F.W. Graft (eds.), *Umstrittene Moderne: Die Zukunft der Neuzeit im Urteil der Epoche Ernst Troeltsch*. Gutersloh: Verlagshaus Gerd Mohn. 133–71.

Patry, R. (1926), *La religion dans l'Allemagne d'aujourd'hui*. Paris: Payot.

Péguy, Charles (1996), *The Portal of the Mystery of Hope*, tr. David Louis Schindler, Jr. Edinburgh: T&T Clark.

Przywara, Eric (1923), 'Gottes in uns oder über uns? (Immanenz und Transcendenz im heutigen Geistesleben)', *Stimmen der Zeit*, no.105, 342–62.

    (1929), 'Neue Religiosität' in *Ringen der Gegenwart*, I. Ausburg: Benno Filser-Verlag. 48–78.

Reymond, Bernard (1985), *Théologien ou prophète? les francophones et Karl Barth avant 1945*. Lausanne: L'âge d'homme.

Ricoeur, Paul (1970), *Freud and Philosophy: An Essay on Interpretation*, tr. Denis Savage. New Haven: Yale University Press.

    (1974), *Paul Ricoeur: Political and Social Essays*, eds. David Stewart and Joseph Bien. Athens, Ohio: Ohio University Press.

    (1976), *Interpretation Theory: Discourse and the Surplus of Meaning*. Fort Worth: Texas Christian University Press.

    (1977), *The Rule of Metaphor*, tr. Robert Czerny. Toronto: University of Toronto Press.

    (1978), 'The Question of Proof in Freud's Writing' in *The Philosophy of Paul Ricoeur: An Anthology of his Work*, eds. Charles E. Reagan and David Stewart. Boston: Beacon Press.

    (1981), 'Metaphor and the Central Problem of Hermeneutics', tr. and ed. John B. Thompson in *Hermeneutics and the Human Sciences*. Cambridge: Cambridge University Press.

    (1984), *Time and Narrative: Volume One*, tr. Kathleen McLaughlin and David Pellauer. Chicago: University of Chicago Press.

    (1986), *Du texte à l'action: Essais d'hermeneutique, II*. Paris: Editions du Seuil.

    (1986a), *Lectures on Ideology and Utopia*, ed. George H. Taylor. New York: Columbia University Press.

    (1991), *From Text to Action*, tr. Kathleen Blamey, eds. Kathleen Blamey and John Thompson. Evanston: Northwestern University Press.

    (1992), *Oneself as Another*, tr. Kathleen Blamey. Chicago: University of Chicago Press, 1992.

Ritschl, Dietrich (1988), 'How to Be Most Grateful to Karl Barth Without Remaining a Barthian' in Donald Kim (ed.), *How Karl Barth Changed My Mind*. Grand Rapids: Wm. B. Eerdmans. 86–93.

Roberts, Richard H. (1992), *A Theology on its Way: Essays on Karl Barth*. Edinburgh: T&T Clark.

Rose, Gillian (1978), *The Melancholy Science: An Introduction to the Thought of Theodor Adorno*. London: Macmillan.

Ruddies, Hartmut (1987), 'Karl Barth und Ernst Troeltsch: Aspekte eines unterbliebenen Dialogs' in H. Renz and F.W. Graft (eds.), *Umstrittene Moderne: Die Zukunft der Neuzeit im Urteil der Epoche Ernst Troeltsch*. Gutersloh: Verlagshaus Gerd Mohn. 230–58.

Rupp, George (1977), *Culture-Protestantism: German Liberal Theology at the Turn of the Twentieth Century*. Missoula, Mont.: Scholars Press.

Said, Edward (1988), Foreword to Ranajit Guha and Gayatri Chakravorty Spivak (eds.), *Selected Subaltern Studies*. New York: Oxford University Press.

Schildmann, Wolfgang (1991), *Was sind das für Zeichen? Karl Barths Träume im Kontext von Leben und Lehre*. Munich: Chr. Kaiser Verlag.

Schindler, Ronald Jeremiah (1998), *The Frankfurt School Critique of Capitalist Culture: A Critical Theory for Post-Democratic Society and its Re-education*. Aldershot: Ashgate.

Schleiermacher, F. (1998), *Hermeneutics and Criticism*, tr. Andrew Bowie. Cambridge: Cambridge University Press.

Schwöbel, Christoph (1981), 'Einleitung' to *Karl Barth – Martin Rade: Ein Briefwechsel*. Gutersloh: Verlagshaus Gerd Mohn. 9–56.

Searle, John R. (1983), *Intentionality: An Essay in the Philosophy of Mind*. Cambridge: Cambridge University Press.

Selinger, Suzanne (1998), *Charlotte von Kirschbaum and Karl Barth: A Study in Biography and the History of Theology*. Pennsylvania: Pennsylvania State University Press.

Sennett, Richard (1977), *The Fall of Public Man*. New York: Knopf.

Shanks, Andrew (1991), *Hegel's Political Theology*. Cambridge: Cambridge University Press.

Steiner, George (1967), 'To Civilize our Gentlemen' in *Language and Silence*. London: Faber and Faber. 75–89.

Sydney, Sir Philip (1965), *An Apology for Poetry*, ed. Geoffrey Shepherd. London: Thomas Nelson.

Tanner, Kathryn (1997), *Theories of Culture: A New Agenda for Theology*. Minneapolis: Fortress Press.

Taylor, Charles (1985), *Human Agency and Language: Philosophical Papers: Part I*. Cambridge: Cambridge University Press.

(1985a), *Philosophy and the Human Sciences: Philosophical Papers 2*. Cambridge: Cambridge University Press.

(1989), *Source of the Self*. Cambridge, Mass.: Harvard University Press.

(1992), 'The Politics of Recognition' in Amy Gutmann (ed.), *Multiculturalism and 'The Politics of Recognition'*. Princeton: Princeton University Press.

(2003), *Modern Social Imaginaries.* Durham, N.C.: Duke University Press.

Torrance, Thomas (1962), *Karl Barth: An Introduction to His Early Theology, 1910–1931.* London: SCM.

(1990), *Karl Barth: Biblical and Evangelical Theologian.* Edinburgh: T&T Clark.

Vattimo, Gianni (1991), *The End of Modernity,* tr. Jon R. Snyder. Cambridge: Polity Press.

Vorgrimler, H. (1985), *Karl Rahner verstehen: Eine Einführung in seine Leben und Denken.* Freiburg: Verlag Herder.

Ward, Graham (1991), 'Biblical Narrative and the Theology of Metonymy', *Modern Theology,* Vol. 7 no.4 (July), 335–50.

(1997), 'Postmodern Theology' in David Ford (ed.), *Modern Theologians,* 3rd edn. Oxford: Blackwell. 585–602.

(2000), *Theology and Contemporary Critical Theory,* 2nd edn. Basingstoke: Macmillan.

(2001), *Cities of God.* London: Routledge.

(2002), *True Religion.* Oxford: Blackwell.

(2002a), 'Theology and Cultural Sadomasochism', *Svensk Teologisk Kvartalskrift.* Arg. 78, 1–10.

(2003), 'The Commodification of Religion', *The Hedgehog Review: Critical Reflections on Contemporary Culture,* vol. 5, no.2 (Summer), 50–65.

(2005), *Christ and Culture.* Oxford: Blackwell.

Ward, W.R. (1979), *Theology, Sociology and Politics: The German Protestant Social Conscience, 1890–1933.* Bern: Peter Lang.

Webb, Stephen H. (1991), *Re-figuring Theology: The Rhetoric of Karl Barth.* Albany, N.Y.: State University of New York Press.

Williams, Raymond (1959), *Culture and Society: 1780–1950.* London: Chatto and Windus.

Wood, Allen (1991), 'Introduction' to Hegel's *Elements of the Philosophy of Right,* tr. H.B. Nisbet. Cambridge: Cambridge University Press. vii–xxxii.

Wuthnow, Robert (1998), *After Heaven: Spirituality in America Since the 1950s.* Berkeley: University of California Press.

Wylie, Alison (1987), 'The Philosophy of Ambivalence: Sandra Harding on *The Science Question in Feminism*' in Marsha Hanen and Kai Nelson (eds.), *Science, Morality and Feminist Theory.* Calgary: University of Calgary Press. 59–74.

Xingjian, Gao (2003), *One Man's Bible,* tr. Mabel Lee. London: Flamingo.

Zaret, David (1992), 'Religion, Science, and Printing in the Public Spheres in Seventeenth Century England' in Craig Calhoun (ed.), *Habermas and the Public Sphere.* Cambridge, Mass.: MIT Press. 212–35.

Žižek, Slavoj (1997), *The Plague of Fantasies.* London: Verso.

Index